Changing Family Values

'The family' has become the controversial focus for many important issues facing Western societies at the turn of the 21st century. It has become commonplace to talk about a 'crisis' in the family which threatens the very fabric of society and for politicians to prescribe a return to 'family values'. But what does any of this actually mean?

Informed by feminist insights, *Changing Family Values* explores these questions from a wide variety of perspectives. Ranging across politics, social policy, the law, sociology, and history, the contributors focus on symbolic constructions of the family and the diverse realities of contemporary family life. Issues covered include the recent backlash against single mothers, lesbian and gay families and the law, men, masculinities and the chánging family, the family in political theory and social policy, and the future of the 'nuclear family'.

This collection offers a comprehensive review of contemporary debates surrounding the family and 'family values'. Making an important contribution to family studies, it will appeal to students and scholars in a range of disciplines including sociology, social policy, and gender and women's studies.

Gill Jagger is senior lecturer of Cultural Studies at Leeds Metropolitan University. **Caroline Wright** is lecturer at the Centre for the Study of Women and Gender at the University of Warwick.

Changing Family Values

Edited by Gill Jagger
and Caroline Wright

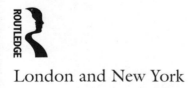

London and New York

First published 1999
by Routledge
11 New Fetter Lane, London EC4P 4EE

Simultaneously published in the USA and Canada
by Routledge
29 West 35th Street, New York, NY 10001

Typeset in Galliard by Routledge
Printed and bound in Great Britain by Redwood Books,
Trowbridge, Wiltshire

British Library Cataloguing in Publication Data
A catalogue record for this book is available from the British Library

Library of Congress Cataloging in Publication Data
Changing family values/edited by Gill Jagger and
Caroline Wright. Includes bibliographical references and index. 1. Family.
2. Family policy. 3. Single-parent family. 4. Work and family. 5. Gay fathers
– Family relationships. 6. Lesbian mothers – Family relationships.
7. Fathers – Psychology. 8. Feminist theory. I. Jagger, Gill. II. Wright,
Caroline.
HQ518.C48 1999   98–36492
306.85–dc21   CIP

ISBN 0 415–14958–4 (hbk)
ISBN 0 415–14957–6 (pbk)

Contents

Contributors

Richard Collier is Reader in Law at the University of Newcastle-upon-Tyne. He has published widely in the area of gender and law and is the author of *Masculinity, Law and the Family* (Routledge, 1995) and *Masculinities, Crime and Criminology: Men, Heterosexuality and the Criminal(ised) Other* (Sage, 1998). He is currently writing a book on heterosexuality and family law.

Lorraine Fox Harding is a Senior Lecturer in Social Policy at the University of Leeds. She has specialised for many years in teaching and researching child and family policy, including lone mothers, parental responsibility and children's rights. Her publications include *Perspectives in Childcare Policy* (Longman, 1991 and 1997) and *Family, State and Social Policy* (Macmillan, 1996).

Elizabeth Frazer is Fellow, Tutor, and Lecturer in Politics at New College Oxford. She is currently working on a book in the fields of political theory and political sociology, on the relationship between politics and community.

Paul Gilbert teaches Philosophy at the University of Hull. His publications include *Human Relationships* (Blackwell, 1991), *Terrorism, Security and Nationality* (Routledge, 1994), and *The Philosophy of Nationalism* (Westview, 1998). He is currently working with Kathleen Lennon and Steve Burwood on a book to be entitled *Philosophy of Mind*.

Gill Jagger is a Senior Lecturer in the School of Cultural Studies, Leeds Metropolitan University, where she teaches feminist theory and sociology. Her research interests include deconstruction, gender/sexual difference and the body, and she has published articles in these areas. She is a member of the editorial board of the *Journal of Gender Studies* and the *Women's Philosophy Review*.

Sue Lees is Professor of Women's Studies at the University of North London. Her publications include *Losing Out* (Unwin, 1986), *Sugar and Spice: Sexuality and Adolescent Girls* (Penguin, 1993), *Carnal Knowledge: Rape on Trial* (Penguin, 1997) and *Ruling Passions: Sexual Violence, Reputation and the Law* (Open University Press, 1997). She was a founder member of the Women's Studies Network (UK) of which she was Chair 1988–91. She has a son and a daughter.

Kirk Mann is Senior Lecturer in Social Policy at the University of Leeds. He has written extensively on social divisions and welfare for a number of years (see *The Making of an English 'Underclass'?*, Open University Press, 1992). His most recent work is concerned with two distinct research fields, pensions policy and masculinities.

Kath O'Donnell is a Lecturer in Law at the University of Hull where she teaches Family Law. She has published in the field of the legal regulation of family life and has particular interest in the construction of family relationships.

Sasha Roseneil is University Research Fellow in Sociology and Director of the Institute of Interdisciplinary Gender Studies at the University of Leeds. She is author of *Disarming Patriarchy: Feminism and Political Action at Green-ham* (Open University Press, 1995) and *Common Women Uncommon Practices: The Queer Politics of Greenham* (Cassell, 1998). She is co-editor of *Stirring It: Challenges for Feminism* (Taylor & Francis, 1994), *Practising Identities: Power and Resistance* (Macmillan, 1999) and *Consuming Cultures: Power and Resistance* (Macmillan, 1999).

Judith Stacey, the Streisand Professor of Contemporary Gender Studies and Professor of Sociology at the University of Southern California, has written and lectured extensively on the politics of family change. Her publications include: *In the Name of The Family: Rethinking Family Values in the Post-modern Age* (Beacon Press, 1996); and *Brave New Families: Stories of Domestic Upheaval in Late Twentieth-Century America* (Basic Books, 1990). She is a founding member of the Council on Contemporary Families, a group committed to challenging the research and politics behind contemporary campaigns for family values.

Jo VanEvery teaches and researches in the areas of family, gender and sexualities from a feminist perspective in the Department of Cultural Studies and Sociology at the University of Birmingham. Her book *Heterosexual Women Changing the Family: Refusing to be 'A Wife'!* was published by Taylor & Francis in 1995.

Caroline Wright teaches in the Centre for the Study of Women and Gender at the University of Warwick. Her research interests include gender and development and gender and migration and she has published several articles in these fields. She was a member of the editorial board of the *Journal of Gender Studies* from 1993–98.

Acknowledgements

Much is owed to friends and colleagues at the Centre for Gender Studies in Hull, which hosted the series of seminars on the family that provided the impetus for this collection. Particular appreciation goes to Kathleen Lennon for her friendship and her inspiration. Thanks also go to Vic Seidler, who initially fostered the idea of the collection, and to Mari Shullaw at Routledge for her commitment to the project and her forebearance in the face of delays. We also thank our reviewers, whose comments we (finally!) came to appreciate. Carol Wolkowitz and Terry Lovell offered useful advice along the way, and for help with the compilation of the final manuscript we thank Gilma Madrid. Many thanks must go to our contributors, who submitted promptly and, in many cases, completed revisions at short notice.

Finally, we are grateful for permission to reprint Chapter 5. This is an extended version of an article that appeared under the title 'Some Mothers Do 'ave 'em: backlash and the Gender Politics of the Underclass Debate', in *Journal of Gender Studies*, Vol. 3, No. 3, pp. 317–331, 1994. We also thank Beacon Press, for permission to reprint a version of Chapter 10, which first appeared under the title 'Virtual Social Science and the Politics of Family Values', in 'In the Name of the Family: rethinking Family Values in the Postmodern Age' 1996.

Introduction

Changing family values

Gill Jagger and Caroline Wright

The 'family' has become the controversial focus of many important issues, cast at centre stage in contemporary collective *fin-de-siècle* angst as we reach a new millennium. All the major political parties denigrate what they see as contemporary trends towards 'selfish individualism' and offer in their place a return to 'family values'. The question is *why* has the family become the focus, in political circles, media proclamations and common sense parlance alike, for concerns about social morality, and economic decline? And not only why but how has this state of affairs come about? As Foucault might have asked, what are the conditions of possibility for this situation to arise? What are the unacknowledged power relations here? Whose interests are being served and whose dissimulated? What forms of knowledge are being produced and promulgated to enable this situation? These are the issues with which we are concerned in this collection, which maps out what Judith Stacey refers to in Chapter 10 as the 'family values terrain'.

But what exactly are 'family values'? At the core of contemporary concerns about the family are changes in family living and household composition. These include the growth of domestic partnerships and decline in the popularity of marriage, as well as growth in the number of divorces, remarriage (serial monogamy), re-formed or step-families, single parenthood, joint custody, abortions, and two-career households. The debates around family values centre on the perceived implications of these changes and their causes and consequences. The main concerns of the 'family values' lobby in Britain and the USA, as identified by Lorraine Fox Harding (in Chapter 6), are stable marriage and child rearing, a gender division of roles, the confinement of sexuality to the permanent married heterosexual unit and the support of these patterns through government policy. In other words, contemporary changes in the family and gender relations are viewed negatively. Social problems tend to be blamed on these changes, in particular the shift from a model of the family in which there is a male breadwinner and an economically dependent female home-maker.

However, family values rhetoric does not stop here. Alongside the attempts of right-wing campaigners to ground policy and political debates in the rhetoric of 'back to basics' family values, the family has also become the focus for those on the patriarchal left, such as Halsey (1993) and Dennis and Erdos (1993).

Drawing on communitarian notions of the family they aim to employ notions of community service, personal responsibility and family obligation to found what is described as 'ethical socialism' (Rodger 1996).

Indeed, the rhetoric of family values conceals many and varied positions on the nature of families, both in terms of what does and what should constitute a family, which families are worthy of support, and the values families produce. Similarly, the appropriate way to help families varies between and within broad political positions. The neo-conservative view encompasses a 'back to basics approach', advocating little or no material assistance (such as welfare provision, social services, etc.) since, it is argued, this merely serves to weaken families by depriving them of their responsibilities and creating a dependency culture feeding off a 'nanny' state. At the same time, however, 'family values' lobbyists on the right assert that government policies should work in favour of the traditional nuclear family, deemed the best possible model of family life. On the 'new' left, Tony Blair insists that calling for traditional values is not inherently Conservative and, at least on his part, does not involve returning to the hypocrisy of Victorian morality, homophobia and women being located 'only' in the kitchen. It is, he insists, rather about linking rights to duties in a social morality based on reason rather than bigotry, and such a project might encompass single-parent families (Radio 4 World at One, reported in *The Guardian* 15 October 1996). On the other hand, gay and lesbian families, rendered 'pretend' by Conservative legislation in the 1980s, are often prominent by their absence from pronouncements about the family from the 'new' left. Yet Stonewall, the London-based group working for gay and lesbian equality, is keen to play the family card. The theme for their annual 'Equality Show' in 1996 was 'We are family' (*Stonewall Newsletter* 1996: 2).

It must be clear by now that 'family values' is something of a catch all, cure all phrase in contemporary social life, on a whole range of levels, and the precise definition of those values varies according to the political and moral sentiments of the user. We argue that whether drawn from the left or the right of the political spectrum, the conceptualisations and idealisations of the family in contemporary politics are exclusionary and theoretically inadequate. Our aim is both to demonstrate this and, using broadly feminist perspectives, to displace family values from a narrow usage which involves celebrating and defending the traditional nuclear family.[1] We seek to examine and challenge the prescriptive, normative status of the patriarchal, heterosexist, white, middle-class, nuclear family, both to emphasise intra-family differentiation and to revalue a whole range of families that take other forms. This project involves highlighting and opposing the patterns of structured inequality – racism, classism, patriarchal power relations and gender-based inequalities – that are inherent in the construction of the nuclear family form as natural, normal and ideal. Revaluing alternative family values and alternative family forms are important strategies in this project.

There are four particular clusters of family values that are the foci of this collection. First, there are the 'traditional family values' that are expounded by the anti-feminist, pro-family lobby which we want to challenge and oppose. Second, there are the family values that are institutionalised in the legal system. These are considered in the context of contemporary changes in family law and the possibilities they present for changing traditional family values. Third, there are the concepts of the family that underpin recent turns to the family in political theory, both left and right, as a means of rethinking the relationship between the individual, the nation and the state in a contemporary context. Fourth, there is the postulated shift from modern to postmodern families and family values.

Our starting point is that the family is neither a pan-human universal nor a stable or essential entity. The groupings that are called families are socially constructed rather than naturally or biologically given. Families and family relations are, like the term itself, flexible, fluid and contingent. They encompass a whole variety of historically and culturally specific types of domestic arrangements and kinship systems. There simply is, as Barrett and MacIntosh (1991) put it, no such thing as *the* family. Following David Morgan's recent work in *Family Connections*, we consider 'family' in the sense of family practices, rather than as a particular entity (1996: 10). Moreover, we take as our project the need to 'see definitions and understandings of the term "family" as topics of inquiry in their own right and part of the process of analysis' (Morgan 1996: 93). A focus on the exclusionary effects and practical implications of a narrow definition of 'the family' is a major theme that resonates throughout the book.

It is also necessary to make clear the difference, and disparity, between the idealisation of one particular family form in the ideology of the family and the diversity of concrete families made up of 'real' people. The former often bears little resemblance to the latter. As Diana Gittins argues:

> The symbolic importance of the family cannot be underestimated, for it goes beyond political allegiances of left or right and has arguably come to be seen as the most important institution of modern industrial society. The problem, however, is that it is seen to be grounded in reality rather than as a symbol system or ideology.
>
> (Gittins 1993: 59)

Barrett and MacIntosh (1991) make a similarly useful move in distinguishing between (the) family as a social and economic institution and (the) family as an ideology. Both of these aspects can then be distinguished from the empirical realities of individuals and their 'families', however composed. This is not to suggest, however, that these three elements are autonomous. It is rather to suggest that understanding 'the family' involves understanding both the inter-implication of all of these aspects and the distinction between them. The point is not to take 'the family' simply as a starting point or 'as a manifest reality, but as a moving resultant, an uncertain form whose intelligibility can only come from studying the system of relations it maintains with the socio-political level' (Donzelot 1980: xxv).

Decades of feminist scholarship on the family make firm foundations for our endeavours. It is worth reviewing this body of work, however briefly, both by way of situating our approach and to illustrate the diversity of feminist positions on the family.

Feminism and the family

Feminists concerned with eliminating gender-based inequalities have long been concerned with the role of the family in establishing, perpetuating and legitimating women's secondary status. What is specific to feminist analyses is that they are developed from the perspective of women, in all their diversity; inequality, in all its manifestations; and power.

The chief concern of feminists, whatever their theoretical affiliation, is with gender-inflected inequalities and power imbalances. Their broad aims are to describe, expose, challenge and redress them in all areas of social life, and to reveal their basis in patriarchal heterosexist conceptions of gender and sexual difference that are socially constructed rather than biologically or naturally given.

It has been shown, for example, that both the patriarchal nuclear family (Edholm 1982) and motherhood (Smart 1996) are historically and culturally specific social institutions. Yet their naturalisation assumes an enormous importance in the organisation of social and cultural life, the acquisition of male and female gender identities, and the moral order. Contemporary changes are perceived as a threat to the social order, and women's gains and the possibility of women's autonomy are perceived as a threat to men and (patriarchal) masculinities. Moreover, these changes are frequently blamed on feminism without taking into account the accompanying social and economic change that facilitated such transformations. Indeed, Judith Stacey (1987) points out that emphasis on the negative aspects of marriage and motherhood in early second-wave feminism attracted the label anti-family and anti-natalist. Yet, she argues, it wasn't this that precipitated the 'irreversible decline' of the family. It was rather that there was a profound crisis of the nuclear family system in the West which helped to generate second-wave feminism in the 1960s. 'The massive increase of female participation in higher education and the labour force are both cause and effect of this family crisis; they both facilitate and are made necessary by family change' (Stacey 1987: 238).

A major problem, however, for feminist analyses of the family arises from the heterogeneity of women as a group; the diversity of family forms; and women's varied experiences within families, which intersect with other factors such as class, race, 'ethnicity', age, disability, etc. It has become evident that women's position within the family and gender-based inequalities in social practices and organisation, despite their structural elements, are not explicable in universal terms (Collins 1994; Mama 1984; Delphy and Leonard 1992). Moreover, the erosion of the more formal aspects of male power in the family in Britain this century, and equal opportunities legislation in terms of sex, 'race' and class, have revealed that formal equality within the law does not result in the abolition of gender-based inequalities, whether within the law itself, in paid employment, or in the family, not to mention in respect of heterosexuality as it is currently conceived.

One reason for this lies in the fact that although the family, both as an institution and in practice, may sustain gender-based inequalities, it is often also the main source of love, identity and succour for many women. This means that addressing gender-based inequalities in heterosexual family relationships, and the sexual division of labour from which they spring, involves changing prevalent understandings of femininity and masculinity and the construction of gender identities. In particular, as Lynne Segal (1990) argues, identities based on 'macho values' need to be displaced.

This argument is not intended, however, to trivialise the importance of formally granting women equal or equivalent rights. Nor is it to under-estimate the significance of what is popularly known as first-wave feminism in getting those rights established. It is rather to suggest that formal equality is perhaps a necessary but nevertheless not sufficient condition for establishing equality empirically. Indeed, just how equality is to be established, and to what extent it involves the recognition of difference, remains one of the pressing concerns for feminism today, and there is still no widespread agreement or easy answer to this problem.

Early feminist approaches to 'the family'

Early feminists, indeed feminists *avant la lettre*, saw the sexual division of labour within the family and women's relegation to the domestic sphere as the root of women's inequality. Although precisely how to rectify this was and indeed remains a contentious area in the main, they campaigned in various ways for equal educational opportunities for women and men, and equal civil and political rights. Mary Wollstonecraft (1970/1792), for example, was concerned with the 'separation of spheres' (men in the public world, women in the home) and the ways that the incarceration of women in the private realm of the home and family excluded them from the public realm of education and work, and in so doing denied them access to rationality. It was this assumed lack of rationality that legitimated women's dependent status and exclusion from political and citizenship rights, as well as property rights, in the political thought of the day. (Women did not gain property rights until 1882.)

Broadly speaking, the middle-class 'Woman Movement' in the nineteenth century espoused such a Liberal view. The suffragists campaigned in the 1890s for the enfranchisement of women on the grounds that liberal sovereign subjects could not include women without the franchise, and/or by pointing to the material contribution women as mothers and workers made to society (Rowbotham 1992: 9). The basic aim was to achieve women's equality through universal rights and reform and to improve family life for women (and men). This included, for example, redressing women's loss of property rights on marriage, indeed women's status as property, their lack of control of sexual access to their own bodies on marriage and their lack of citizenship rights. It did not, in the main, involve challenging the centrality of marriage and motherhood to women's lives and the sexual division of labour on which marriage was based (Eisenstein 1993).[2]

Early liberal feminists were much criticised in retrospect for generalising across all women from the experiences of white, middle-class women, who generally had servants to take care of the domestic work. Indeed, early liberal feminists also met with some dissent in their own time. More radical feminists, such as Emma Goldman in nineteenth-century North America and Alexandra Kollontai in early twentieth-century Russia, rejected liberal feminist reformist campaigning in favour of wholesale social transformation, and wanted to do away with the patriarchal nuclear family altogether, advocating 'free love' instead (Rowbotham 1992).

By the 1920s, as Rowbotham points out, some of the demands for political and voting rights for women had begun to be met in Britain and the US and there was some agreement among liberal and socialist feminists that political rights were not enough. Although gaining the suffrage meant that at least in principal women could influence laws and policies, in practice it did little to address the economic and social dependence of the bulk of working-class and middle-class women. The secondary status of women was still pervasive in the home, the economy, and the wider culture, although there was little agreement about how to rectify this or how to attend to class differences. Many campaigners argued that women's role as mothers needed recognition and public support. Some argued for the collectivisation and socialisation of domestic labour; others, such as Eleanor Rathbone, campaigned for the endowment of motherhood. Margaret Sanger and others campaigned for access to information on birth control as an aid to women gaining control of their own bodies and limiting the size of their families (Rowbotham 1992); it was not until 1991 that rape in marriage was acknowledged in law in Britain. And campaigns around women's working conditions and employment rights continued; it was not until 1971 that the Sexual Discrimination Act ended the marriage bar which excluded married women from formal employment (Silva 1996).

Second-wave feminist approaches to 'the family'

It wasn't really until second-wave feminism in the 1960s that the institution of the family and the sexual division of labour on which it is based came under sustained attack as the cornerstone of male power. Certain radical feminists began overtly to challenge heterosexuality and/or to reject it altogether as a political move. Revolutionary feminist Sheila Jeffreys (1990), for example, currently subscribes to this view. She argues that social transformation is required to end gender-based inequalities and, as a step along the way, feminists should reject heterosexuality.[3] Other feminists wanting to problematise heterosexuality without giving it up build on the distinction between heterosexuality as an institution and heterosexual practice (Jackson 1995). Indeed, heterosexuality has become a central focus in contemporary feminist theory and the (heterosexual) family has come to be seen as one site amongst many in the production and reproduction of gender-inflected inequalities. It is increasingly recognised by contemporary feminists that change at the legal and institutional level also requires change at the level of individual identities and the construction of meanings and desire. Though again, just how this is to be operationalised is a matter of much debate (see, for example, Benhabib *et al.* 1995).

How the specificity of women is to be recognised and valued without essentialising what it means to be a woman or making motherhood a defining feature of womanhood, and without further devaluing what is conceived as 'women's' caring work, continue to be central concerns for feminists. The implications of women's caring roles are highlighted by Sylvia Walby (1997) in the context of citizenship rights, further demonstrating the shortfall between formal equality and actual social and economic equality, and the problem of women's 'difference'. Walby (1997) argues that despite great strides forward in the quest for equality this century, conceptually and practically, social studies reveal that women still do not necessarily have equal access to citizenship with men, due to women's position in the family as carers. This is because welfare provision in the form of pensions, etc. remains tied to paid employment. The caring role is currently identified as a major cause of women's lack of autonomy and financial and economic independence.

How to counteract this dependency presents a serious dilemma for feminists today, as in the past. Providing women with the opportunity to enter the workforce on an equal footing with men, though not itself unproblematic to establish, is one way to address women's economic dependency. Nevertheless, it is only a partial solution, perhaps a necessary but nevertheless not sufficient condition, for it does nothing to (re)value the specificity of women or women's work as carers. Thus Walby (1997) argues that calls for returns to traditional family values need to be accompanied by interventions to support women as individuals in the caring role, recognising the social utility of such work. Perhaps, she suggests, recognising the social utility of the caring role and rewarding it financially would also help to create the conditions of possibility for shifting it from being an almost exclusively female province.

Indeed, women's economic dependence on men is one of the results of the sexual division of labour within the family that second-wave feminists have sought to challenge. The patriarchal nuclear family defines men as breadwinners and women as their dependants with responsibility for domestic servicing. Feminists have challenged this and the way that domestic work and caring are regarded as women's natural roles. Initially challenges were made in terms of the domestic labour debates and wages for housework campaigns of Marxist and socialist feminists in the 1970s (see Seccombe 1974; Molyneux 1979). However, these debates and the solutions they presented, although providing insight into the utility of domestic work for families, men and capital, tended to present their analyses largely in terms of political economy and neglected issues of (the social construction of) identity and desire (Delphy and Leonard 1992).

Fundamentally, then, addressing asymmetrical gender relations in the family involves confronting the construction of gendered identities. Once we see that the ' "war over the family"...is at its root a debate over gendered identities', as Marshall (1994: 132) suggests, then we can see, to reiterate our earlier point, that changing the family and family values also involves changing men, gender identities and their link to 'macho' values. In particular it involves transforming the denial of emotion in men and their non-participation in 'women's work' and child care (Segal 1990). Of course, the idea that change requires involving men in caring work is not new. Not only was it the substance of object relations theory and Chodorow's seminal work in the 1970s, Crystal Eastman, a US socialist who came over to Britain, was arguing in the 1920s that women's entry into paid work would need to be accompanied by men's entry into women's work.

> It must be womanly as well as manly to earn your own living, to stand on your own feet. And it must be manly as well as womanly to know how to cook and sew and darn and take care of yourself in the ordinary exigencies of life.
> (Eastman 'Now we can begin' in *The Liberator* December 1920, cited in Rowbotham 1992: 242)

Family values and economic change

Recent feminist analysis has also highlighted the extent to which calls for a return to traditional family values belie contemporary economic circumstances. As Crompton *et al.* (1996) argue, calls on both the political right and the communitarian left for a return to traditional family values and the male as breadwinner model of the family are clearly incompatible with the changes in the nature of work that have accompanied changes in the family and 'family values' this century. Crompton *et al.* characterise these changes in terms of three main themes: changes in the shift to a service economy; the impact of technological change and information technology; and the decline of the male breadwinner or single earner model of employment and household (1996: 37). This amounts to a number of changes in the gender division of labour, most notably an increase of married women in employment in all Western countries, both in terms of standard full-time employment and, more frequently, in terms of part-time or 'non-standard' employment. Therefore, rather than a return to 'family values', what is required is a renewal and restructuring of institutions which regulate employment and 'mediate between employment and the household over the domestic lifecycle' (Crompton *et al.* 1996: 7).

Two areas for change cited are national insurance principles, premised as they are on a family wage (so women only benefit indirectly through their status as wives and mothers) and 'the assumption that caring work can be left to the household (i.e. women)' (ibid.). It is argued that the reform of social institutions to incorporate these changes would involve two main aspects. First, the recognition of caring work within the household as work. They give the example of Norway where this kind of work attracts pension rights. Second, the 'normalisation' of non-standard work, so that, for example, it too would be associated with national insurance benefits, pension rights, etc.

Family values and 'domestic violence'

Finally, no review of feminist perspectives on the family would be complete without mentioning the 'dark side' of the family. Feminist analyses of so-called 'domestic violence' have highlighted the role of family values in dissimulating the extent of male violence and sexual abuse of women and children within the family. They seek to expose the ways in which the widespread romanticised ideal of the family and family values is systematically skewed to empower men and disempower women and children; and the ways that this ideal informs the way that welfare and legal institutions respond to sexual violence to the detriment of women and children, in the main denying female victims protection or redress.[4]

Indeed, feminist studies are only just beginning to show the biases inherent in the Crown Prosecution Service's handling of 'domestic violence' cases, highlighting in particular the difficulties women face in attempting to carry through a prosecution. For example, the bailing of violent offenders who then return to terrorise their victims into dropping charges, and the commutation of serious charges to the relatively trivial one of common assault, even for the most horrific cases of attempted murder and grievous injury.

This is not, of course, to suggest that all families harbour violent and aggressive men. Nevertheless the focus in feminist analyses on inequitable gender relations in general, and the social construction of masculinity in particular, are a welcome corrective to the apparent neutrality of terms such as 'domestic violence'. They highlight the need for changing the kind of family values that are complicit in the dissimulation and perpetuation of this form of the abuse of male power.

As will be clear by now, feminists tend to view traditional family values with suspicion. However, although there are some more radical feminists who want to jettison the family altogether, others, recognising the apparently natural appeal the family has for many women, want to challenge its patriarchal, heterosexist and homophobic basis, broadening out the possibilities that are held within it for women, children and men. This involves challenging and rejecting the family's basis in patriarchal, 'macho values' and the traditional sexual division of labour. It also involves highlighting and challenging the cultural resilience of the ideal of the heterosexist nuclear family.

Contesting traditional 'family values'

In keeping with these aims, one of our concerns in engaging with family values debates in this volume is to extend Judith Butler's (1992) notion of heterosexual hegemony, to contribute to unpacking what we might call 'heterosexist familial hegemony'.[5] It is argued that the ideal of the heterosexist nuclear family remains a constitutive element in social institutions such as the law (see O'Donnell, Chapter 4; Collier, Chapter 2) social policy (see Harding, Chapter 6), even, as Jo VanEvery shows (Chapter 9), sociological research practices that explicitly attempt to avoid it; as well as in individual identities.

One of the most salient themes in the family values debates is the notion of crisis. In Chapter 1 we examine contemporary calls for a reaffirmation of 'family values' amidst evocations of crisis and compare them with the rhetoric of crisis and degeneration in the family at the end of the nineteenth century. We find a number of similarities including an association of the health of the family with the health of the nation, a rethinking of the intersection of state, individual and family responsibilities, a concern with the definition and value of gender roles and a moral panic around the inadequate mothering of the lower classes in the 1890s which has resonances with the moral panic around the increase in lone motherhood in the 1990s. We highlight the following: there is nothing new about the idea that the family is in crisis; the perceived state of the family has long been associated with moral order; and there is a long history to what Cheal (1991) refers to as the disjunction between the idealisation of one type of family – the heterosexist nuclear family – and the diversity of actual family forms and living arrangements.

One difference highlighted in our comparative analysis concerns the contemporary focus on men, masculinity and fatherhood; this was completely absent at the end of the nineteenth century. This brings us to the second theme we want to highlight in the contemporary family values terrain: the association of changes in family life, employment practices and gender relations with various forms of crisis for men. Richard Collier (Chapter 2) examines the thread within the family crisis scenario that links the crisis of the family to a crisis of masculinity. He suggests that at the core of the crisis of masculinity is a reconceptualisation of fatherhood. He argues that this reconceptualisation of fatherhood involves not only shifting relations between women and men but also changes in the concept of parenthood and parent–child relationships.

His analysis focuses on the recent changes in family law policy occasioned by the Children Act 1989, the Child Support Act 1990, and the Family Law Act 1996. He argues that recent political-theoretical engagements with sexuality and identity, in particular Queer Theory's concern with the hetero/homosexuality binary, are more helpful for understanding the relationship between the family and the social, and hence debates about the social and legal status of fatherhood, than traditional functionalist approaches to the family. Following Judith Butler, he argues for an understanding of fatherhood as performative. It might be helpful to note here that Butler employs this term not to denote the performance of a role but rather the constitution of gender identities and gendered selves in and through gender specific practices. In this case, then, fatherhood is not simply a matter of role playing but rather, as Collier argues, an intrinsic part of the discursive production of the heterosexed male subject. Examining the role of the legal regulation of the changing family in the production of the heterosexed male subject problematises the sociality of the heterosexuality of parenthood. This highlights the role of assumptions about parental presence/absence, heterosexual marriage, economic status, emotionality and the nature of sexual difference/ontology in the constitution of the normative model of fatherhood that recent changes in family living and gender relations have rendered problematic.

Sue Lees (Chapter 3) is also concerned with changes that contribute to the family/male crisis scenario. She considers the loss of young men's monopoly on the breadwinner role in the context of rising male unemployment, increased female employment, and the decline in marriage rates in the last two decades. Her concern is with the effects of these changes on the attitudes of young women and young men to marriage and the family. She argues that while interview data indicate significant changes in the attitudes, aspirations and educational achievements of girls from a diverse range of backgrounds, and a disaffection with marriage, no corresponding shift in the attitudes of boys is indicated. She relates this to the intractability of the construction of hegemonic masculinities.

Another strand in the crisis scenario concerns the high public profile of gay and lesbian campaigns for formal equality and the emergence, or rather the visibility, of gay and lesbian 'pretended families' which are seen as 'threatening' the nuclear family by traditional family values campaigners (Brosnan 1996). But how far does increased social acceptance of lesbian and gay relationships extend to recognising them as family relationships? This is the question raised by Kath O'Donnell in Chapter 4. O'Donnell explores the perceived link between heterosexual marriage and the procreation of children, and the implications of this for the family as a legal construct. Since the legal perception of the family is based primarily upon the status of marriage, and the legal status of marriage is denied to those in lesbian and gay partnerships, the latter are not considered to be 'family' and are denied access to the mechanisms of family justice. However, O'Donnell argues, the growth and acceptance of differently structured family units has resulted in a change in legal perspective. Rather than developing a more inclusive definition of marriage, the law is instead turning to the presence of children as a determinant of family relationships. This means that access to the adjustive functions of family law is no longer determined by the relationship between the adult partners but instead by their relationships with children living within the family unit. O'Donnell examines the implications of this change for lesbian and gay partnerships.

Lone mothers

Another, highly salient, element in the crisis debates has been the rise in the number of lone mothers, in particular never-married mothers, both in Britain and the USA, and their association with a growing 'underclass'. Family values campaigners' calls for a remoralisation of society through a strengthening of the patriarchal nuclear family are often linked to a 'remoralisation' of welfare which involves restigmatising 'illegitimacy' and refusing benefits to 'undeserving' causes, such as lone mothers and young homeless people (Murray 1990). Kirk Mann and Sasha Roseneil (Chapter 5) examine the gender politics of these debates. They examine the 'powerful and widespread' discourse that links lone mothers, juvenile crime, and the fiscal crisis of the welfare state. Tracing the development of this discourse in its various forms from 1993, they argue that a consensus developed that united politicians and commentators in their hostility to never-married mothers and suggest that this can all be understood as part of a wider backlash against feminism, and that it locks into the restructuring of the welfare state.

The next three chapters examine the detail of recent constructions of family values in the contemporary political rhetoric of the 'New Right' and communitarianism. What is involved here are attempts, in both camps, to theorise the link between the individual and the state through the filter of the family in order to place increased individual rights in the context of family responsibilities and obligations.

Lorraine Fox Harding (Chapter 6) outlines the development of the 'family values' lobby in the late 1970s, 1980s and 1990s, its relationship to the 'New Right' and the main arguments and policy recommendations involved. She raises the question of whether 'family values' are necessarily right-wing and concludes that while such arguments have sometimes been convenient to right-wing government, the family values lobby and the New Right should not necessarily be identified. She examines the influence of the family lobby on government policy in Britain in the Thatcher years and through to the end of the Conservative reign in 1997, concluding that the policies were conflicting and did not necessarily match the government's rhetoric.

Family values remain a constitutive element in the 'New Labour' government's thinking and policy making. But to what extent do these 'family values' mirror the New Right understanding of the family? Do they involve some kind of socialist communitarianism? What is involved in communitarian notions of the family? How do communitarian notions differ from those of the New Right? Paul Gilbert (Chapter 7) examines these questions through an examination of the link between the family and the nation in both New Right thinking and that of New Labour. He examines the New Right view of the family as both model of the nation and a mechanism for its reproduction, involving the construction of the family as a natural unit, based on non-contractual biological relationships. He argues that this construction can then be taken to justify the minimalism of the state and to provide a basis for national loyalty. Such a family is inescapably patriarchal 'for without patriarchy the minimal state would be impossible'. He asks whether the family can be rescued from the New Right and outlines an alternative communitarian notion of a communal family based on socialist values. However, he argues, the nationalism of New Labour is too steeped in New Right assumptions to accept the consequences of a socialist communitarianism.

In a rather different move, Elizabeth Frazer (Chapter 8) examines the strengths and weaknesses of communitarian conceptualisations of family life. Attention is paid to relatively recent 'political communitarianism', as exemplified by the work of Amitae Etzioni and the US communitarian agenda, which has excited a good deal of interest in the UK mass media. Frazer argues that the communitarian conception of families under-emphasises and under-theorises conflict between men, as such, and women, as such, and that the emphasis on 'community' is normatively dubious as well as sociologically inadequate. Political theory and policy making must have a more nuanced grasp of the complexity of social relations that connect individuals and groups, including households and families.

Postmodern family values

Finally, changes in the family are sometimes defined in terms of the emergence of postmodern family forms. As Judith Stacey puts it in an earlier work cited by Jo VanEvery in Chapter 9, 'the postmodern family revolution is here to stay'. But is it? There are two main issues in these debates. First, do contemporary changes amount to the emergence of postmodern families? Second, are theoretical approaches rooted in postmodernism or poststructuralism more appropriate than traditional functionalist or structuralist approaches in analysing contemporary family life?

The term 'postmodern' is used to capture the apparent flux and fluidity of contemporary family life and changing family forms whilst avoiding ideas of 'breakdown', 'crisis', etc. Similarly, it is argued that theoretical approaches rooted in postmodernism, or poststructuralism, can accommodate cultural (or empirical) and theoretical pluralism (Bernardes 1997; Cheal 1996; Rodger 1996).

Jo VanEvery (Chapter 9) argues that postmodern approaches are helpful in focusing on diversity because they can accommodate 'difference' rather than homogenising it. She argues that family sociology remains implicated in the link between the putative 'breakdown' of the family and breakdown of social cohesion because it has not sufficiently embraced the tools of postmodernism to provide alternative explanations. She examines recent sociological family research in the UK, as published in a number of academic journals, and finds that despite empirical changes in the family on the one hand, and protestations to the contrary on the other, there was an overwhelming tendency to privilege the nuclear family as an object of study. VanEvery argues that these studies thereby contribute to current concerns over contemporary changes and living arrangements. Sociology as it is practised has the unintended consequence of constructing a reality in which only nuclear households 'exist' and in which other kinds of living arrangements are deemed transitional.

Judith Stacey (in Chapter 10) analyses the elements in 'the postmodern family condition' and various responses to it in the USA. She describes 'the messy improvisational patchwork of postmodern family life' and argues that part of the problem for family values campaigners is that the decline of the modern family era has left in its wake a normative vacuum and definitional crisis that postmodern families can not and will not fill. Contemporary changes are thought to amount to an end to the era of the modern family, replacing this family form and its attendant certainties with normative instability and definitional crisis – both of which are defining features of 'the postmodern condition'. Moreover, there are significant differences as well as important resonances between the family values lobby in Britain and that in the US. Judith Stacey discusses the power and knowledge shifts that underpin the family values terrain in the US and provides a comparative perspective.

Notes

1   Although our project as editors is a feminist one we do not mean to imply by this that all the contributions are themselves explicitly feminist. It does mean however that we think that the arguments that they make and the insights that they provide contribute to our overall project.

2   For a more detailed review of women's campaigning and the spectrum of campaigners and their relationship to feminism see Rowbotham's *Women in Movement* (1992). Her work ranges from the late eighteenth century to the late twentieth century and provides an international focus.

3   There were also feminists around with radical views about the transformation of society earlier than this, although they tended not to be the most dominant voices. There were also women who rejected the label 'feminist' but espoused the cause of women, and those who rejected calls for equality as 'masculinism' in favour of celebrating women's difference, precipitating one of the central issues that would divide later feminists. Again, see Rowbotham (1992). For a broad overview of recent feminist approaches to the family see, for example, Segal (1995).

4   See Elliot (1996: Chapter 5) for an overview of work in this area.

5   Butler (1992) uses the phrase heterosexual hegemony to suggest the pervasiveness of heterosexism and its role in shaping the cultural imaginary. She argues that what she calls presumptive heterosexuality coupled with phallogocentrism characterises the contemporary epistemological and ontological regime. In other words, it shapes the production of knowledge and the construction of what is, as well as individual identities. It seems to us that the heterosexist nuclear family is the social exemplar of this regime. Our analysis of the family is concerned with the effects of certain idealisations of this particular family form and the gender/power relations it sustains at the practical and institutional level. As such it complements the work of queer theorists such as Butler in their concern to expose the constructedness and normativity of heterosexuality, and its pervasive role in shaping and producing social institutions. The various chapters in this book contribute to this by revealing the pervasiveness, constructedness and normativity of the heterosexist nuclear family.

Bibliography

Barrett, M. and MacIntosh, M. (1991) *The Anti-Social Family* (second edition), London, New York: Verso.

Benhabib, S., Butler, J., Cornell, D. and Fraser, N. (1995) *Feminist Contentions: A Philosophical Exchange*, with an introduction by Linda Nicholson, New York and London: Routledge.

Bernardes, J. (1997) *Family Studies: An Introduction*, London: Routledge.

Brosnan, J. (1996) *Lesbians Talk: Detonating the Nuclear Family*, London: Scarlet Press.

Butler, J. (1992) *Bodies that Matter, On the Discursive Limits of 'Sex'*, New York and London: Routledge.

Cheal, D. (1991) *Family and the State of Theory*, Hemel Hempstead: Harvester Wheatsheaf.

Collins, P. C. Hill (1994) 'Shifting the Centre: Race, Class, and Feminist Theorizing about Motherhood', in D. Bassin, M. Honey and M. M. Kaplan (eds) *Representations of Motherhood*, New Haven and London: Yale University Press.

Crompton, R., Gallie, D. and Purcell, K. (eds) (1996) *Changing Forms of Employment: Organisations, Skills and Gender*, London and New York: Routledge.

Delphy, C. and Leonard, D. (1992) *Familiar Exploitation: A new Analysis of Marriage in Contemporary Western Societies*, London: Polity.

Dennis, N. and Erdos, G. (1993) *Families Without Fatherhood* (second edition), London: Institute of Economic Affairs.

Donzelot, J. (1980) *The Policing of Families*, trans. R. Hurley, London: Hutchinson.

Edholm, F. (1982) 'The Unnatural Family' in E. Whitelegg, M. Arnot, E. Bartels, V. Beechey, L. Birke, S. Himmelweit, D. Leonard, S. Ruehl and M. A. Speakman (eds) *The Changing Experience of Women*, Oxford: Martin Robertson.

Eisenstein, Z. R. (1993) *The Radical Future of Liberal Feminism*, Boston: Northeastern University Press.

Elliot, F. R. (1996) *Gender, Family and Society*, London: Macmillan.

Gittins, D. (1993) *The Family in Question: Changing Households and Familiar Ideologies* (second edition), London: Macmillan.

Halsey, A. H. (1993) 'Foreword' to N. Dennis and G. Erdos *Families Without Fatherhood*, London: Institute of Economic Affairs.

Jackson, S. (1995) 'Gender and Heterosexuality: A Materialist Feminist Analysis' in M. Maynard and J. Purvis (eds) *(Hetero)sexual Politics*, London: Taylor and Francis.

Jeffreys, S. (1990) *Anticlimax: A Feminist Perspective on the Sexual Revolution*, London: The Women's Press.

Mama, A. (1984) 'Black Women, The Economic Crisis and the British State', *Feminist Review* 17.

Marshall, B. L. (1994) *Engendering Modernity: Feminism, Social Theory and Social Change*, Cambridge: Polity.

Mitchell, J. and Goody J. (1997) 'Feminism, Fatherhood and the Family in Britain' in A. Oakley and J. Mitchell (eds) *Who's Afraid of Feminism: Seeing Through the Backlash*, Harmondsworth: Penguin.

Molyneux, M. (1979) 'Beyond the Domestic Labour Debate', *New Left Review* 116: 3–27.

Morgan, D. (1996) *Family Connections: An Introduction to Family Studies*, Cambridge: Polity Press.

Murray, C. (1990) *The Emerging British Underclass*, London: IEA Health and Welfare Unit.

Rodger, J. J. (1996) *Family Life and Social Control: A Sociological Perspective*, London: Macmillan.

Rowbotham, S. (1992) *Women in Movement: Feminism and Social Action*, New York and London: Routledge.

Seccombe, W. (1974) 'The Housewife and her Labour under Capitalism', *New Left Review* 83: 3–24.

Sedgwick, E. K. (1990) *Epistemology of the Closet*, Harmondsworth: Penguin.

Segal, L. (1990) *Slow Motion: Changing Masculinities, Changing Men*, London: Virago.

—— (1995) 'A Feminist Looks at the Family', in John Muncie, M. Wetherell, R. Dallos and A. Cochrane (eds) *Understanding the Family*, London: Sage.

Silva, E. B. (ed.) (1996) *Good Enough Mothering*, London and New York: Routledge.

Smart, C. (1996) 'Deconstructing Motherhood' in E. B. Silva (ed.) *Good Enough Mothering*, London and New York: Routledge.

Stacey, J. (1987) 'Are Feminists Afraid to Leave Home?: The Challenge of Conservative Pro-Family Feminism' in J. Mitchell and A. Oakley (eds) *What is Feminism?*, Oxford: Blackwell.

—— (1998) 'Families against "The Family": The Transatlantic Passage of The Politics of Family Values', *Radical Philosophy* 89: 2–7.

Stonewall Newsletter (1996) 4: 4.

The Guardian 15 October 1996.

Walby, Sylvia (1997) *Gender Transformations*, London and New York: Routledge.

Wollstonecraft, M. (1970) *A Vindication of the Rights of Women*, London: Dent (first published 1792).

1 End of century, end of family?

Shifting discourses of family 'crisis'

Caroline Wright and Gill Jagger

In all countries the purity of the family must be the surest strength of a nation.

(Reverend W. Arthur 1885, cited in Showalter 1992: 3)

Introduction

According to the voices that make up the chant of traditional 'family values', insistent in contemporary Britain as well as in the United States, the turn of our century is marked by a growing crisis in the family, a crisis that may prove terminal unless decisive action is taken. The tabloid press in Britain talk about 'the collapse of marriage and family life', discuss 'the extent of the crisis' and run a headline 'End of Family Life in Britain' (*Daily Express* cited in Selman 1996: 2 and Walker 1996: 49). Authors writing under the auspices of the Institute of Economic Affairs speak of the threat to freedom and stability posed by the unmistakable decline in traditional family life (Davies 1993: vi, 7), equating 'fatherless families' with rising crime and educational disadvantage (Dennis 1993).

The perceived crisis in the family may be but one example in the 1990s, an age which is, according to several commentators, replete with the language of crises and anxieties (Furedi 1997; Stokes 1992; Dunant and Porter 1996). As Showalter argues in *Sexual Anarchy*, it need not surprise us that there is so much talk of crisis as the twentieth century closes and the next millennium awaits. She writes:

> The ends of centuries seem not only to suggest but to intensify crises...more intensely experienced, more emotionally fraught, more weighted with symbolic and historical meaning, because we invest these crises with the metaphors of death and rebirth that we project onto the final decades and years of a century.
>
> (Showalter 1992: 2)

If the ends of centuries share a weighing down of the popular imagination by crises, we might nonetheless expect the themes of the crises to be very different. Yet there are some important parallels between *fin-de-siècle* angst in the late nineteenth century and now, as Showalter suggests. Both embody fears for the health of the family and the nation; there is nothing new in today's talk of a crisis in the family. Moreover, the definition and roles of gender are very much to the fore in both cases; it is clear that the concern with the family is a concern with the roles and values of women and men, and with 'the longing for strict border controls around the definition of gender, as well as race, class, and nationality' (Showalter 1992: 4).

Our purpose in this chapter is to explore the eschatological ideas of family crisis in the 1990s in the light of the invocation of family crisis and degeneration in the 1890s. Such a project opens up several avenues of analysis at once. Primarily, perhaps, it helps to disrupt today's all too ubiquitous 'once upon a time there were happy, healthy families' myth, subverting the monolithic version of 'the past' on which it depends. At the same time, it allows us to highlight important differences as well as similarities in the content of the debates between the two periods. In seeking to make sense of these, we need to map out some of the shifting and contested notions of 'the family' and of individual, family and state responsibilities across the intervening century. Such an account remains inevitably partial, drawing out themes we consider pertinent (many of which are pursued in more depth elsewhere in this collection) rather than attempting to say all that could be said.

Our first section begins by pursuing the dominant intellectual and political concerns with 'the family' in the late nineteenth century. We then turn to the late twentieth century and the lobby for traditional family values, with its echoing idealisation of the family and lament of family degeneration and social decline. Thereafter we begin to compare and contrast these two 'end of century, end of family' refrains. In the second section we seek to make sense of the privileging of the family in social commentary, exploring the political spaces that it opens up at the close of both centuries and the place of the family in political narratives about the role of the state. We also look at dimensions of 'race'/ethnicity, social class and gender in state practices on, and narratives of, family life. Our final section focuses on the gender politics of family values. The prescriptive visions of motherhood that characterised late nineteenth-century angst about the family are set against the moral panic about lone/single mothers in the late twentieth century, and the absence of debate about fatherhood as the twentieth century dawned is contrasted with today's obsessive anxiety with fatherhood and with men's role in society more broadly. We argue that in both periods it is through a focus on the family that struggles over gender roles and relations have in part been played out, ensuring that the family looms large in government rhetoric and policies.

Two tales of family crisis

Constituting family 'crisis' in late nineteenth-century Britain

As the nineteenth century drew to a close in Britain, claims in political circles of social crisis and degeneration abounded. These were asserted on the basis of the following 'evidence': women having children outside marriage, or not having children at all, prostitution, including child prostitution, homosexuality, sexually transmitted diseases (Showalter 1992: 3–4) and the indiscipline of working-class youth (Gittins 1993: 143–4). Portrayed by many establishment commentators as symptoms of sexual decadence and degeneracy, there were calls to guard against such 'evils' by shoring up the family (Showalter 1992: 3) and, where necessary, substituting for deficient families.

High infant mortality rates among the propertyless majority were also invoked as part of the crisis. With the view coming to the fore in parliament that working-class (male) children were a national asset, the soldiers and workers who would populate and consolidate the British empire, so their welfare came to be reflected in state practices (Davin 1978: 10). Poor child health was connected not to structural inequalities but to 'inadequate' and 'immoral' mothers who neglected their children by going out to work and who had to be 'corrected' (Dyhouse 1989: 84).

Of interest is how tightly the borders were drawn around what constituted the hegemonic family, whose bolstering was deemed so urgent. To be sanctioned and reinforced was a single family form established by a married man and woman and their legitimate children. In other words, a heterosexist concept of the family was invoked: the sexual relations between spouses, for the purposes of bearing children, were the only legitimate expression of sexuality. Moreover, the convention of the family to be championed was also class-specific; it was the bourgeois family form of the new middle classes, with its particular gender division of labour and its particular demarcation of a child's years into distinct periods of childhood and adolescence.

Within this family, the 'proper' role of the woman was deemed to be the full-time care of her children and husband, and children were deemed to require a 'childhood' that inculcated them with appropriate moral values and prepared them for adulthood, all in gender specific ways. Men's role was as economic providers, as representatives of the family in the public sphere and as a source of moral authority. The new middle classes used this gender division of labour within the family as the basis for their claim to moral superiority. They asserted the virtues of husbands taking financial and moral responsibility for wives who were busy creating a regulated domestic sphere, as against the profligacy and excesses of the aristocracy and the dangers of the undomesticated working classes (Gittins 1993: 157; Collier 1995: 219–20). Although this specific model of family life achieved wide currency, this is not to suggest that there were not alternative, competing notions of family life in circulation. For example, Dyhouse (1989) details a range of feminist work of the period that is critical of the Victorian bourgeois family and celebrates alternative visions, expressed through women's fiction as well as in political pamphlets and platforms.

Constituting family 'crisis' in late twentieth-century Britain

In the 1980s and 1990s a vocal lobby has also espoused the virtues of one 'normal' and 'traditional' heterosexual nuclear family form and warned of the perils for society of departure from it (see Fox Harding, Chapter 6).[1] Dissent is vigorous, a clamour of voices seeking to repudiate such narrow and prescriptive assertions of one 'natural' family form. And as busy as some academics, politicians and church leaders are, using public platforms to espouse a plurality of family forms, even busier are the many people creating and recreating the wide variety of social relationships they claim as family (see Stacey 1990). However, the lobby for traditional family values is certainly not without influence. It was very active during the latter years of Thatcher's New Right premiership and throughout the Major years, although, as Fox Harding shows in Chapter 6, its success in terms of legislative impact was mixed. It is perhaps to the level of ideas that we must look to gauge the full significance of this lobby in the late twentieth century. We will suggest that the often crude connections asserted between 'deviant' family forms and social ills, as well as a particular vision of individual, family and state responsibilities, are reflected in the debates and policies of the New Left as well as the New Right.

As in the United States (see Stacey, this volume), policy units and think tanks, most notably the Institute of Economic Affairs (Health and Welfare Unit) and the Social Affairs Unit, as well as newspapers, have proved more receptive publishing outlets for the 'family values' lobby than the academic presses.[2] Prominent members of the lobby include the 'ethical socialist' academics Professor Halsey and Norman Dennis and the journalists Melanie Phillips and Janet Daley. Their self-declared calling is as lobbyists on behalf of what they call the 'normal' family, argued to have been deserted by traditional supporters like the Church of England and to be actively threatened by government policies, feminist ideology, 'conformist intellectuals' and reproductive technology (Anderson and Dawson 1986: 9–11; Dennis 1993: 48).

Two crises, same difference?

The evidence relied upon in the 1990s to 'prove' the crisis in the family bears a striking resemblance to that invoked in the 1890s: lone/single motherhood; rising crime rates; indiscipline in schools; sexually transmitted diseases (with the emphasis on HIV/AIDS rather than syphilis); and lesbian and gay relationships. To these might be added rising divorce rates and the concern that cohabitation is replacing marriage. Again, a particular heterosexual, nuclear family form, with a very specific history, is idealised and universalised. Indeed, the 'crisis' in the family in both cases can be seen as no more than the 'gap' between the ideological construction of 'the family' and the diverse realities of family life (Gittins 1993: viii).

There are also important differences in the two narratives, however. In the 1990s, the rigid gender division of labour of male breadwinner and female home-maker cannot be so unambiguously idealised by the lobby for traditional family values. Paid work, albeit often part-time and poorly paid, has become the norm for women across all classes in Britain. Indeed, it could be argued that the economy now relies more than ever on the 'cheap' labour of women workers. Moreover, amidst high levels of male unemployment and increasing demands for families to pay their own way and take financial responsibility for areas of need no longer adequately provisioned by the state (such as dental care, health care, education, care of the elderly), women's wages are crucial to the very maintenance of family life. In this context, advocating that women be forced out of paid employment would be untenable. This is not to say, however, that the lobby for traditional family values does not express a preference for women to be in the home, particularly when they have young children.

If a rigid gender division of labour cannot be so forcefully decreed, we suggest that there is also a shift from the 1890s to the 1990s in the mode of despatch of relationships and family forms which differ from the nuclear ideal. What was pathologised in the late nineteenth century, to be stamped out at all costs, is more likely to be tolerated in the liberal democracy of the 1990s, at least rhetorically. However, the lobby for traditional family values typically asserts that such tolerance must be accompanied by moral censure. The role of the contemporary state should, in their view, be to mark out and reward nuclear families as morally superior to any other form, and do nothing to encourage diversity.

State regulation of lesbian and gay sexualities provides a good example of the difference between the late nineteenth century and the late twentieth century in this respect. In 1885 a new offence of gross indecency outlawed sexual acts of any kind between men, and in 1895 the celebrated playwright Oscar Wilde was convicted of gross indecency and sentenced to two years of hard labour in prison. As the century closed, and with the Wilde trial fuelling the newly emerging stereotype of 'the homosexual' as a personality, displacing the emphasis on sodomy as a practice, the position of the Crown was clear: practising homosexuals were criminals. It was also clear that homosexual acts were defined as between men only. Lesbian practices, although subject to censure, have never been illegal and have more often been ignored.[3]

In the late twentieth century, in contrast, lobbying on the state regulation of lesbian and gay sexualities, by those espousing the 'traditional' family, attempts to combine (rhetorical) tolerance with censure. A good example is some of the lobbying in the run up to the legislation passed in the House of Commons in June 1998 to lower the age of consent for homosexual sex from 18 to 16, making it equivalent to the age of consent for heterosexual sex. The Maranatha Community, a national movement of Christians based in Manchester, despatched a lengthy document to MPs making the case against lowering the age of consent on medical, social and religious grounds. Introductory remarks include the 'need to accept individuals as they are, without condition', and profess to recognise 'the deep hurts and often sense of injustice carried by many men and women who consider themselves to be homosexual' (The Maranatha Community 1998, no page numbers). Yet the tenor of the document as a whole is clear: it stereotypes homosexuals as deviants with confused identities whose promiscuous sexual practices are a major health risk, who are unsuitable to raise children, whose personal relationships are of poor quality and whose sexuality is an abuse of God's gifts. Since the House of Commons vote was later over-turned in the Lords, such lobbying may have found its mark. It remains to be seen whether, as widely predicted, new legislation will prevail.

Meanwhile, past 'successes' of the campaigners for traditional family values still endure. Witness Section 28 of the Local Government Act 1988, the first explicitly anti-gay and lesbian legislation of the twentieth century, which makes it illegal for local authorities to intentionally promote homosexuality or the acceptability of homosexuality as a pretended (sic) family relationship (Powell 1998: 16).[4] Although the Labour government has promised to repeal this legislation, at the time of writing (June 1998) it remains on the statutes and a recent attempt to bring the first prosecution under Section 28 has been reported (see Sanderson 1998).

To reiterate, the idea that there is one 'right' family form, and that deviation from it carries great risks for society and nation, characterises both the 1890s and the 1990s. This is not to say that this notion of an ideal family type is not contested, nor that there are not important differences between the two periods in the ways in which this idea finds expression. Indeed, a concern throughout this chapter is to draw out the resonances and dissonances therein. In the following section we seek to unravel the political salience of concern with the family at the ends of both centuries, tracing shifting ideas about the relationships between individual, family and state. It is suggested that in both periods the narrative of family crisis accompanies a primarily 'moral' or 'moralising' state, concerned with inculcating the 'right' sort of values and cultivating individual responsibility to meet needs.

The politics of traditional family values in Britain

David Morgan has written of the need to 'see definitions and understandings of the term "family" as topics of inquiry in their own right and part of the process of analysis' (1996: 93). So how can we make sense of the attention paid to the family and to ostensible family crisis in the 1890s and the 1990s? As suggested earlier, the impending turn of the century, invested with hopes and fears for the future, may itself be relevant. It certainly enhances the appeal that lies in the (false) promise that getting the family 'right' would bring about a better world. Adherence to the notion that there is one true blueprint for all families makes for apparently easy diagnosis and prognosis of social problems: if the family form differs from the blueprint, that is the problem, and in its 'regularisation' must lie the solution.

Politics is, of course, the art of the possible, and so we must also ask why it is that appeals to one family form as panacea have had and continue to have such currency. The ideal of one family form is, as Cheal explains, inherently suited to the pursuit of modernity, with its insistence that there is only one true way to progress (Cheal 1991: 22). Moreover, because we associate family life with what we might take to be universal and natural experiences – emotion, sexuality, birth, ageing, death – perhaps we are open to the suggestion that 'the' family itself is natural and universal (Morgan, 1996: 194).

We would suggest that invoking the family as both problem and solution holds out the promise of important political resources on several levels. First, it can legitimate surveillance of and intervention in families deemed problematic; not all families are equal and not all families deserve to have their sanctity in the 'private' sphere, otherwise so beloved of the liberal state, preserved. Second, it promises cheap and feasible politics. With the emphasis firmly on individual and family morality, governments can be seen to be 'solving' societal problems without incurring additional expenditure, even whilst cutting expenditure. Third, invoking the family in a general sense may bring rhetorical advantage; we all 'know' about family and can project onto its invocation our own preferred vision of it (see Frazer, Chapter 8). Finally, by obscuring the complexities of social change, also obscured is any unwillingness or inability of politicians to tackle the problems facing society. In the 1990s, as Britain's power on the world stage continues to wane and globalisation renders politicians increasingly impotent in the face of economic problems, the politics of the family, firmly embedded in the domestic sphere, may take on a new salience (Morgan, 1996: 196).

These political resources may help to explain why, as we show below, the family can be found at the heart of political discourse whether or not the government of the day ascribes to the notion that there is only one healthy family form. As broader ideas about the role of the state in relation to individuals have shifted, recourse to the family has proved to be politically expedient.

Family and state in the 1890s

The late nineteenth century saw the emergence of a British state taking on the management of populations (Westwood 1996: 23). Through the construction of a direct association between the health of the nation and the health of its families, the family was opened up as a terrain on which the practices of the state might legitimately be exercised. Only a very particular form of family, the heterosexual bourgeois family, was deemed healthy, and this health was above all a moral health, apparently intrinsic to a particular structuring of gender roles and relations within the family. Management of the bourgeois family was deemed neither necessary nor desirable, except perhaps by way of rewarding its assumed morality. On the other hand, families which did not conform to this normative type could be portrayed as a national risk, their women in particular subject to censure, surveillance and moral re-education. National interests were invoked in the name of a particular project: working on individual lives in order that they might approximate to bourgeois family practices, rather than attending to the constraints against which those lives are led. The state was constructing a responsibility for inculcating the 'right' sort of values, but not for the provision of resources to meet needs.

Family and state in an age of welfare

As the twentieth century got underway, social 'problems' were increasingly subject to a new field of measurement and quantification. The weight of accumulating data served to configure the structural features of poverty and ill-health, displacing the emphasis on the 'pathology' of families and individuals. A concern for the efficiency and health of the nation came to require national and regional interventions, if still with some emphasis on re-educating the 'degenerate' then also with an agenda to begin to safeguard access to the means of survival for all. In the name of Empire, some of the interventions long advocated by socialists were born: school meals and medical programmes for children, the first national insurance schemes against old age and unemployment, and maternity benefit (Davin 1978: 16–17, 44). These measures proved to be precursors of much more comprehensive legislation after the Second World War in the fields of education, health, family allowance, national insurance, and child welfare. Socialist agendas came to the fore in this new welfare state, building on the state planning that had characterised the war years, and, ironically, founded at least in part in the name of capitalism, amidst concerns about the possible spread of communism (Elliot 1997: 17). What characterised this new age of welfare was the invocation of a *collective* responsibility to meet the basic needs of all those defined as citizens of the nation-state, displacing the hegemony of the liberal conception that well-being is a matter of *individual* responsibility.

As feminist commentators have made clear, post-war measures to combat poverty were predicated on the normativity of the heterosexual family form and its associated gender relations. It was assumed that men's needs were to be met through paid work, with a state safety net in case of unemployment, and that the needs of women and children were to be met through dependency in the family (see Abbott and Wallace 1992: 25–7; Muncie and Wetherell 1995: 43–4). However, it is also argued that the welfare state had contradictory effects in terms of family life. Despite underlying assumptions of female dependency, the availability of benefits paid out to individuals facilitated women's defamilialisation, that is, their escape from financial dependency within the family (Millar 1996: 63; Dean and Thompson 1996: 148).

Family and state in the 1990s

It is widely agreed that the 1990s have witnessed a shift away from state provision and a new emphasis on 'the family' as a source of support for individuals, backed up by legislation as well as rhetoric. Much of the impetus for this shift has come from the New Right thinking that characterised the years of Tory government (1979–97), and which is sometimes, although not always, coincident with the valorisation of the 'traditional' family. However, we will suggest that 'refamilialisation' has thus far also been an important characteristic of the new Labour government.

A far-reaching tenet of New Right thinking is that the scale and extent of the activities funded and implemented by the state is a key determinant of the health of the economy, polity and society. In pursuit of a 'small is beautiful' mantra, great attention is paid to the size of the budget and institutions of state welfare, deemed bloated and unhealthy. It is argued that state benefits threaten freedom, are inefficient, promote dependency, destabilise the family by eroding individual responsibility for self and family, and reduce incentives to work (see Vic and Wilding 1994: 21–34).

Invoking such 'bads' sanctioned a steady curtailment of collective responsibility for individual welfare throughout the 1980s, albeit amidst considerable outcry, as universal benefits were eroded and entitlement to means-tested benefits curtailed (Land 1995: 102–5). The end of the cold war accelerated this trend, as capital no longer needed to support the welfare state by way of staving off the threat of communism (Elliot 1997: 17). A re-moralisation of welfare was underway (Deakin 1994: 196), whereby wider social transformations were reduced in popular discourse to symptoms of individual moral decline (Smart 1997: 303), thus resonating with nineteenth-century discourses of the 'deserving' and 'undeserving' poor. With the stigmatisation of unemployed (male) 'benefit scroungers', so it became possible once more to attribute poverty to individual apathy and degeneracy, and to obscure its links to recession, the widespread restructuring of the economy, and the feminisation of employment. In the late 1980s and early 1990s moral panic about the (male) benefit scrounger shifted to the (female) lone parent on benefit (see below).

Concomitant with this emphasis on individuals making provision for their own needs, legitimated through the conjuring up in the popular imagination of undeserving beneficiaries of state handouts, came renewed emphasis on families as a source of support. Indeed, while celebrated as *reducing* dependence on the state, many measures served only to *increase* dependency within the family, of young people on their parents, of the elderly on their children, of people with physical and mental disabilities on the community, by which we can read the family. We would suggest that the rhetoric of traditional family values helped smooth the way for the state to back away from some of the fiscal responsibilities it had previously shouldered. It was acceptable to do so because 'the family' could be called upon to pick these up; indeed it was deemed healthier for society all round if family rather than state provision was relied upon.

Legislative changes have reflected this concern to make families a principal means of support, and where deemed necessary to reconstitute families in a nuclear form. For example, the Child Support Act of 1991 paved the way for the Child Support Agency, which has powers to assess and collect child maintenance from absent parents, setting these against benefit payments made to the parent with care of the child(ren). The impetus for the Act was partly financial, given the then Prime Minister Thatcher's concern that the cost of benefits paid to lone-parent households had increased more than four-fold in the decade since 1982–3. However, there was also a moral agenda of refamiliali-sation, of attempting to reattach men to their children[5] at least in financial terms (Smart 1997: 314). Thereby an economic form of the nuclear family is reconstituted even after divorce or relationship breakdown (see further discussion below).

Plus ça change...?

What does a Labour government mean for this tendency to refamilialise? Little more than a year into their term of office it is too early to answer this question. However, early indications suggest that the tendency to refamilialise and to tackle social problems by giving more 'work' to the family has not abated. Moreover, a preference for the nuclear family form can be discerned, although the Labour government may be more cautious than its Conservative predeces-sor about prescribing this family for society's ills.

The Labour Party Manifesto for the 1997 General Election emphasised a commitment to strengthening family life and, despite a brief textual reference to diversity, the accompanying images reinforced the sense that what is meant by family is the nuclear family constituted through marriage (The Labour Party 1997: 24–7).[6] The word 'family' was the third commonest 'buzzword' in the manifesto, appearing 36 times (*The Guardian* 4 April 1997: 13) and provoking the comment that Labour was 'fully engaged with the Conservatives over which is the party of the family' (*The Guardian* 3 April 1997: 1). In government, Labour makes much of the family's role in society, focusing in particular on parental responsibilities for children. Although acknowledged by Labour to be failing (*The Guardian* 10 February 1998), abolition of the CSA has not been countenanced. Instead, opening hours have been extended, a telephone-based operation pursued, and more reforms are promised in a bid to tackle the backlog of cases (*The Guardian* 11 March 1998).

Meanwhile, a plank in Labour's education policy involves holding parents responsible for ensuring that their primary school children practise their reading at home, get enough sleep and do not truant (*The Guardian* 29 July 1997; Elliot 1997: 17). Parents deemed to be failing to comply with the latter risk fines or even prison sentences (*The Guardian* 22 September 1997), and withdrawal of child benefit has also been mooted (*The Guardian* 25 March 1998). There are moves to make parents legally responsible for children under probation orders and curfews, giving courts powers to order parents to attend parent education classes and to control their children in particular ways, with fines and possible jail terms for non-compliance (*The Guardian* 26 September 1997: 10). In one case a mother whose son was found smoking cannabis at home was herself arrested and given a two year probation order (*The Guardian* 26 September 1997).

Clearly a recurrent theme in New Labour policy initiatives is an emphasis on the family as a mediating structure between the individual and the state. It might even be argued that the tenor of some initiatives is that children are parental property (sitting very uneasily alongside the discourse of children's rights), and that there are resonances here with right-wing agendas to 'off-load every responsibility for socialisation onto parents' (Grant 1998). In fact, New Labour has its own ideological inspiration for a focus on the family, namely communitarianism. As Liz Frazer argues in Chapter 8 of this volume, popular communitarianism involves 'an insistent emphasis on "the family" as *the* relevant and significant institution', together with 'the insistence that rights must be correlated with duties, obligations and responsibilities' (see p. 152). Thus, what began during the years of Conservative rule, parental accountability for children's actions being voiced in the White Paper on Young Offenders back in 1980 (Cannan 1992: 9), and was legally inscribed in the 1991 Criminal Justice Act and the 1994 Public Order Act (Lister 1996: 26), is being consolidated and extended under a new Labour government.

Family values as discourses of 'race'/ethnicity, class and gender

The political privileging of family provision, a reification even of the family in society, may make for powerful rhetoric. It carries with it the idea that all families matter and matter equally, and that 'strong' and 'capable' families are necessarily good for all their members. In fact, as we have seen, it typically refers to and deems authentic and healthy only one particular type of family, the modern nuclear family. Moreover, particular narratives of 'race'/ethnicity, class and gender are woven into this valorisation of family life.

It is very clear that not all families are equal in the eyes of the state: if the family and family provision matters so much, how is it that UK immigration laws have been continuously amended to make the reunification of British Asian and African-Caribbean families ever more difficult? (Lister 1996: 27; Westwood 1996: 24). Moreover, racial stereotyping of British Asian and African-Caribbean families has, in different ways, served to render them less eligible for state support. For example, so much is made of the ostensible cohesiveness and fierce independence of the extended British Asian family that its members are presumed to be less in need of state sponsored benefits and services than white British families (Campion 1995: 245–6; Nasir 1996: 28). Given the contrasting preoccupation with the perceived breakdown in British African-Caribbean family life, we might expect such families to be explicitly targeted for state support. In fact, invoking essentialist fictions of the middle-income black superwoman, strong, single and independent, and her antithesis the low-income black lone mother, motivated by promiscuity and welfare greed, serves to disqualify the British African-Caribbean family from state support (see Reynolds 1997).

Alongside 'race', the intersection of particular families with particular state practices is also differentiated by social class. Working-class families have generally been subject to a higher degree of state surveillance and state regulation than have middle-class families, in part because working-class families tend to be more overtly reliant on state welfare but also because predominantly middle-class professionals are more comfortable surveilling groups they see as different (Campion 1995: 34).

If blanket invocations of 'the family' fail to address the ways in which state practices differentiate between families, on the grounds of 'race' but also of class, also ignored are the gendered dynamics of family life. Given the prevailing gender divisions of labour, more 'work' for the family, whether caring for the sick and the elderly or monitoring children's home-work, generally means more work for women. This is not recognised when the family is spoken of as an aggregate unit. Nor is the extent to which income may be unevenly distributed within the family along gender lines. What tends to be missing, both from New Right models of family life drawing on the market and from New Left versions drawing on political communitarianism, is an analysis of the relations of power and conflict intrinsic to the family. Not only does this leave the 'dark side' of family life too often undisturbed – domestic violence, child abuse, dependency – it also obscures the extent to which, even when gender conflict is cooperative, gender roles may be separate but not equal.

We have suggested in this section that the terrain of the family may offer the illusion of a cheap and feasible political programme. Setting the family 'to work' in the 1980s and 1990s may be one way of legitimating the goal of reduced public expenditure, of moving away from the valorisation of collective provision by the state and back to the valorisation of individual and family provision that marked the end of the nineteenth century. This may help to explain the salience of campaigns espousing traditional family values and their capacity to set the context for debate, even among politicians who would be unlikely to subscribe to the 'nuclear family good, other families bad' mantra. This section has also begun to illustrate the gender projects that underpin the rhetoric of traditional family values. As we suggest below, what is actually at stake are the relations between women and men.

Gendering the politics of traditional family values

What is interesting about the clarion call to the nuclear family at the ends of both centuries is that it involves the construction and scapegoating of a particular stereotype of women, blamed for producing 'deviant' and dangerous family forms. In both cases it is women's role as mothers that is the focus of attention. So much of the crusade to save the 'traditional' family is about claiming that if women don't change their ways then children, men, and society in general are at risk.

Surveilling motherhood: the 1890s

With responsibility for the health and welfare of working-class children laid firmly at the door of the family and, specifically, at the door of mothers, high infant mortality rates were assumed in much political discourse to indicate that something was wrong in the working-class family, and, specifically, that something was wrong with mothers. Campaigns to 'improve' mothers came to the fore, with much proselytising about 'good mothering', 'mothercraft' and the need for mothers to remain in the home and eschew paid work, without regard to the paucity of family income or the extent to which it was unevenly divided between family members (Davin 1978). Thus, public concern for the nation's children typically brought not poverty alleviation measures but the surveillance of motherhood. Women who bore children outside marriage were blamed unilaterally and typically condemned to the work-house (Smart 1996: 49). Where mothers were deemed absent or inadequate the rounding up of children from the streets, to be despatched 'for their own good' to institutions or to the colonies, was legitimated (Cannan 1992: 54).

Important class differences between women lay at the heart of this surveillance of working-class motherhood. It was in part the political activism of early middle- and upper-class feminists that made it possible to blame working-class mothers for the poor welfare of their children. As Smart argues, in pursuit of an autonomous status within family law, such women 'constructed an ideology of motherhood that rendered mothers as caring, vital, central actors in the domestic sphere, as well as persons with an identity and source of special knowledge that was essential to the good rearing of a child' (Smart 1996: 45).[*] Moreover, the attempt to inculcate these new norms of bourgeois motherhood among working-class women was a task embraced by many middle- and upper-class women (Davin 1978: 36–43). Somewhat ironically, wealthier women had time on their hands for such philanthropic quests precisely because they had off-loaded so much of their own domestic duties on to poorer women (Gittins 1993: 123–4). Through their work managing the lives of poorer women, elite women could secure legitimate entry into the world beyond their family, and were building the foundations for their entry into professional life in the decades to come, as teachers, nurses, health visitors, etc.

It is notable that while the content of motherhood was subject to scrutiny, to be valorised or policed accordingly, no such attention was paid in the 1890s to the content of fatherhood. The 'rights' that fathers had over women and children were generally taken for granted, presented as 'natural rights' that emanated from men's superior strength and superior rationality. The struggle by early feminists to draw attention to the way in which such 'rights' were discharged could be resisted by disallowing the content of fatherhood as a topic of inquiry in the first place.

Surveilling motherhood: the 1990s

By the 1990s, the conditions of family life in the UK had become a major political issue and motherhood, notably lone and single motherhood, once again lay at its heart (see Mann and Roseneil, Chapter 5). (By lone motherhood we mean mothers parenting without the father of their child(ren) following marital breakdown and by single motherhood we mean parenting by never-married mothers.) One narrative – that lone and single mothers are a threat to society – has received particular prominence, but there are competing narratives. Lone and single mothers are also portrayed as a social problem; as an aspect of lifestyle change; and as an example of women escaping patriarchy (Duncan and Edwards 1997: 55).

Articulations of lone/single mothers as a social threat vary in form, some more popular, others more academic. Both draw on the eugenic thesis of US commentator Charles Murray, so succinctly portrayed by Bea Campbell: 'the morals of mothers are to blame for fatherless families whose bitter harvest is boys who are bad and girls who breed' (Campbell 1998). Attention is paid in social threat accounts to the perceived causes and consequences of, and the perceived solution to, the increasing number of women with children who are no longer marrying (or staying married to) men.

The cause is generally argued to be the availability of (preferential) state benefits to women raising children alone. These are held to encourage women to make 'selfish' choices and 'marry' the state instead of marrying men,[7] or to divorce men in order to 'marry' the state, their children thus being raised at the tax-payer's expense rather than at their father's expense. Such a situation is decried by those espousing the narrative that lone/single mothers are a social threat as a costly exercise responsible for nothing less than unruly and ill-educated children, rising crime, and a crisis in masculine identity.

It is argued that while women and children suffer poverty in the absence of male earnings, the sheer scale of the benefit payments, however meagre, means that state resources are drained at an unacceptable rate. It is assumed that the educational outcomes, socialisation and conduct of children, especially boys, brought up 'fatherless' are necessarily inferior to those of children raised in a nuclear family. Moreover, on finding their role as economic provider usurped by state provision, it is argued that young men are no longer disciplined employ-ees, motivated to hard work by the needs of their family, but inclined to dissent and unrest, and to forging new identities through violence, crime and predatory sexual behaviour (Morgan, cited in Jones and Millar 1996: 2).

The narrative of lone/single mothers as a social threat serves both to casti-gate women and to offer a political programme of action: benefits for single parents [read mothers] need to be withdrawn or reduced in order to stop encouraging women's 'selfish choices'. Thereby, men's 'rightful' position in the family would be restored[8] and a host of other problems in society, from truanting children to poverty to violent crime, ostensibly resolved. We would suggest that this agenda has helped to set the terms of reference for government policies, but it has also been hotly contested and has by no means determined legislative outcomes.

With the decline in real terms of maintenance from absent fathers (see Land 1995: 109), and the economic participation rate of lone/single mothers at the lowest level in Europe (see Millar 1994: 70; Land 1994: 111),[9] the extent of state benefits to support children in lone/single parent families has come under scrutiny. In the 1991 Child Support Act we see an attempt to reinforce parental (financial) responsibility for children and shift some of the financial burden from the state to the absent parent (father) (Wasoff and Morris 1996: 78). The Act gave the Secretary of State new powers to initiate and pursue applications for maintenance, regardless of the wishes of the resident lone/single parent concerned.

The CSA has been decried on several counts by women's interest groups and academic feminists. They argue that because payments are offset against benefits it leaves many lone/single parent families no better off (Wasoff and Morris 1996: 70–1; Hooper 1996: 153) and that it reinforces women's dependency on men (ibid.: 157), denying 'that mothers are entitled to state benefits for the work of raising children' (Mitchell and Goody 1997: 205), putting pressure on lone mothers to name the father(s) of their children and making 'clean-break' settlements for women in violent and abusive relationships an impossibility (Smart 1997: 317–18).

The CSA has also been hotly contested from within the camp espousing traditional family values. Welcomed by some as reinforcing men's (financial) responsibilities to family life, there has been vociferous and well-organised pressure from others who feel that the CSA scapegoats 'innocent' men, who are only absent parents in the first place because of an unwanted divorce/separation initiated by their wife/partner (see Mitchell and Goody 1997: 204–7). One interpretation of men's fury is that the Act poses economic constraints on their ability to pursue serial monogamy as a form of intimacy, limiting the extent to which they can walk away from one family to make another in the name of what Giddens has termed 'confluent love' (Giddens 1992: 61; Smart 1997: 315).

As well as measures to make absent parents pay more for their children, the 1990s have also witnessed measures allowing the state to pay less. During the final months of the last Conservative government, legislation was mooted to remove the benefit premium paid to lone parents. Although vigorously opposed by Labour in opposition, a cut in benefit for new claimants was pursued by Labour once in government and passed by the House of Commons on 10 December 1997. The revolt within Labour's own ranks was by far the largest the new government had witnessed – 61 Labour MPs abstained or voted against the government (*The Guardian* 18 December 1997) – and the issue caused great controversy. Thereafter the budget of March 1998 arguably gave back in child-care tax credits and increased child benefit what had been taken away from new lone-parent claimants.

Reducing state benefits to lone/single parents is entirely in line with a pro-nuclear family position, so what does it say about new Labour and the family?

Some discern a moral agenda in Labour's policies, arguing that they establish 'the superior social morality of couple-based upbringing' (*The Guardian* 9 December 1997). Others favour a pragmatic interpretation, arguing that it is more popular politically to redistribute money via the taxation system than via the post office benefit book (*The Guardian* 16 February 1998). It is still too early to identify the variety of positions vis-à-vis lone/single mothers within New Labour, or decide which position is most influential in terms of legislation. But a social security spending cut is so uncharacteristic of a Labour government that we might ask to what extent it was made possible by the idea that lone/single mothers are a social threat?

New Labour has also sought to make employment of the resident parent a key source of income for lone-/single-parent families. Here there is a very marked departure from the agenda of traditional family values. Lone-/single-parent families find themselves subject to Labour's flagship welfare-to-work programme, which emphasises the responsibility that all benefit claimants have to find work if possible, and holds that paid work is the best, indeed perhaps the only, way out of poverty. It is intended that many lone/single parents – mostly women whose children have reached school age – will receive a personal consultation to help them find work and, with affordable child care deemed the major constraint, child-care tax credits and new money for out of school clubs have been announced (*The Guardian* 20 November 1997, 27 November 1997). Moreover, the government has refused to rule out making benefit payments conditional upon the participation of lone/single parents in the welfare-to-work programme. In total contrast to the rhetoric that prevailed at the end of the nineteenth century, and through much of the twentieth, the government message in the late 1990s is that a good mother is a working mother.

We have suggested that the ends of both centuries are characterised by claims (and counter-claims) that the 'wrong' kind of mothering is at the root of multiple social ills, and that mothering should be 'corrected'. While it is clear that such views have not determined policy outcomes, they have nonetheless contributed to the terms of reference for debate. An important difference between the two periods is the attention paid to fatherhood. In contrast with the 1890s, great anxiety is expressed in the 1990s about the extent to which many men are perceived to be failing to fulfil their family responsibilities (see Collier, this volume: Chapter 2, for a more sustained discussion of men, masculinity and fathering). However, what does not look so different is that women still get the blame; 1990s fatherhood is understood to be in jeopardy at least in part because of the way women behave. In 'choosing' to do without men women are made to bear responsibility not only for disadvantaging their 'fatherless' children but also for the acts of violence and the crime perpetrated by young men; these are argued to be the logical and inevitable fall-out of women's failure to 'domesticate' men through family life.

Conclusion

As Stokes has pointed out, 'Fin-de-si cle myths can be particularly danger-ous...because they feed on data in order to confirm fears' (1992: 1). In this context the fears are of decline and degeneration, the myth that of family crisis, the data invoked that deemed indicative of short-lived and unstable families, and a proliferation of the 'wrong' kind of families. Our concern here has been to compare and contrast the political projects that are opened up by the telling and retelling of the myth at both 'ends of centuries'.

We have argued that there are striking similarities between the 1890s and the 1990s in terms of the 'evidence' cited to support the myth of family degenera-tion and the type of family that is idealised: the heterosexual nuclear family. There are also important differences between the two periods: diverse family forms are more possible and more prevalent in the 1990s, hostility more likely to take the form of moral censure and social and legal discrimination rather than the absolute vilification of the 1890s. At the ends of both centuries there is a strong attachment to the idea that the health of the nation is defined by the health of the family. In trying to make sense of this we have concentrated on its political potential. If a government can be seen to 'work' on the national good by 'working' on families, and if 'working' on families is both a cheap and feasible form of politics, it may have particular salience amidst an ideology of 'small' state and individual rather than collective provision.

We have suggested that the attention paid to the family form and its impact on society is an often ill-concealed quest to engage in gender politics. In particular, to hark after the 'traditional' family is actually to lament changes in gender relations – not (apparently) of themselves but because of the threats they are supposed to pose to society. So, just as poverty, ill-health, high infant mortality and, ultimately, the fate of the empire, were deemed the outcome of the nineteenth-century's 'bad' mother, so poverty, children's apparent indiscipline, crime, and, ultimately, the fate of the economy, is laid at the door of the twentieth-century's 'single' mother. These narratives of motherhood also work to conceal other dynamics of social and political change and conflict. Just as the late nineteenth-century discourse of 'bad' motherhood drew the gaze of many social commentators away from the monopolisation of wealth, health and opportunity by the bourgeoisie (Davin 1978: 30–2), so today's discourse of lone/single motherhood as a social threat helps to resist close scrutiny of the content of hegemonic masculinity and fatherhood (Lister 1996: 18–19) and conceals the fear that if men lose their relevance to family life they also lose control over women and children (Abbott and Wallace 1992: 135; Cannan 1992: 159).

As we sit on the cusp of the twenty-first century, collective fears for the future of social life are written into a myth of family crisis and decline, just as they were as the twentieth century was dawning. The content of this myth is not arbitrary, but indicative of the contestations around class and gender and the role of the state that mark out social life. In the meantime, precisely because the family does not and cannot exist outside social, cultural and economic currents, it will not stand still as the rest of the world changes. Far from being at risk of extinction, it will continue to be transformed by new family values.

Notes

1   It is, of course, not only at the close of the twentieth century that concerns about family form and morality come to the fore again. See, for example, Fletcher's account of the moralists in the 1960s, who he finds determined that 'All the ills from which our sick modern society is suffering – crime, delinquency, the disreputable behaviour of some teenagers – are laid at the door of the growing instability of marriage, the continual increase of divorce, and the decline of the family' (1966: 234).

2   The titles of recent Institute of Economic Affairs publications speak for themselves: *Rising Crime and the Dismembered Family* (Dennis 1993); *The Family: Is It Just Another Lifestyle Choice?* (Davies 1993); *Farewell to the Family? Public Policy and Family Breakdown in Britain and the USA* (Morgan 1995).

3   Where lesbian women were brought to trial in the past this was for presenting themselves as men, and thus fraudulently claiming the rights and privileges of men (Reynolds 1993: xvii). An attempt in 1921 to criminalise lesbian sex was passed in the House of Commons but then defeated in the House of Lords.

4   It has also been suggested that Section 28 was motivated by economic and political factors; in the name of 'family values' it 'enabled Thatcher to slash the spending of Labour-run councils and education authorities' (Powell 1998: 17).

5   The Child Support Agency is also concerned to collect maintenance from absent mothers, and the number of mothers it has targeted has trebled since 1995. However, it remains the case that 95 out of every 100 absent parents sought are fathers (*The Guardian* 25 May 1998).

6   The two most prominent images in the section on strengthening family life being of two adults of different sex with two children (p. 24) and a 'white' wedding (p. 27).

7   Recent feminist scholarship has refuted the idea that the rise in single and lone motherhood has been caused by the availability of state benefits. Attention is directed instead to shifting meanings of motherhood and their reflection in state practices and in family law (see Neale 1995; Smart 1996).

8   'Restoring Marriage by Recognising Men' was the title of a conference held in London in the mid-1990s, initiated, *inter alia*, by Patricia Morgan and Norman Dennis.

9   For explanations of the decline in maintenance see Land (1995: 110, 115) and Brown (cited in Fox Harding 1996: 141) and of the decline in employment see Land (1994: 111) and Edwards and Duncan (1996).

Bibliography

Abbott, Pamela and Claire Wallace (1992) *The Family and the New Right*, London: Pluto Press.

Anderson, Digby and Graham Dawson (eds) (1986) *Family Portraits*, London: The Social Affairs Unit.

Campbell, Beatrix (1998) 'It's Sexual Toryism', *The Guardian* 3 March.

Campion, Mukti Jain (1995) *Who's Fit to be a Parent?*, London: Routledge.

Cannan, Crescy (1992) *Changing Families, Changing Welfare: Family Centres and the Welfare State*, Hemel Hempstead: Harvester Wheatsheaf.

Cheal, David (1991) *Family and the State of Theory*, Hemel Hempstead: Harvester Wheatsheaf.

Collier, Richard (1995) *Masculinity, Law and the Family*, London: Routledge.

Davies, Jon (ed.) (1993) *The Family: Is It Just Another Lifestyle Choice?*, London: Institute of Economic Affairs.

Davin, Anna (1978) 'Imperialism and Motherhood', *History Workshop* 5: 9–65.

Deakin, Nicholas (1994) *The Politics of Welfare: Continuities and Change*, Hemel Hempstead: Harvester Wheatsheaf.

Dean, Harley and Di Thompson (1996) 'Fetishizing the Family: The Construction of the Informal Carer' in Helen Jones and Jane Millar (eds) *The Politics of the Family*, Aldershot: Avebury: 145–65.

Dennis, Norman (1993) *Rising Crime and the Dismembered Family: How Conformist Intellectuals Have Campaigned Against Common Sense*, London: Institute of Economic Affairs.

Dunant, Sarah and Roy Porter (eds) (1996) *The Age of Anxiety*, London: Virago.

Duncan, Simon and Rosalind Edwards (eds) (1997) *Single Mothers in an International Context: Mothers or Workers?*, London: UCL Press.

Dyhouse, Carol (1989) *Feminism and the Family in England, 1870–1939*, Oxford: Basil Blackwell.

Edwards, Rosalind and Simon Duncan (1996) 'Rational Economic Man or Lone Mothers in Context: The Uptake of Paid Work' in Elizabeth Bortolaia Silva (ed.) *Good Enough Mothering? Feminist Perspectives on Lone Motherhood*, London: Routledge, 114–29.

Elliot, Larry (1997) 'Bone of Contention over Risk', *The Guardian* 8 December: 17.

Fletcher, Ronald (1966) *The Family and Marriage in Britain*, London: Pelican Books.

Fox Harding, Lorraine M. (1996) ' "Parental Responsibility": The Reassertion of Private Patriarchy?' in Elizabeth Bortolaia Silva (ed.) *Good Enough Mothering? Feminist Perspectives on Lone Motherhood*, London: Routledge: 30–147.

Furedi, Frank (1997) 'Why Do We Live in Terror?', *The Guardian* 26 July (*The Week*: 1–2).

Giddens, Anthony (1992) *The Transformation of Intimacy: Sexuality, Love and Eroticism in Modern Societies*, Cambridge: Polity Press.

Gittins, Diana (1993) *The Family in Question: Changing Households and Familiar Ideologies* (second edition), London: Macmillan.

Grant, Linda (1998) 'Now Eat Your Apple Pie', *The Guardian* 17 March (Tabloid: 8).

Hooper, Carol Ann (1996) 'Men's Violence and Relationship Breakdown: Can Violence Be Dealt With as an Exception to the Rule?' in Christine Hallett (ed.) *Women and Social Policy: An Introduction*, Hemel Hempstead: Prentice Hall Europe and Harvester Wheatsheaf in association with the Social Policy Association Women and Social Policy Group: 132–45.

Jones, Helen and Jane Millar (1996) 'Introduction', in Helen Jones and Jane Millar *The Politics of the Family*, Aldershot: Avebury: 1–10.

Land, Hilary (1994) 'The Demise of the Male Breadwinner – In Practice but not in Theory: A Challenge for Social Security Systems' in Sally Baldwin and Jane Falkingham (eds) *Social Security and Social Change*, Hemel Hempstead: Harvester Wheatsheaf: 100–15.

—— (1995) 'Families and the Law' in John Muncie, Margaret Wetherell, Rudi Dallos and Allan Cochrane (eds) *Understanding the Family*, London: Sage: 81–123.

Lister, Ruth (1996) 'Back to the Family: Family Policies and Politics under the Major Government' in Helen Jones and Jane Millar (eds) *The Politics of the Family*, Aldershot: Avebury: 11–31.

Millar, Jane (1994) 'Lone Parents and Social Security Policy in the UK' in Sally Baldwin and Jane Falkingham (eds) *Social Security and Social Change*, Hemel Hempstead: Harvester Wheatsheaf.

—— (1996) 'Women, Poverty and Social Security', in Christine Hallett (ed.) *Women and Social Policy: An Introduction*, Hemel Hempstead: Prentice Hall Europe and Harvester Wheatsheaf in association with the Social Policy Association Women and Social Policy Group: 52–64.

Mitchell, Juliet and Jack Goody (1997) 'Feminism, Fatherhood and the Family in Britain' in Ann Oakley and Juliet Mitchell (eds) *Who's Afraid of Feminism?: Seeing Through the Backlash*, London: Hamish Hamilton: 200–23.

Morgan, David (1996) *Family Connections: An Introduction to Family Studies*, Cambridge: Polity Press.

Morgan, Patricia (1995) *Farewell to the Family? Public Policy and Family Breakdown in Britain and the USA*, London: Institute of Economic Affairs.

Muncie, John and Margaret Wetherell (1995) 'Family Policy and Political Discourse' in John Muncie, Margaret Wetherell, Rudi Dallos and Allan Cochrane (eds) *Understanding the Family*, London: Sage: 40–80.

Nasir, Shafquat (1996) ' "Race", Gender and Social Policy' in Christine Hallett (ed.) *Women and Social Policy: An Introduction*, Hemel Hempstead: Prentice Hall Europe and Harvester Wheatsheaf in association with the Social Policy Association Women and Social Policy Group: 15–30.

Neale, Bren (1995) 'Negotiating Parenthood: A Framework for Research', *Gender Analysis and Policy Unit Research Working Paper 3*, University of Leeds: 1–31.

Powell, Vicky (1998) 'Looking Back in Anger', *Diva*, May.

Reynolds, Margaret (1993) 'Introduction' in Margaret Reynolds (ed.) *The Penguin Book of Lesbian Short Stories*, Harmondsworth: Penguin Books.

Reynolds, Tracey (1997) '(Mis)representing the Black (Super)woman' in Heidi Safia Mirza (ed.) *Black British Feminism*, London: Routledge: 97–112.

Sanderson, Terry (1998) 'God is My Co-Pilot', *Gay Times*, April.

Selman, Peter (1996) 'The Relationship Revolution: Is the Family Collapsing or Adjusting to a New World of Equal Opportunities?' in Robin Humphrey (ed.) *Families Behind the Headlines*, Newcastle upon Tyne: British Association for the Advancement of Science, Sociology and Social Policy Section/Department of Social Policy, University of Newcastle upon Tyne: 1–17.

Showalter, Elaine (1992) *Sexual Anarchy: Gender and Culture at the Fin-de-Si cle*, London: Virago.

Smart, Carol (1996) 'Deconstructing Motherhood' in Elizabeth Bortolaia Silva (ed.) *Good Enough Mothering? Feminist Perspectives on Lone Motherhood*, London: Routledge: 37–57.

—— (1997) 'Wishful Thinking and Harmful Tinkering? Sociological Reflections on Family Policy, *Journal of Social Policy* 26(3): 301–21.

Stacey, Judith (1990) *Brave New Families: Stories of Domestic Upheaval in Late Twentieth Century America*, New York: Basic Books.

Stokes, John (ed.) (1992) *Fin de Si cle/Fin du Globe*, London: Macmillan.

The Labour Party (1997) *New Labour. Because Britain Deserves Better*, London: The Labour Party.

The Maranatha Community (1998) *Homosexuality. The Medical, Social and Religious Implications*, Manchester: The Maranatha Community.

Vic, George and Paul Wilding (1994) *Welfare and Ideology*, Hemel Hempstead: Harvester Wheatsheaf.

Walker, Janet (1996) 'Changing Families: Great Expectations in Hard Times' in Robin Humphrey (ed.) *Families Behind the Headlines*, Newcastle upon Tyne: British Association for the Advancement of Science, Sociology and Social Policy Section/Department of Social Policy, University of Newcastle upon Tyne: 49–59.

Wassoff, Fran and Sue Morris (1996) 'The Child Support Act: A Victory for Women?' in Helen Jones and Jane Millar (eds) *The Politics of The Family*, Aldershot: Avebury: 65–81.

Westwood, Sallie (1996) ' "Feckless Fathers": Masculinities and the British State' in Mairtin Mac an Ghaill (ed.) *Understanding Masculinities*, Buckingham: Open University Press: 21–34.

2 Men, heterosexuality and the changing family

(Re)constructing fatherhood in law and social policy

Richard Collier

Introduction

Within a series of what might be termed 'traditional' functionalist approaches to the relationship between law and the family the institution of marriage has been understood to be central to ideas of social stability and cohesion (Eekelaar 1984, 1978). Recently, however, and from a broad range of very different perspectives, the position has emerged within the social sciences in which the idea of the *heterosexual* family has itself surfaced as a contested terrain, a site of competing discourses. This chapter[1] seeks to explore the discursive construction of the heterosexual family 'in crisis'. It does so, specifically, via an engagement with what I shall argue has been the reconceptualisation of fatherhood which has taken place within recent family law policy in Britain. What follows is, in a sense, about the unspoken 'heterosexuality' of fatherhood itself. It seeks to unpack assumptions about the relationship between male heterosexuality and fatherhood which, I shall suggest, have not simply been contained within but have been *central to* the debates which are presently taking place around the meaning of the 'changing family' and shifting 'gender relations' between women and men. In order to move beyond the dominant paradigms through which family change has been conceptualised by reference to ideas of 'collapsing', 'reforming' or 'reconstituted' families, this chapter seeks to engage with the complex – and under-researched – nature of the *mutual constitution* of heterosexuality, marriage and fatherhood within a range of discourses concerned with constituting the inside/outside of the boundaries of 'family'. In so doing it seeks to challenge the ways in which a particular male subject has historically been encoded as, simultaneously, both 'masculine' and 'heterosexual'. As the model of heterosexuality which this masculine subject has come to signify has become, I shall argue, increasingly problematic within recent debates, so too has the concept of fatherhood itself emerged as emblematic of some broader concerns, anxieties and tensions around the idea of the social at the end of the twentieth century.

The schema of the chapter, which is structured around five sections, is as follows. In the first section I contextualise the argument to follow by outlining some of the associations which are presently being made, both in Britain and elsewhere, around the relationship between male heterosexuality and father-hood. The second section explores further the discursive production of male heterosexuality/ies in the context of family law policy in Britain by focusing on the way in which a particular correlation has been made between a crisis of *fatherhood* and a crisis of the *family*. This discussion will take place via a consideration of three recent major legislative reforms in this area (the Child Support Act 1991, the Children Act 1989 and, especially, the Family Law Act 1996). The third section explores what I shall suggest are the inherent contradictions within the 'new fatherhood' idea. The fourth section presents an alternative reading of family policy in Britain, one which shifts the focus away from the fatherhood/family relationship and towards an analysis of changing conceptions of childhood and, in particular, of shifting understandings of the relationship between *men and children*. Finally, and by way of conclusion, I shall address some of the implications of the 'rethinking' of heterosexuality presented in this chapter for developing an understanding of the production of the (hetero)sexed subject in the context of more general debates around the legal regulating of the changing 'family'.

Contexts: heterosexuality, fatherhood and 'family'

The relationship between gender, law and the family has produced a vast literature, much of which, though by no means all, has sought to engage in both a conceptual and a practice-based critique of law from a range of feminist perspectives. Yet notwithstanding the now well-established nature of this 'gender' frame of analysis, and of critical discussion of legal constructions of motherhood, it continues to be rare to speak specifically of the *heterosexuality* of the 'family' and 'family law'. This may, in part, be due to what appears to be the tautological nature of the relationship. Marriage in Britain is, after all, an institution reserved for 'biological' men and women and can thus be seen as the institutional embodiment of heterosexuality (Section 11(c), Matrimonial Causes Act 1973). Within social and political theory more generally little attention has been given to *theorising* heterosexuality per se as an historically, culturally specific concept (Richardson 1996). Thus, although heterosexuality is clearly deeply embedded in accounts of social and political participation, and is 'of the essence' to the institution of marriage (and thus, it could be argued, to popular understandings of what constitutes a 'family') it is rarely acknowledged or problematised in these terms. The broader 'heterosexual frame' of family law and social policy, as it were, has been largely unspoken and taken-for-granted (Carabine 1996a). When social policy and sexuality *are* addressed in Britain it has tended to be taken to be a 'handy euphemism' for discussion of the relationship between lesbian, gay and bisexual studies and the subject matter in question (in relation to law, see Stychin 1996).

In recent years, both across disciplines and from different perspectives, the study of heterosexuality *in its own right* has emerged as, in the words of one recent text, 'a new research agenda' (Richardson 1996; Segal 1994; Steinberg *et al.* 1997; cf. Maynard and Purvis 1995; Wilkinson and Kitzinger 1993). And what has emerged from a now rich body of work more generally has been an engagement with heterosexuality, and in particular a consideration of its relationship to the ever-present Other of homosexuality, which, I wish to argue, is of considerable potential analytic use in seeking to understand the nature of the present debates taking place around the social and legal status of (about what is happening *to*) contemporary fatherhood. For, what has emerged from within a diverse body of scholarship around the relationship between subjectivity, corporeality and gender(ed) identities is an, albeit sometimes implicit, theorisation of the heterosexual subject as a fluid 'performative practice', an understanding of being 'straight' as a dynamic 'project of the self' whereby the idea of the gendered self is itself conceptualised as a series of constantly shifting practices and techniques (Butler 1990; Probyn 1993). Specifically, within one strand of political-theoretical work on sexuality and identity – that informed by the different variants of 'queer theory' (Butler 1990, 1993; Sedgwick 1994; Stychin 1996; Warner 1993; Wittig 1992) – the idea of there being a (hetero)sexed subjectivity, a distinctive process of being 'sexed' as heterosexual, as having, or rather obtaining or taking up a heterosexual sensibility, has itself been seen as a process not merely defined by private sexual acts but as (to quote one recent text) 'a public process of power relations in which everyday interactions take place between actors with sexual identities in sexualised locations' (Bell and Valentine 1995: 146; see also Smart 1996a, 1996b). Within this emerging 'heterosexual problematic' it is now no longer simply counter-hegemonic or subordinate sexualities which are thought of as 'marking' their bearers in some way. The 'straight sensibility' of heterosexuality, and the radical instability of the hetero-homo (sexual) distinction itself, have each become meaningful objects of concern in analyses of how sexual borders are patrolled and constructed, sexual identities assigned and sexual politics formulated (Collier 1996; Robinson 1996; Waldby 1995).

For my present concerns, and to locate these developments in the context of recent debates around the changing status of fatherhood, this raises the interesting question of what it might mean for the study of family policy in relation to fatherhood to fuse this emerging problematisation of the sociality of heterosexuality (understood as an always, already, contingent and performative practice) with a critical analysis of the pervasive, and oft-expressed, idea that Western societies are now experiencing a contemporary *crisis* in relation to the shifting boundaries of 'family life' in which the changing demands on, and experiences of, men and their 'masculinity/ies' have assumed a particular significance. These are purported 'crises' of 'masculinity' in which a number of contestations around the concept of *fatherhood* have increasingly assumed centre-stage; fatherhood, indeed, has become the very battleground around which some more general conversations about the changing relationship between men, the family and the social are taking place. Thus, whether it be from the perspective of neo-liberal or 'ethical socialist' underclass theory (Dennis and Erdos 1993; Morgan 1995; Murray 1984, 1990), from within sociological and historical research (Burgess 1997; Lewis 1986; Lewis and O'Brien 1987), in feminist, pro-feminist or explicitly anti-feminist thought (Campbell 1996; Mitchell and Goody 1997; cf. Coward 1996), in media and popular cultural texts (Lupton and Barclay 1997: Chapter 3), in personal accounts, as the subject of empirical studies (e.g. Dench 1996; Speak *et al.* 1997; Utting 1995) and, of particular significance for my present concerns, at the level of social and family policy rhetoric (Burgess and Ruxton 1996; Burghes *et al.* 1997) the relationship between 'men and their children' has emerged as a high-profile, pressing and unquestionably politically contentious issue. This is a conversation or debate which has also been, in a most fundamental way, about the changing contours of heterosexual relating and meaning of family in which key aspects of what has in the past been taken to be a normative model of fatherhood is being rendered problematic. Increasingly, and in diverse contexts, questions are asked about the nature of 'responsible' fathering. Do 'families need fathers'? What is a father's 'role'? What, ultimately, are fathers 'for' at a time of profound economic, cultural and technological change which is demanding new adaptations, new forms of attachment and, of course, the mobilisation of new subjective commitments to modes of belonging and integration such as legal 'marriage' and the heterosexual 'family'? (Giddens 1992).

Having established something of the theoretical and political context for this discussion of heterosexuality and fatherhood it is necessary, in order to begin to address these questions, to explore in more detail the nature of the specific policy changes which have taken (and are taking) place in Britain at the present moment; to consider further, in particular, the ways in which – and reasons why – these shifting contours of heterosexual relating should then be represented as involving a reconceptualisation of the idea of the 'good father' whilst *also*, importantly, being constituted as undermining the social and legal institution of heterosexual marriage and the family.

Making the 'father figure': social policy, legislative change and family law

What is taking place in Britain in the late 1990s is, Carol Smart (1997) has argued, no less than a clear and determined attempt to effect social engineering in the area of the family by using the law to 'change the very nature of post-divorce family life' (Smart 1997: 301). Making a distinction between the *rhetoric surrounding* and the *realities of* lived experiences of 'family' life, Smart sees the core provisions of three major pieces of legislation, the Children Act 1989 (henceforth CA), the Child Support Act 1991 (CSA) and the far-reaching divorce law reforms contained in the Family Law Act 1996 (FLA) as each, far from facilitating any adaptation to complex and rapid social change, actively promoting a return to the 'traditional' family. And the way in which this reformation of the heterosexual family is taking place, it is argued, is through a reconceptualisation of fatherhood. In relation to both post-divorce and separation family *economics* (the CSA) and in relation to understandings of *parenthood* as a largely gender neutral (ungendered) practice (CA and FLA), an ideological shift has taken place in which what is in effect a new or reconstituted notion of 'fatherhood' has emerged. This 'new' father (as he might be termed) is (a) to be economically responsible 'for life' for his 'first' family – financially, he is not to 'move on' unencumbered (the provisions of the CSA); and (b) is considered, as part of the 'good father' ideal the law seeks to promote, to be active in joint-parenting after divorce or separation. Together, the CSA, the CA and the FLA thus each contain measures which, Smart suggests, can be seen as being premised on this ideological commitment to *keeping fathers in touch* with children – even though, importantly, this may, as developing case law has illustrated, be at times against the wishes of a mother who is deemed to be 'implacably hostile' (Re R (A Minor) (Contact) [1993] 2 FLR 762).

The increasing centrality of the father within family policy has been secured, perhaps above all, by a shift in relation to understandings of the 'welfare of the child'. This has involved a conception of the child which is subtly different from previous interpretations of welfarism in this context. Indeed, and as a number of commentators have noted, there has occurred a growing consensus on the part of policy makers around the belief that children suffer through lack of contact with both parents. In the vast majority of cases this entails ensuring that post-divorce contact with the otherwise 'absent' father is to be maintained as, central to making the 'father figure' in this way, a range of psychological and social arguments have highlighted the importance of 'father-presence' as desirable. Yet the idea of the 'modern', progressive fatherhood underlying these changes – the father of the egalitarian 'symmetrical' family – has itself, I have argued elsewhere, been constituted through reference to some socially and economically specific ideas of the 'respectable' masculine and sexual propriety which have their roots in ostensibly more archaic authoritarian and traditional notions of paternal masculinity (Collier 1995). What interests me here, and what is particularly important about the more recent period in family law policy, notably from around the mid-1980s through to the present day, is the way in which a number of social and economic changes affecting the status of this 'good father' ideal have not simply been interpreted as involving a rethinking of men's 'role' in the family. They have, importantly, done so through recourse to a language which suggests that what has happened during this recent period can best be made sense of in terms of a transition in *gender relations*. And this is a 'gender-shift' (or 'genderquake') which has, increasingly, been conceptualised as raising some profound questions about men and their 'masculinity', questions which have themselves then served to *politicise* aspects of the paternal (presumed heterosexual) masculinity of the father. Developments such as rising rates of cohabitation and the increasing numbers of births outside marriage, the increased 'visibility' (and thus it is assumed legitimacy) of gay, lesbian and bisexual practices and cultures, the construction of the idea of 'family crisis' across diverse discourses (Midgley and Hughes 1997), as well as a range of concerns around the implications of technological changes transforming reproductive practices (Callahan 1997; Morgan and Lee 1997; Stanworth 1987; Steinberg 1997), have each been interpreted as, variously, undermining, threatening, reconstituting or (more rarely) as providing new opportunities for the 'gendered' practices of men and their 'masculinities' in their role of fathers in the family.

These changes in gender relations, and in particular a much-heralded 'crisis of fatherhood', provide one important context for locating the ways in which recent legal reforms affecting the status, rights and entitlements of fathers have then been played out through reference to this 'crisis of the family' (equals) 'crisis of paternal masculinity' association (cf. Fineman 1995: 201–13). In such a context, and in the light of the above, it may be tempting to interpret the major family law reforms of the recent period as having involved the promotion of a 'new' kind of fatherhood, a model of the 'father as active parent' more in tune with contemporary demographic changes, cultural shifts and gender ideologies. Yet such an interpretation of recent family policy reforms would be, I now wish to argue, at best misleading in a number of respects. What we appear to be dealing with is the emergence of a (largely, it is presumed, benign) 'new fatherhood', an idea of the father as being somehow an 'improvement' on earlier practices and values (such as the father as disciplinarian, the father as emotionally distant, the father as the primary 'breadwinner' and so forth). On closer examination, however, this 'new fatherhood' is revealed as not so much, or not simply, pervaded by a number of profound contradictions and tensions. He is also, on closer examination, perhaps not so 'new' after all.

Sex difference and parental 'responsibility': the inherent contradictions of the 'new' fatherhood

Central to the construction of the paternal (hetero)normativity underlying the new fatherhood ideology is an ambiguous and ultimately contradictory notion of men's familial 'responsibility', the tensions around which can be seen at a number of levels.

Parenthood–fatherhood

First, the relationship between the concepts of 'parenting' and 'fatherhood' is far from clear. In theory the new post-divorce paternal presence underlying the FLA and CA is based on a model of parenting in which some of the tradition-ally gender-specific attributes of fatherhood (authority, discipline, of man as economic 'breadwinner') have each been, if not effaced, then downgraded in importance. Purported gender-neutrality 'cuts' these associations off from the sexed-specificity of it being a *man's* familial presence which is seen necessarily to provide these particular qualities in constituting the familial, whether in relation to household economic provision and/or the socialisation of children. Yet, as

Fineman (1995) has warned, differences in the discursive constructions of motherhood and fatherhood, alongside the fact that men and women come before/to the law as already 'gendered' subjects living 'gendered lives' (Fineman 1995: 47–51), means that family law itself can never be gender neutral. Equality of rules, as feminist scholarship has shown, do not unproblematically map onto equality of outcomes, and the 'myth' of gender-neutrality has itself historically served to reinforce existing inequalities by assuming an equality which does not necessarily exist in practice (Fineman 1991). What we can see in the context of this shifting regulation of post-divorce fatherhood in Britain is in fact something of a tension in this regard. For, at the very moment gender-neutrality is being propounded in the form of a discourse of 'parenting', the familial presence of the father continues to be constituted as desirable in 'official' family law policy (as, indeed, it is within fathers' rights discourse: Collier 1996) in ways which *continue* to rest on reductionist notions of ontological (sexual) difference and normative (hetero)sexuality. Perhaps the clearest manifestation of this continues to be the way in which, within the reformed welfare principle underscoring recent family policy, certain deleterious consequences attached to 'father-absence' continue to be invoked in the name of the well-being of children in some sex-specific ways. Fathers' presumed utility as appropriate 'role models' continues, for example, to be constructed, particularly in cases where there are boy children, in such a way that father-presence, mediated by certain clear sex/gendered assumptions, remains wedded to a functionalist frame and the making of social constructionist presumptions around family, gender and identity; presumptions which have, of course, become increasingly problematic within other discourses.

Parenthood–(hetero)sexuality

Second, there exists a potential contradiction in the legislation (and in particular the FLA) with regard to the relationship between parenthood and heterosexuality. An overarching heteronormativity is both being reasserted and undermined by the recent reforms. On one level heterosexual marriage continues to be central to the privileged and enforced foundational imperative of family law policy. Indeed, it is a clearly articulated and arguably *heightened* support for the institution of marriage which underscores the divorce law reforms of the FLA (Smart and Neale 1997). At the same time, however, in theory at least, this gender-neutral 'new fatherhood' is itself 'divorced' from the heterosexual frame in a number of respects. Within the privileging of active parenting envisaged in the legislation the combination of masculine ontology, sexual division and normative heterosexuality – the trinity which has been so central historically to the discursive constitution of father-presence as socially desirable (Collier 1995) – is displaced as the door is opened to readings of 'transformations of intimacy' which *cannot* be confined to changing contours of heterosexuality and which, importantly, embrace forms of 'confluent love' which do not *have* to be heterosexual (Giddens 1992). Importantly, if it is the case that the 'space' of the heterosexual family is itself being fractured and reformed, and a different kind of space, open to new possibilities and new familial subjects, is being constituted, then the presence of the 'family man' as historical signifier of the familial per se can himself no longer be taken for granted. It is perhaps no wonder, therefore, that both fathers' rights organisations and right-wing 'pro-family' agendas should have each sought to criticise such developments as involving no less than an attack on the institution of heterosexual marriage per se (see, for example, Cheltenham Group 1994).

Parenthood and the 'sexed' negotiation of divorce

Third, and perhaps most significantly in view of the clear social engineering dimensions to these reforms, there exists a further tension within the new fatherhood ideology in relation to a disjuncture between what research suggests would appear to be the *rhetoric surrounding* and the *realities of* parenting. The recent attempts to encourage and regulate post-divorce parenting contained in the CA, FLA and CSA can be seen as running counter in a number of respects to what has been widely identified within sociological scholarship as the pervasive *dissociation* of men from the domain of the familial. By this I do not mean simply that divorce has historically functioned to physically 'separate out' men from a familial sphere in which they had already been, in many ways, constituted as an 'absent' partner (be it physically, because of the demands of work and the cultural pull of the homosocial, or else absent in an emotional sense). Men can be seen as having been dissociated from the familial because of the very ways in which male heterosexuality has *itself* been historically institutionalised in the form of marriage.

To clarify. The provisions of the FLA envisage a sense of reciprocal obligation, duty and familial responsibility which is made manifest in the commitment to legal marriage and, it is assumed, shared parenting. In terms of the discursive structuring of post-divorce fathering, however, this is a commitment which sits uneasily with the sexed/gendered nature of the negotiation of divorce which, empirical studies of fatherhood and family life suggest, tends to entail distinct and differential strategies of 'coping' for women and men. For example, what appears to emerge from the research of Arendell (1995), Lupton and Barclay (1997), Smart and Neal (1997) and others is the existence of a male subject which tends to be configured as unified, solitary and autonomous, a man who ascribes in many ways to 'traditional' notions of gender relations both in and outside marriage relationships, a man who is marked not so much by a connection *to* the familial but by a dissociation *from*, not simply from the expression of individual feelings of vulnerability and powerlessness but also, importantly, the range of material practices associated with the 'everyday living out' of the 'dependencies' which, in Fineman's (1995) terms, inevitably mark the familial sphere. It appears to be, above all, in relation to a differential relationship to/with children in particular that these sexed *as different* negotiations of heterosexual relationships are experienced. Research on 'family life', marriage and divorce suggests a distinct (though by no means clear-cut) contrast between men's and women's experiences in this regard, with it being – importantly – precisely the material and emotional dependencies surrounding child care (and, increasingly, elder care) which tend to mediate women's negotiations at moments of conflict within and at the end of heterosexual relationships (see further Smart 1997, following Griffiths 1995).

In short, although the law may at present be seeking to 'reconstitute' the relationship between men and children in a number of ways, it remains the case that other economic, legal, cultural and social discourses continue to position men as social agents who are, if not effectively free, then at least dissociated in a number of important respects from a range of familial, emotional and material encumbrances in relation to children. Without under-estimating the economic imperatives of advanced capitalist societies, as mediated in specific national and governmental contexts, this cannot be reduced to questions of public provision of child care. Experience across jurisdictions suggests that it is by no means clear that men do assume a greater share of child-care responsibilities even when specific public provision is established (for example, in the form of parental leave). In the UK context, where such structural support is notably lacking, considerable evidence attests to the pervasive and deep-rooted nature of attitudes and behaviour which, notwithstanding the very real changes which have taken place in women's and men's familial roles, continue to reproduce quite traditional sexual divisions of labour. At the very least this pervasive dissociation from the dependencies of the familial calls into question the material realities underlying the rhetoric of the new fatherhood. Current family law policy envisages and seeks a relationship between men and children based on a model of shared parenting. However, the rhetoric and realities of paternal responsibility are by no means the same thing.

Fatherhood as performative practice: men, children and the 'crisis' of the social

Approaching fatherhood as a material, embodied practice in terms of sex difference, as above, involves surfacing the ways in which the gendered experiences of parenting are themselves discursively produced. To integrate questions of sexual difference is *not* to argue that women are somehow inherently or biologically more 'connected' or 'relational' than men. It is, however, to surface the complex, contingent and contested nature of the overarching frame of heterosexual relating in which men and women have *already* been positioned differentially within the material, cultural and emotional discourses which surround ideas of 'family life' (ideas of marriage, parenthood and divorce, for example). Problematising the sociality of the 'heterosexuality' of parenthood, as it were, surfaces the ways in which a particular normative model of fatherhood has itself been constituted via reference to the making of certain assumptions about such issues as paternal presence/absence, about heterosexual marriage, economic status, emotionality and the nature of sexual difference/ontology.

At this point, it becomes possible to (re)read what I have suggested above are some of the inherent contradictions within recent family policy in a way which might seek to transcend the dominant suggestion that such legal reforms can usefully be conceptualised as being either 'pro' or 'against' the 'family', fatherhood or motherhood, men or women; as either (and as necessarily) 'empowering' or 'disempowering' specific groups and/or individuals. To approach family policy in this way is not to efface the undoubted political dimensions of the reforms. Far from it, it is to seek to reconceptualise the very categories and systems of thought through which ideas of change (be it of progress, regress) have been understood historically in the field of family law. Far from the new family policy 'pulling away from' or failing to recognise, as it were, complex social change in an 'unhelpful' 'tinkering', one consequence of which is then seen to be a defence of the 'traditional' family – broadly, Smart's (1997) argument – it is possible to see these tensions as resulting from a profound shift not so much (or not just) in the concept of fatherhood, but also in relation to a broader and multi-layered reconceptualisation of both heterosexuality and *childhood* itself. And such a change in the concept of the child has had a particularly heightened resonance for men who, we have seen, have already been positioned as 'masculine' within modernity as being in many ways apart from the familial sphere. One result has been the surfacing of some profoundly difficult questions about fatherhood at a time when a series of contradictory demands are increasingly being placed on men as fathers – to both 'provide' for and to 'nurture', to 'work *on*' and 'be with' (as active parent) and yet to 'work *for*' (as breadwinner) – the experiences of each of which are then mediated by a 'gendered life' in which not only has the meaning of the 'masculine' increasingly come to float free from established sources of heterosexual masculine identity (with all the attendant ontological insecurities this entails) but in which the transition into and status secured by 'being a father' has itself become, in so many ways, an uncertain site from which to ground men's experiences 'as a man'.

On 'doing' fatherhood: ontological (in)security and the postmodern child

To clarify the nature of this reconceptualisation of the childhood/fatherhood association. In the negotiation of or straining towards what is seen as being a 'good father', and in seeking to establish and assert identities *as men*, the notion of gender performativity (Butler 1990, 1993) within postmodern theories of the subject can be seen as linking in some respects to Giddens (1991) suggestion that, within late modernity, a prerequisite of what he terms 'confluent love' is an engagement with the 'project of the self'; that is, a making and re-making of the self at different stages of the life-course. Conceptualising men negotiating fatherhood (whether as first-time fathers,

fathers in ongoing relationships with partners or as fathers on divorce) as subjects 'in process' engaged in a gendered reflexive project is lent a further resonance when it is recognised that contemporary changes around the idea of fatherhood are taking place at a time of heightened anxieties around the meaning and status of the 'masculine' per se within Western cultures. For the individual man the experience of fatherhood may be inextricably bound up with the desire for authenticity and for a 'true' masculine self (a 'proof' of manhood) which may well have a particular ontological resonance (a resonance further mediated by issues around class, 'race'/ethnicity, sexuality, fertility, 'potency' and physical ability).

Yet, crucially, this is a gendered performative project which is taking place at a time in which the figure of the child has itself come to assume a particular importance within a range of discourses concerned with the maintenance and security of the social bond. Indeed, the concept of the child within postmodern cultural configurations has been increasingly identified as being the site for the relocation of a variety of discourses concerned with questions of stability, integration, and the maintenance of sociality (note, in particular, the work of Beck 1992; Beck and Beck Gernsheim 1995; James and Prout 1990; Qvortrup 1995: see, more generally, Brannen and O'Brien 1995; Gittins 1998; James *et al.* 1998; Jenks 1996; Qvortrup *et al.* 1994). Given the demographic changes presently taking place in household structures at the end of the twentieth century, and the many dimensions to the 'crisis of the family' discussed above, it is perhaps unsurprising that an acceleration in the intensity, purchase and currency of emotions centred round the idea of the 'fragmenting' heterosexual family should have then assumed such a central significance in understandings of how women's and men's experiences of the 'social' are grounded in the first place. In such a context the heightening of a range of economic, cultural and sexual anxieties around men's and women's respective 'gender roles', both within and beyond 'the family', can be seen as not only reflecting the privileged position of the heterosexual family per se within modernity as 'the locus for the confluence of politics and individual psychology...the primary unit for, and also the site of, governmentality; that is, it both absorbs and, in turn, distributes social control' (Jenks 1996: 14; Donzelot 1980; Rose 1996; Collier 1995, 77–80). What is *also* becoming apparent is that a complex range of diverse social, cultural and economic reconfigurations are also presently connecting this fragmenting family with a set of more general concerns around the issues of men, masculinity and heterosexuality as discussed above. And, in so doing, the reconceptualisation of the child-childhood has *itself* become inextricably bound up with the discursive constitution of the 'family crisis' *as* 'paternal masculine' crisis idea because of the ways in which both fatherhood and childhood have been *mutually* discursively constituted in the first place. Within the conditions of postmodernity, and as the relationship between adults and children becomes seen as contested a terrain as the breach of the social itself, between a more general search for ontological security and existential anxiety (Jenks 1996: 17; Giddens 1991) what appear as contestations around childhood are thus reformed as questions about the (re)constitution of the social (on the James Bulger murder trial, see King 1995; Morrison 1997). No wonder, perhaps, that 'father-absence' should then assume such iconic status, be it in relation to broader concerns around child welfare, crime and delinquency, family breakdown and social (dis)order.[2]

To return to the question of sexual difference, gendered performativity and the embodiment of fatherhood, it is in the context of this reconceptualisation of childhood that changes within the ideology of 'care' implicit in the now dominant notion of gender-neutral parenting can be seen as playing out differently for men and women. Men and women have been positioned very differently in relation to both children and child care within the discourses of modernity, their experiences of 'inevitable dependencies' (Fineman 1995) differentially constituted in terms of sexed embodiment and gendered lives. This is not to argue that the parenting practices of men and women may not significantly 'overlap' in terms of form, function and emotionality (see further, on the 'feminine' qualities of fatherhood, Lupton and Barclay 1997). It is to argue, however, that in the gendering of this ideology of care what emerges is a masculine subject which, as we have seen above, has already been constituted in many ways as Other to children/child care, beyond the primary men/child nexus of economic provider and socialising role model. It is not 'adults' but primarily mothers who have been (and continue to be) routinely depicted as 'sacrificing everything' for their children, women who are judged, held responsible and who are seen as having 'failed' or 'succeeded' in the acting out of this duty of care. Fathers, in contrast, have been constituted 'as' familial in other ways and through reference to other discourses.

There is, in effect, a fundamental paradox at the heart of the 'new fatherhood' ideology. The values of autonomy, control and separateness through which cultural understandings of the 'masculine' continue to be made sit most uneasily with the qualities of the 'everyday' nurturing and sacrifice implicit in the 'new fatherhood' ideology. It should not surprise, therefore, that the reconfiguration of the meaning of the 'familial' is surfacing as problematic that which has hitherto been unspoken, natural, inviolable, and unquestioned: *the relationship between men and children*. In so doing, social problems which had hitherto been understood within modernity in terms of 'broken' families, broken communities and broken solidarities are themselves re-emerging as questions about such issues as father-absence, the 'crisis' of masculinity and questions of 'What are fathers for?' (and, for some, 'What are *men* for?') The crisis of the family (equals) crisis of fatherhood association may have deep historical roots. Yet what we appear to be witnessing at the present moment is a fundamental challenge to both a model of fatherhood and an ideology of care which, throughout the twentieth century, has been premised on a sexual division of labour which 'lubricated and legitimised the investment of economic and cultural capital in the "promise" of childhood' (Jenks 1996: 15). At the present moment both the concepts of the *child* and *fatherhood* are being transformed in the face of changing sexual subjectivities, employment structures, cultural formations and political realignments. Given the centrality of the figure of the child to the constitution of gendered experiences of the material and emotional dependencies which surround heterosexual relating more generally, it is perhaps also unsurprising that it has been in negotiations around conflicts over children at the point of relationship breakdown that the nature of these shifting 'gender differences' should have surfaced as one of the most contested and problematic issues of family law reform. In a context in which 'the enhanced interest in men's relationship to children and of men in children' grows (Jenks 1996: 20), and where the construction of both fatherhood and (hetero) masculinities are being subjected to increasing critical scrutiny, it is the iconic status of the (postmodern) child which has become the disputed territory in which this more general assessment of the contribution of men to the social is taking place.

Conclusions: what is the 'family' – on fantasising the 'family' man

In this chapter I have explored some of the contours of the reconfiguration of heterosexual social relations which are presently taking place within British family law policy. Particular attention has been paid to the changing signifi- cances accorded to the relationship between men and children. I have sought to counterpose readings which have privileged the idea of a 'crisis of the family' (equals) 'crisis of masculinity' association with an approach which has sought to problematise the mutual discursive constitution of heterosexuality, fatherhood and the familial. I have argued that a reconfiguration of the child has been central to the construction of the 'new' fatherhood implicit in this family law policy. Within the context of current debates taking place around divorce reform (FLA), child support (CSA) and parental rights and responsibilities (CA) the concept of fatherhood has assumed an emblematic status. Yet disputes around fatherhood have long been a cipher for other anxieties, fears and concerns around the changing contours of heterosexual relating. In engaging with the discursive construction of the heterosexual subject it becomes possible to identify some of the significant contradictions which exist within the recent family policy, tensions which, I have argued, serve potentially (and ironically) to undermine some quite traditional conceptions of marriage and fatherhood, at the very moment they are seeking to reassert them.

It is ultimately around the question of 'What constitutes the familial?' that the family policy/legal arena can usefully be conceptualised as a site of confrontation on a number of different issues around heterosexuality. Just as 'law desires' 'the production through discourse of the figure of the homosexual – sadomasochistic, polluted, addicted to his desires, self-destructive, and yet terrifyingly seductive' (Stychin 1996: 139) – so too (though in very different ways) does the discursive constitution of a 'heterosexual' norm reveal at the very moment of its constitution the contingency of heterosexual identity and the sociality of the hetero-/homosexual binary itself (Stychin 1996: 53). In constructing, in *fantasising* (Walkerdine 1995: 325) the 'family man', the law continues to 'desire' the 'good father' as the embodiment of a 'masculine' heterosexual norm. And in so doing male heterosexuality continues to be disciplined and regulated through a discursive inscribing of sameness and difference in terms of the naturalised binary divisions of modernity.

To conclude and summarise the main points of my argument. First, the concept of fatherhood is inherently vague. It is fluid and open-ended. It has historically signified different things at different moments and in differing contexts. Within the family policy debates which have taken place during the past thirty years or so fathers have appeared within a range of discourses as, variously, 'Casanova's' and 'Lotharios' (*c.* 1969–73: see further O'Donovan 1993), as 'beleaguered' and 'put upon' husbands, as 'wholesome' and 'errant fathers', as 'good fathers', 'absent fathers', 'feckless fathers' and 'deadbeat dads' (on the CSA see Collier 1994; Diduck 1995; Mitchell and Goody 1997; Smith 1997; Wallbank 1997; Westwood 1996) and, less visibly though increasingly, as 'dangerous' or 'abusing' fathers (Morgan, 1994). These changing ideas of men's familial and paternal subjectivities draw on and map onto shifts in wider cultural understandings of 'masculinity', discourses which are themselves located in the market imperatives of advanced capitalism (Mort 1996).

Second, and following on from the above, the contemporary cognitive, ethical and aesthetic reconfiguration of the men/gender relation – indeed, the individual and collective experience of *being* a man in Western society – increasingly appears to bespeak crisis, contestation and resistance at a number of levels. Refigurations of the 'family man' within recent debates around family policy are no exception. Across Western countries at the end of the twentieth century judgements of heterosexual 'manliness' have become increasingly dispersed, fragmented and de-traditionalised as the meaning of the masculine has come to float free from some established sources (the 'good father', the breadwinner, the sexually potent man). The 'male role' of modernity has, in short, become an unreliable position from which to ground emotion as men's achievement and status (Hearn 1996) – those previously indelible markers of social experience – have become relativised through the pressure of economic and cultural shifts (not the least of which has been the impact of feminism and women's increased entry into the work place).

Third, the analysis of the 'heterosexuality' of 'fatherhood' presented in this chapter reveals a male subject encoded *as familial* produced and sustained by interwoven discourses of sexuality and gender which are themselves rooted in the dualistic configurations pervading liberal legal thought. The model of the 'new' fatherhood which has emerged during the 1980s and 1990s continues to embody normative presumptions about 'family', marriage and sexuality which only make sense in terms of the hierarchic binaries which have constituted (hetero)sexual difference in the first place. In seeking to move beyond the theoretical parameters of current debates I have sought in this chapter to locate the present central, iconic status of fatherhood in relation to some broader transformations taking place around the relationship between men and children.

'Masculinity' and 'fatherhood' do not exist on desert islands; they are defined relationally and discursively, always in relation to femininities, motherhood and, I have suggested, childhood. Importantly, this 'fatherhood' in/of legal discourse actively participates in the construction of 'men', involving a 'way of seeing' that is constructed hegemonically through the mobilisation and consolidation of various practices and the exclusion of others. In exploring the 'good father' in law this chapter has sought to explore how legal struggles over meanings about gender are reproduced, legitimised and refashioned.

Fourth, and finally, let us be clear. Underlying present family policy is not a concern to challenge those existing social structures which continue to sustain and promote such separations. In Britain there has been little attempt to structure support for joint-parenting *in* marriage, let alone any attempt to enhance the possibilities to combine work and family through any comprehensive system of public services. Fathers in Britain work longer hours than in any other European country (*The Times* 9 June 1997). Nor, importantly, has there been any engagement with the conceptual basis of the 'private' family itself in any way which might seek, in moving beyond the traditional hierarchical meanings of fatherhood to

> forge social and political meanings that are corollaries to the challenges presented by single mothers...and to recognize the need for systemic societal reform to address inevitable dependencies. To be a nurturing father is to concede the importance of mothering.
>
> (Fineman 1995: 205)

Far from engaging in any 'deconstruction' of the family the aim is, as the FLA 1996 makes all too clear, to reproduce quite traditional norms of heterosexual monogamous marriage and the dominance of heterosexuality in public discourse and institutional arrangements through the use of what is in effect moral invective and individualist explanation.

What we continue to be dealing with, in short, is a model of a familial legal unit premised on the privileging of the sexual affective relationship between a biological man and a woman over and above all others. It is not, for example, as Fineman (1995) observes, the mother–child dyad which is taken as ascribing any privileged legal status in denoting the meaning of the familial. It is, rather, a (hetero)sexual relationship which continues to constitute a 'proper' legal marriage, the 'proper' and 'natural' family. However, and in speaking of the hitherto hidden pains and suffering of this heterosexual familial, it is other, dissident voices which continue to surface hitherto subjugated knowledges and, in so doing, fundamentally challenge, undermine and reconfigure understandings of what the 'safe' 'normal' and familial heterosexual male subject has historically been taken to signify in the first place. These may be voices far from the mainstream of political debate; and, certainly, family law, social policy and legal studies remain places in so many ways set apart from those forms of politics which seek to break down the fixed boundaries which presently

constitute the contours of the 'familial',[3] of 'family law'. And yet, I have argued
in this chapter, it may well be that it is in looking 'outwith' these taken for
granted understandings of 'family values', towards the boundaries of 'law' and
the 'family', that it might ultimately be possible to seek to dissolve the
categories of 'the family' itself, insisting that 'queer' itself is not some bounded
community, or not only so, but is 'everywhere' (Johnson 1997: 9). In seeking
to question the meaning of 'family values' at the end of the twentieth century
such a 'queering' of the heterosexual family may, I have suggested, be a most
productive place to start.

Notes

1 An earlier version of this paper was presented to the 'Gendered Persons and
   Communities in Nordic Legal Discourse' conference, Helsinki, Finland, November
   1997 and the 'Socio Legal Studies Association Annual Conference', Manchester,
   England, April 1998. I would like to thank all who participated in discussion for their
   comments. I am particularly indebted to conversations with, and the written comments provided by, Shelley Day Sclater on aspects of the argument.
2 A recurring theme in this work has been to surface the emblematic status of the child
   as the 'last remaining, irrevocable, unexchangable primary relationship. Partners
   come and go. The child stays. Everything that is desired, but is not realisable in the
   relationship, is directed to the child....The child has become the final alternative to
   loneliness that can be built up against the vanishing possibilities of love. It is a private
   type of re-enchantment, which arises with, and derives its meaning from, disen-
   chantment' (Beck 1992: 118, quoted by Jenks 1996: 20).
3 One text which does seek to break down the boundaries between the sociology of
   the family and other areas of sociological study is Morgan's *Family Connections*
   (1996), which argues that not only can families and what goes on inside them be
   better understood by using insights from other areas of sociology, but that an
   exploration of family practices is essential for the development of a fuller understanding of other areas of social life. Whilst it is feminism which has opened up the study
   of families in this way, it remains the case that the various sub-divisions of 'legal
   studies' remain broadly impervious to such issues.

Bibliography

Archbishop of Canterbury's Group (1966) *Putting Asunder: A Divorce Law For
    Contemporary Society*, London: SPCK.
Arendell, T. (1995) *Fathers and Divorce*, London: Sage.
Beck, U. (1992) *Risk Society: Towards a New Modernity*, London: Sage.
Beck, U. and Beck Gernsheim, E. (1995) *The Normal Chaos of Love*, Cambridge: Polity.
Bell, D. and Valentine, G. (1995) 'The Sexed Self: Strategies of Performance, Sites of
    Resistance' in S. Pile and N. Thrift (eds) *Mapping the Subject: Geographies of Cultural
    Transformation*, Routledge: London.
Berotia, C. and Drakich, J. (1993) 'The Fathers' Rights Movement: contradictions in
    rhetoric and practice', *Journal of Family Issues* 14(4): 592–615.
Bonnett, A (1996) ' "White Studies" The problems and projects of a new research
    agenda', *Theory, Culture and Society* 13(2): 144–55.

Brannen, J. and O'Brien, M. (1995) (eds) *Childhood and Parenthood: Proceedings of the International Sociological Association Committee for Family Research Conference*, London: Institute of Education.

Brittan, A. (1989) *Masculinity and Power*, Oxford: Blackwell.

Burgess, A. (1997) *Fatherhood Reclaimed*, London: Vermilion.

Burgess, A. and Ruxton, S. (1996) *Men and Their Children: Proposals for Public Policy*, London: Institute for Public Policy Research.

Burghes, L., Clarke, L. and Cronin, N. (1997) *Fathers and Fatherhood in Britain*, London: Family Policy Studies Centre.

Butler, J. (1990) *Gender Trouble: Feminism and the Subversion of Identity*, London: Routledge.

—— (1993) *Bodies That Matter: On the Discursive Limits of Sex*, London: Routledge.

Callahan, S. (1997) 'Gays, lesbians and the use of alternate reproductive technologies' in H. L. Nelson (ed.) *Feminism and Families*, London: Routledge.

Campbell, B. (1996) 'Big Bad Dad', *The Guardian* 25 June 1996.

Carabine, J. (1996a) 'Heterosexuality and social policy' in D. Richardson (ed.) *Theorising Heterosexuality: Telling it Straight*, Buckingham: Open University Press.

—— (1996b) 'A straight playing field or queering the pitch? Centring sexuality in social policy', *Feminist Review* 54 (Autumn): 31–64.

Carrigan, T., Connell, R. and Lee, J. (1985) 'Towards a New Sociology of Masculinity', *Theory and Society* 14: 551–604.

Cheltenham Group (1994) *Restoring Legal Marriage*, Cheltenham: The Cheltenham Group.

Collier, R. (1994) 'The Campaign Against the Child Support Act 1991: "Errant Fathers" and "Family Men" ', *Family Law* July: 384–7.

—— (1995) *Masculinity, Law and the Family*, London: Routledge.

—— (1996) ' "Coming Together?": Post-Heterosexuality, Masculine Crisis and the New Men's Movement', *Feminist Legal Studies* 4(1): 3–48.

—— (1998) *Masculinities, Crime and Criminology: Men, Heterosexuality and the Criminal(ised) Other*, London: Sage.

Coltrane, S. and Allan, K. (1994) ' "New" fathers and old stereotypes: representations of masculinity in 1980s television advertising', *Masculinities* 2(4): 43–66.

Connell, R. W. (1987) *Gender and Power*, Cambridge: Polity Press.

—— (1995) *Masculinities*, Cambridge: Polity Press.

Coote, A. (1994) *Families, Children and Crime*, London: IPPR Publishers.

Coward, R. (1996) 'Make the father figure', *The Guardian* 12 April 1996.

Crockett, L. J., Eggebeen, D. J. and Hawkins, A. J. (1993) 'Fathers' presence and young children's behavioural and cognitive adjustment', *Journal of Family Issues* 14(3): 355–77.

Dench, G. (1996) *Exploring Variations in Men's Family Roles: Joseph Rowntree Foundation Social Policy Research Findings No. 99*, London: Joseph Rowntree Foundation.

Dennis, N. and Erdos, G. (1993) *Families Without Fatherhood*, London: Institute of Economic Affairs.

Diduck, A. (1995) 'The unmodified family: The Child Support Act and the construction of legal subjects', *Journal of Law and Society* 22(4): 527–48.

Dingwall, R., Greatbach, D. and Ruggerone, L. (1996) 'Divorce Mediation: Micro-Studies and Macro-Issues', Paper delivered to the Law and Society Association Annual Meeting, Glasgow, 10–13 July.

Donzelot, J. (1980) *The Policing of Families*, London: Hutchinson.
Doyle, R. F. (1996) *The Men's/Fathers Movement and Divorce Assistance Operation Manual: History, Philosophy, Operation*, New York: Men's Defence Association, Poor Richard's Press.
Eekelaar, J. (1978) *Family Law and Social Policy*, London: Weidenfeld and Nicolson.
—— (1984) *Family Law and Social Policy* (second edition), London: Weidenfeld and Nicolson.
Fineman, M. A. (1991) *The Illusion of Equality: The Rhetoric and Reality of Divorce Reform*, Chicago: University of Chicago Press.
—— (1995) *The Neutered Mother, The Sexual Family and Other Twentieth-Century Tragedies*, New York: Routledge.
Fineman, M. A. and Karpin, I. (1995) (eds) *Mothers in Law: Feminist Theory and the Legal Regulation of Motherhood*, New York: Columbia University Press.
Foster, P. (1993) 'Are men now suffering from gender injustice?' in A. Sinfield (ed.) *Poverty, Inequality and Justice: New Waverly Papers, Social Policy Series No. 6*, Edinburgh: University of Edinburgh Press.
French, S. (1992) (ed.) *Fathers and Sons*, London: Faber.
Gardiner, J. K. (1998) 'Feminism and the future of fathering' in T. Digby (ed.) *Men Doing Feminism*, New York: Routledge.
Giddens, A. (1991) *Modernity and Self-Identity*, Cambridge: Polity.
—— (1992) *The Transformation of Intimacy*, Cambridge: Polity.
Gittins, D. (1998) *The Child in Question*, London: Macmillan.
Griffiths, M. (1995) *Feminisms and the Self: The Web of Identity*, London: Routledge.
Hall, W. (1994) 'New fatherhood: myths and realities', *Public Health Nursing* 11(4): 219–28.
Harrison, F. (1987) *A Winter's Tale*, London: Collins.
Hearn, J. (1987) *The Gender of Oppression: Men, Masculinity and the Critique of Marxism*, Brighton: Harvester Wheatsheaf.
—— (1996) 'Is masculinity dead? A critique of the concept of masculinity' in M. Mac an Ghaill (ed.) *Understanding Masculinities*, Buckingham: Open University Press.
Henriques, J., Hollway, W., Urwin, C., Venn, C. and Walkerdine, V. (1984) *Changing the Subject: Psychology, Social Regulation and Subjectivity*, London: Methuen.
Hollway, W. (1989) *Subjectivity and Method in Psychology: Gender, Meaning and Science*, London: Sage.
—— (1995a) 'A second bite at the heterosexual cherry', *Feminism and Psychology* 5(1): 126–30.
—— (1995b) 'Feminist discourses and women's heterosexual desire' in S. Wilkinson and C. Kitzinger (eds) *Feminism and Discourse*, London: Sage.
—— (1996) 'Recognition and heterosexual desire' in D. Richardson (ed.) *Theorising Heterosexuality: Telling it Straight*, Buckingham: Open University Press.
Jackson, S. (1996) 'Heterosexuality and Feminist Theory' in D. Richardson (ed.) *Theorising Heterosexuality: Telling it Straight*, Buckingham: Open University Press.
James, A., Jenks, C. and Prout, A. (1998) *Theorizing Childhood*, London: Polity.
James, A. and Prout, A. (1990) (eds) *Constructing and Reconstructing Childhood*, London: Falmer Press.
Jenks, C. (1996) *Childhood*, London: Routledge.
Johnson, R. (1997) 'Contested Borders, Contingent Lives' in D. L. Steinberg, D. Epstein and R. Johnson (eds) *Border Patrols: Policing the Boundaries of Heterosexuality*, London: Cassell.

King, M. (1995) 'The James Bulger Murder Trial: Moral dilemmas, and social solutions', *The International Journal of Children's Rights* 3: 167–87.

Law Commission (1966) *Report on the Reform of the Grounds of Divorce: The Field of Choice*, No. 6, London: HMSO.

Lewis, C. (1986) *Becoming a Father*, Milton Keynes: Open University Press.

Lewis, C. and O'Brien, M. (1987) *Reassessing Fatherhood: New Observations on Fathers and the Modern Family*, London: Sage.

Lord Chancellor's Department (1998) *Court Procedures for the Determination of Paternity: The Law on Parental Responsibility for Unmarried Fathers – Consultation Paper*, London: Lord Chancellor's Department.

Lupton, D. and Barclay, L. (1997) *Constructing Fatherhood: Discourses and Experiences*, London: Sage.

Maynard, M. and Purvis, J. (1995) *(Hetero)Sexual Politics*, London: Taylor and Francis.

McKee, L. and O'Brien, M. (1982) 'The father figure: some current orientations and historical perspectives' in L. McKee and M. O'Brien (eds) *The Father Figure*, London: Tavistock.

Messner, M. (1997) *The Politics of Masculinities: Men in Movements*, London: Sage.

Midgley, M. and Hughes, J. (1997) 'Are families out of date?' in H. L. Nelson (ed.) *Feminism and Families*, London: Routledge.

Mitchell, J. and Goody, J. (1997) 'Feminism, fatherhood and the family in Britain' in A. Oakley and J. Mitchell (eds) *Who's Afraid of Feminism? Seeing Through the Backlash*, London: Hamish Hamilton.

Morgan, D. (1994) 'The "Family Man": A Contradiction in Terms?', *Fifth Jacqueline Burgoyne Memorial Lecture*, February: Sheffield Hallam University.

—— (1996) *Family Connections: An Introduction to Family Studies*, Oxford: Polity Press.

Morgan, D. and Lee, R. G. (1997) 'In the name of the father? Ex Parte Blood: Dealing with Novelty and Anomaly', *Modern Law Review* 60(6): 840–56.

Morgan, P. (1995) *Farewell to the Family?*, London: Institute of Economic Affairs.

Morrison, B. (1997) *As If*, London: Granta Books.

Mort, F. (1996) *Cultures of Consumption: Masculinities and Social Space in late Twentieth-Century Britain*, London: Routledge.

Murray, C. (1984) *Losing Ground*, New York: Basic Books.

—— (1990) *The Emerging British Underclass* (with responses by Frank Field, Joan C. Brown, Nicholas Deakin, and Alan Walker), London: IEA Health and Welfare Unit.

O'Donovan, K. (1985) *Sexual Divisions in Law*, London: Weidenfeld and Nicolson.

—— (1993) *Family Law Matters*, London: Pluto.

Osherson, S. (1996) *The Passions of Fatherhood*, Sydney: Harper Perennial.

Pederson, A. and O'Mara, P. (1990) (eds) *Being a Father: Family, Work and Self*, Santa Fe, NM: John Muir.

Piper, C. (1996) 'Divorce Reform and the Image of the Child', *Journal of Law and Society* 23(3): 364–82.

Prendergast, S. and Forrest, S. (1997) 'Hieroglyphs of the heterosexual: learning about gender in school' in L. Segal (ed.) *New Sexual Agendas*, London: Macmillan.

Probyn, E. (1993) *Sexing the Self: Gendered Positions in Cultural Studies*, London: Routledge.

Qvortrup, J. (1995) 'Childhood and modern society: a paradoxical relationship?' in J. Brannen and M. O'Brien (eds) *Childhood and Parenthood*, London: Institute of Education.

Qvortrup, J., Bardy, M., Sgritta, G. and Wintersberger, H. (1994) (eds) *Childhood Matters: Social Theory, Practices and Politics*, Aldershot: Avebury Press.

Reinhold, S. (1994) 'Through the parliamentary looking glass: "real" and "pretend" families in contemporary British politics', *Feminist Review* 48: 61–79.

Richards, M. P. M. (1986) 'Behind the best interests of the child: an examination of the arguments of Goldstein, Freud and Solnit concerning custody and access at divorce', *Journal of Social Welfare Law* 77–95.

—— (1996) 'The socio-legal support for divorcing parents and their children' in B. Bernstein and J. Brannen (eds) *Children, Research and Policy*, London: Taylor and Francis.

Richardson, D, (1996) (ed.) *Theorising Heterosexuality: Telling it Straight*, Buckingham: Open University Press.

Robinson, V. (1996) 'Heterosexuality and Masculinity: Theorising Male Power or the Wounded Male Psyche?' in D. Richardson (ed.) *Theorising Heterosexuality*, Buckingham: Open University Press.

Roche, J. (1996) 'The politics of children's rights' in J. Brannen and M. O'Brien (eds) *Children in Families: Research and Policy*, London: Falmer Press.

Rose, N. (1987) 'Transcending the Public/Private', *Journal of Law and Society* 14(1): 61–75.

—— (1996) *Inventing Our Selves: Psychology, Power and Personhood*, Cambridge: Cambridge University Press.

Ruddick, S. (1997) 'The idea of fatherhood' in H. L. Nelson (ed.) *Feminism and Families*, London: Routledge.

Samuels, A. (1997) 'Therapy as think tank: from a man's internal family to new political forms' in L. Segal (ed.) *New Sexual Agendas*, London: Macmillan.

Sears, W. (1990) 'Foreword' in A. Pederson and P. O'Mara (eds) *Being a Father: Family, Work and Self*, Santa Fe, NM: John Muir.

Sedgwick, E. (1994) *Epistemology of the Closet*, Hemel Hempstead: Harvester Wheatsheaf.

Segal, L. (1994) *Straight Sex: the Politics of Pleasure*, London: Virago.

—— (1997) 'Feminist sexual politics and the heterosexual predicament' in L. Segal (ed.) *New Sexual Agendas*, London: Macmillan.

Seltzer, J. A. (1994) 'Consequences of marital dissolution for children', *Annual Review of Sociology* 20: 235–66.

Showalter, E. (1992) *Sexual Anarchy* London: Virago.

Silva, E. (1996) (ed.) *Good Enough Mothering? Feminist Perspectives on Lone Motherhood*, London: Routledge.

Smart, C. (1984) *The Ties That Bind*, London: Routledge and Kegan Paul.

—— (1996a) 'Collusion, Collaboration and Confession on Moving Beyond the Heterosexuality Debate' in D. Richardson (ed.) *Theorising Heterosexuality: Telling it Straight*, Buckingham: Open University.

—— (1996b) 'Desperately Seeking Post-Heterosexual Woman' in J. Holland and L. Adkins (eds) *Sex, Sensibility and the Gendered Body*, London: Macmillan.

—— (1997) 'Wishful thinking and harmful; tinkering? Sociological reflections on family policy', *Journal of Social Policy* 26(3): 301–21.

Smart, C. and Brophy, J. (1985) (eds) *Women in Law: Explorations in Law, Family, Sexuality*, London: Routledge and Kegan Paul.

Smart, C. and Neale, B. (1997) 'Good enough morality? Divorce and postmodernity', *Critical Social Policy* 17(4): 3–27.

Smith, R. (1997) 'Paying the penalty: the impact of the Child Support Act', *Critical Social Policy* 53: 111–19.

Speak, S., Cameron, S. and Gilroy, R. (1997) *Young Single Fathers; Participation in Fatherhood – Bridges and Barriers*, London: Family Policy Studies Centre.

Stanworth, M. (1987) (ed.) *Reproductive Technologies*, Cambridge: Polity Press.

Steinberg, D. L. (1997) 'Eugenic reproductions under glass' in D. L. Steinberg, D. Epstein and R. Johnson (eds) *Border Patrols: Policing the Boundaries of Heterosexuality*, London: Cassell.

Steinberg, D. L., Epstein, D. and Johnson, R. (eds) (1997) *Border Patrols: Policing the Boundaries of Heterosexuality*, London: Cassell.

Stowe, D. W. (1996) 'Uncoloured people: The rise of whiteness studies', *Lingua Franca* September/October: 68–77.

Stychin, C. (1996) *Law's Desire*, London: Routledge.

Utting, D. (1995) *Family and Parenthood: Supporting Families, Preventing Breakdown: Social Policy Summary 4*, London: Joseph Rowntree Foundation.

Waldby, C. (1995) 'Destruction: boundary erotics and refigurations of the heterosexual male body' in E. Grosz and E. Probyn (eds) *Sexy Bodies: The Strange Carnalities of Feminism*, London: Routledge.

Walkerdine, V. (1995) 'Subject to change without notice: Psychology, postmodernity and the popular' in S. Pile and N. Thrift (eds) *Mapping the Subject: Geographies of Cultural Transformation*, London: Routledge.

Wallbank, J. (1997) 'The campaign for change of the Child Support Act 1991: Reconstituting the "absent" father', *Social and Legal Studies* 6(2): 191–216.

Walters, S. (1992) *Lives Together/Worlds Apart: Mothers and Daughters in Popular Culture*, Berkeley, CA: University of California Press.

Warner, M. (1993) (ed.) *Fear of a Queer Planet*, Minneapolis: University of Minnesota Press.

Westwood, S. (1996) ' "Feckless fathers": masculinities and the British state' in M. Mac an Ghaill (ed.) *Understanding Masculinities*, Buckingham: Open University Press.

Wilkinson, S. and Kitzinger, C. (1993) (eds) *Heterosexuality: A Feminism and Psychology Reader*, London: Sage.

Wittig, M. (1992) *The Straight Mind and Other Essays*, Brighton: Harvester Wheatsheaf.

3   Will boys be left on the shelf?

Sue Lees

Contemporary moral posturing around the changing family throws little light on why the traditional family is changing. It neglects to take into account the major transformations in the patterns and forms of employment in recent years, with the decline of respectable working-class male employment in manufacturing and the rise of the service sector, where employers find it more profitable to employ women part-time workers. The growth of flexible, part-time work using new technology has replaced the older manual jobs in a growing service-based economy. In real terms young working-class men have lost ground in the past decade and some face permanent unemployment.

This chapter examines the impact of the loss of young men's monopoly of the breadwinner role on young women's and men's attitudes to the family, in the light of the increased economic activity of mothers, wives and single women, in some cases in traditional male spheres of employment (see Lees 1986, 1993; Mirza 1992; Prendergast and Forest 1997; Sharpe 1976, 1994; Stafford 1991; Willis 1977). Drawing on a number of small-scale British studies based on the oral testimonies of adolescent young women and men undertaken in the 1980s, I consider what effect these economic changes have had on the attitudes of young men and, as the other side of the coin, what effect they have had on young women's attitudes and aspirations. This chapter does not attempt to answer these questions definitively, but merely to present some preliminary findings. To what extent changing attitudes lead to a change in behaviour is clearly contentious, but by sketching out some statistical trends regarding changes in marriage and divorce, it does appear that there is a connection. I suggest that young (heterosexual) men in the 1990s may be 'left on the shelf' in two senses: by not being able to find work and by failing to get married.

Background

Parsons and Bales (1956), American sociologists of the 1950s, regarded the family as a crucial stabilising factor in modern capitalist society, with the man's role being seen as 'instrumental' as the breadwinner and the woman's role as 'expressive' in providing domestic and child-care services. Whatever salience this model may once have had, it is not useful in the 1990s. In Britain over the period 1952–92 women have moved from 31 to 45 per cent of the labour force (see Witz 1993). While the trend to increasing female employment runs in the opposite direction to increasing male unemployment, they are, of course, both reflections of a single process of economic change. Willott and Griffin (1996) show that it is the changing patterns of unemployment amongst young working-class women and men which have had profound effects on heterosexual and marital relationships, rather than any breakdown in morality. Work opportunities (albeit in low-paid work) for young women have increased and are consequently changing their expectations of the future roles both of themselves and of men in the family.

Over the last twenty years, the number of marriages has fallen (Haskey 1995). The increase in the proportion of women aged under 50 who have been living outside a partnership increased from under one-quarter in 1979 to almost a third in 1993. The number of women who have cohabited before marriage has also risen tenfold in a generation from about 5 per cent in the mid-1960s to 50 per cent today. The number of first marriages almost halved from a peak of 340,000 in 1970 to 182,000 in 1993, the lowest since 1889, despite a much larger population. Heterosexual couples are marrying later and divorcing sooner. Cohabitation prior to marriage is the norm. Some couples regard their partnerships as a 'trial marriage' but others reject the institution of marriage altogether.

According to HMSO population trends, these changes are already affecting the traditional family and it is the youngest age groups – those in their twenties – which have shown the greatest changes in patterns of marriage and cohabitation. This suggests that the proportions cohabiting will tend to increase whilst those married will tend to decline. More children are born out of wedlock than ever before. Births outside marriage rose from 54,000 in 1961 to 236,000 in 1991, and births within marriage fell from 890,000 in 1961 to 556,000 in 1991. According to Kiernan and Wicks (1990), by the year 2000 it may be that as few as half of all children will have spent their lives in a conventional two-parent family with both their natural parents. This move away from the 'traditional' family is clearly differentiated by gender, as it is wives who are most likely to sue for divorce. It may well be that they are less likely than men to remarry following divorce, although this question needs substantiating.

It is argued that the changing structure of employment is creating an identity crisis for some men who have been encouraged to see the breadwinner role as central to their identity as men. As Tolson (1977) commented, 'the main focus of masculinity is the wage'. Paradoxically, this view fails to take account of the de-humanising and 'unmanliness' of most jobs under capitalism. It also fails to take account of rising unemployment in the face of new technologies. Unemployment and under-employment is chronic in less developed countries and is rising in the developed economies.

Paul Willis (1984), in a series of articles written in the mid-1980s, emphasised how the socialisation of young people into gender roles is tied to the transition from school to work and the acquisition, by males especially, of the wage. He speculated on the consequences of loss of work for the traditional sense of 'working-class masculinity'. He considered two possibilities. One is that the traditional male working-class identity might be 'softened' when the link with wage labour and the dignity and sacrifice of manual work is broken. Alternatively, the loss of the wage might lead young males to a 'gender crisis' to which one solution 'might be an aggressive assertion of masculinity and masculine style for its own sake'.

The latter is the option which appears to have been adopted by a group of unemployed young men studied by Anne Stafford (1991), who spent five months as a participant observer in a government youth training programme in Scotland in the late 1980s. In contrast to Willis's boys, who had been confident that they would find manual jobs, for the young men Stafford interviewed even dead-end jobs were out of reach. She found they appeared to be retreating into aggressive sexism, rather than moderating it:

> In all the times I was with the boys, I do not think I ever heard a girl discussed in terms of anything other than her appearance or as an object of sex. Girls as people were never mentioned....Girls were pieces of anatomy, to be discussed and commented on. Scoring and undermining girls were constant themes.
>
> (Stafford 1991: 60)

Stafford pointed out that the whole culture, both inside and outside the town, was laced with sexism. From television, cinema, porn videos, and from friends and relatives, boys absorbed abusive and objectified images and messages about women. Stafford argued that as the material conditions of young men's lives worsen, these images tend to escalate and be exaggerated. Weiss (1990) has argued that in a de-industrialised America white working-class males are so threatened by their loss of traditional masculinity along with loss of job opportunities that the New Right is rendered very attractive.

We do not know how other young men are responding to these changes and it is a mistake to generalise Stafford's findings to all working-class youth. However, there are signs that unless such problems emanating from long-term unemployment are addressed, the gender divide will widen. Bea Campbell (1993) points out that unemployment and poverty produce a human and economic crisis for both men and women, but that what is perceived as an economic crisis for a woman is seen as an identity crisis for young men. The rising suicide rate among young men under 25 and the high number of accidents, alcohol related illnesses, heart attacks and homelessness is certainly a cause for concern (see Salisbury and Jackson 1996: 217).

Alongside unemployment for young working-class men, what are the likely effects of the increase in female employment, which by 1990 meant almost half the labour force comprised women? The effect on the family of women's employment is only beginning to be investigated but it has been long anticipated that the effects would be profound (see Engels 1940). It may well be that this shift is challenging what Carol Pateman (1988) has referred to as the 'sexual contract', whereby a fraternal patriarchy was able to subordinate women to the needs both of individual men (through the marriage contract) and to men as a group (through political and economic subordination) (Arnot *et al.* 1997).

In her influential book *The Sexual Contract*, Carol Pateman traces the development of relationships based on equality or a *social* contract, and discusses the distinction between social contracts typical of labour relations and sexual contracts, typical of marriage relationships. She shows how sexual contracts were based on a slave type of relationship. Since old domestic contracts between a master and his slave and servants were labour contracts, she points out that the marriage contract can be seen as a kind of labour contract. Indeed, over the past three centuries feminists have compared wives to slaves, servants and workers.

With the separation of production from the family, male domestic labourers became workers. The important point that Pateman makes is that the wage labourer, in contrast to the domestic labourer, stands as a civil equal with his employer in the public realm of the capitalist market. A housewife remains in the private domestic sphere, but unequal relations of domestic life are 'naturally so' and thus do not detract from the universal equality of the public world. The marriage contract reflects the patriarchal ordering of nature embodied in the original contract through which a sexual division of labour is constituted. Pateman perceptively argues that women cannot be inserted into the public sphere without involving a complete upheaval of the private sphere, as women will no longer be prepared to accept the subordination based on a 'sexual' contract and will start demanding equality in the home. One result could be that young women will not find marriage attractive, particularly if young men are not able to be the breadwinners. Certainly, more young men are now remaining single. In the US the number remaining single aged 25–34 increased from one-third to three-fifths between 1968 and 1993, a period which saw rises in crime, and prison population, and drug and alcohol abuse (see Grice *et al.* 1998). Moreover, women's greater dissatisfaction with marriage is indicated by the rising numbers of divorces where women are petitioners. Over two-thirds of divorces are initiated by women and divorce has increased sixfold in England and Wales over the past thirty years, a higher increase than in any other European country.

Other social changes have also been significant in rendering marriage less vital for sexual and reproductive purposes. In the USA, continental Europe and Britain there has been a trend towards earlier and more frequent sexual intercourse among adolescents of both sexes. This was facilitated by the greater availability of abortion (following the Abortion Act of 1967), the availability of the birth control pill since the 1960s and the greater acceptance of illegitimacy culminating in its abolition in the Legitimacy Act 1988. Britain has one of the highest rates of unplanned pregnancies in Europe and promotion of sex- and HIV-related education was one of the five priorities identified by the government in the White Paper 'Health of the Nation' (HMSO 1992). Additionally, there is today far more tolerance of different types of sexual behaviour. It is argued that heterosexuality may well no longer be the norm in future years (Giddens 1992). Advances in reproductive technology, enabling women to have children without sexual intercourse with a man, are significant, although exactly what impact such changes will have is by no means clear.

Research into young women's attitude to marriage

It is likely that young women have for some time been more ambivalent about marriage than the romantic idea of 'living happily ever after' implies. Certainly in examining the oral testimonies of middle- and working-class young women and men interviewed in the early 1980s, almost all wanted to delay marriage as long as possible. This appeared to be one way in which girls could increase their autonomy, if only in a short-lived fashion.

A hundred girls and thirty boys, aged fifteen to seventeen and from a wide range of ethnic and social class backgrounds, at four comprehensive schools in London were interviewed, as described in *Sugar and Spice: Sexuality and Adolescent Girls* (Lees 1993). Three of the schools were mixed, and the remaining one was all girls. Three of the schools had children from a wide range of ethnic backgrounds, and the remaining mixed school was predominantly white working-class. Most of the children from ethnic minority groups had been brought up in this country but a few had recently come from Bangladesh. There were pupils from Greece, Africa, the Caribbean, India, Pakistan, Italy, China, Israel, Spain and Eastern Europe. All the schools were attempting to teach a multi-ethnic curriculum and implement equal opportunity policies.

Non-directive, semi-structured interviews and group discussions, as opposed to more formal quantifiable methods, enabled the subjects' responses to be followed up and allowed the young men and women to be more revealing about intimate material. The young men and women were asked about five areas of their lives: their views of same sex friends, opposite sex friends, school, sex relations and how they saw the future. The focus of the study was on young people's views rather than on their own personal experience, so that questions were not asked, for example, about sexual orientation. Several groups did raise questions regarding homosexuality, views that were both liberal and hostile, but this is not the focus of this chapter. None of the young men or women gave homosexuality as a reason for not marrying.

Attitudes to marriage predictably differed from one ethnic group to another, and views varied as to whether or not marriage could successfully be combined with a career. Social class differences did not appear to be as important as anticipated. Marianne, a lively young white woman, reflected the unromantic realism of working-class women towards the idea of marriage when she said 'I don't want to get married until I've had my life'. At 16, Marianne was out most nights and brimming with plans for the future. She wanted to be an actress and go round the world. A year later she was an assistant at Woolworth's, hardly went out, and was saving to get married. All her ambitions for a future career had dissolved and she was resigned to a life that she described as 'not her own'.

There was a puzzling contradiction in the young women's views of marriage. Marriage was seen as anything but romantic: rather it brought in its train subordination and loneliness. Yet despite the fact that almost half the girls were no longer living with both parents, most of them saw a future without marriage as unimaginable: only three young women said that they did not want to get married. My findings were similar to Sue Sharpe's (1976) study of 200 fourth form girls living in Ealing (Greater London) in the 1970s, a third of whom hoped to be married by the time they were 20 and three-quarters by the time they were 25. They accepted that a husband and family were the most satisfying things in a woman's life.

This discrepancy between the ideal of marriage as fulfilment and the grim reality also emerged from a study of young mothers carried out in Camberwell (South London) by Brown and Harris (1978). They found that two-thirds of married women with a child at home suffered from clinical depression or were borderline cases, compared to 17 per cent of a cross sample of all women in the study. Married working-class women were at a higher risk of depression when they had young children at home. Husbands were not likely to recognise the difficulties of child care, which they saw as a cushy job; this trivialised the women's work and lowered their self-esteem.

Overall the young women in my study viewed marriage as a domestic burden that carried little in the way of reward, accompanied by financial dependency that was both a constriction on the mother and a bone of contention between husband and wife. Sharon, a young black teenager, expressed such a view clearly when she commented:

> My dad won't give in. My mum she sort of goes short now and again and she asks him for extra money and he just won't give it to her. I think other families are like that. If you don't have to rely on a man, they don't feel so tight with their money.

Such views seemed to be realistically based on observations of their parents and the parents of their friends and acquaintances.

Young women were aware that their mothers often suffered treatment from their husbands which no employer would get away with. 'My dad thinks she should be a total wife/mother image be there ready and waiting. The meal should be ready and if he clicks his fingers she should go running'. Illness, drunkenness and physical violence were also mentioned. Several young women had experienced male violence in their home and described the man they would marry as 'someone who would not beat them up'. Many recognised that the marriages around them were based on inequality, organised around the unpaid and often unacknowledged labour of women.

The most important reason young women put forward for marriage was that they saw *no realistic alternative*. As Adrienne Rich (1984) suggested, heterosexuality and marriage are not actively chosen by girls and therefore could be seen as 'compulsory'. In other words, the choice of getting married became a negative one – of avoiding being left on the shelf. The young women saw this as carrying a stigma, a whole battery of neglect, suspicion and derision being directed at the non-married and the childless, who were stereotyped as shirking their duty, selfish, immature, lonely, bitter, abnormal, unattractive or pathetic. Sylvia explained: 'If you don't want to get married and want to live a free life...everyone will call you a tart. Like you've got to go out with a bloke for a really long time and then marry him'.

There was also fear of loneliness, and being single was seen as rendering one vulnerable to male violence. Jasmin, a young woman, said she was scared to sleep alone and explained that she was scared of the dark. She realised a compromise was necessary when she said: 'I wouldn't like to live with my family all my life, but I wouldn't like to live alone either'. The fear of being alone was also linked to the question of security and protection in a male-dominated world with the ever present fear of violence and sexual harassment. As Bridget explained:

> A boy can go out and just enjoy himself, but a girl can't really. She's got to worry. I could go out and be raped but he couldn't. I think that comes up all the time. It's not that a boy is more trusted. He's free.

The inevitability of marriage was cushioned for many through a desire to put it off, usually for as long as ten years. Aged 16, ten years is a lifetime away. As Sylvia put it,

> I don't think about the future at all until it happens. I don't think – oh what am I going to do in ten years' time, for a start. I never think that. I think – what am I going to do to-morrow?

By delaying marriage, many girls thought they would be able to have some fun, often fantasised as travel and seeing the world. Michaela, like Marianne above, explained how marriage was something you ended up with after you had lived.

> I don't really want to get married, 'cos I want to go round the world first like my dad did. They got married when they were 30. *They had their life first* and then they got married and had us. When you're an air hostess you start the job when you're 20, so I want to work until I'm 35.

Another way young women avoided the predicament of marriage was to attribute the unhappiness they saw in marriages around them to the wrong choice of partner. The subordinate position of many women was often attributed to their lack of good sense in choosing the right husband. Alice, looking at the 'mistakes' her mum had made in choosing the wrong man, said 'not all marriages are like that, though, are they? Like if your mum's goes bad, yours might be good, it's what husband you pick'.

Romanticism about choosing the 'right man' could be seen as a way of ignoring structural inequalities. Sharon said:

> I would hate to rely on a husband. I see how my mum depends on my dad and it's turned her against him. I'm not going to marry a husband like my mum did. My dad, he doesn't help at all. I don't know what they see in each other. They must love each other.

This did not lead her to question the ideal of 'true love' and look realistically at the material realities of her mum's life. Instead she assumed that any disadvantages could be avoided by being careful about whom you marry.

Annie had made up her mind whom to avoid when she got married. 'I will get someone who doesn't like drinking a lot and just has a little Coke or something', she volunteered. When asked whether it's common for men to come home drunk she replied:

> Yes. It's like this lady round our flats. She gets beaten every night because her husband goes drinking, comes home about twelve, starts beating her, you know, for nothing saying she's been out with this man, she's done this and done that. He just makes it up, any lies, and starts trouble.

The only two girls who were doubtful about getting married still regarded it as essential for anyone having children. As Sharon, put it:

> Actual marriage, I don't think it's necessary unless you're going to have children and I can't visualise myself having children. Apart from that, I don't think actual marriage, a piece of paper is that important. I'm not religious or anything.

Such negative views of marriage appear to be more common in the 1990s. Sue Sharpe in the 1994 update of her book *Just like a Girl*, first published in 1976, returned to the London schools where she had interviewed 200 15-year-old girls and compared them with girls today. The most remarkable change she found in the oral testimonies related to the girls' changed views of marriage, which had dramatically dropped in popularity. Over three-quarters of the girls she interviewed had said 'yes' to marriage in 1972. By 1991 this had dropped to under half. Most girls did not want to get married, and saw it as something to be approached with extreme caution.

Other studies found that a more conservative attitude to marriage was still predominant. Studies of white girls in Britain (Mirza 1992) and in Canada

(Gaskell 1992) portrayed girls in the mid-1980s as not expecting to be the main breadwinner, taking it for granted that child rearing and lower earning capacity would combine to force them to give up work while their children were young, even though this is not necessarily what they wanted. In an Australian study of Melbourne girls (Wyn 1990) young women expressed similar views. They were not romantic about marriage and relationships with men but saw marriage and child rearing as an important feature of their future lives.

Social class and ethnicity did make a difference in my own research (Lees 1993). For example, strong religious affiliation appeared to be associated with more traditional attitudes to marriage among Greek and Muslim families. However, virtually all girls planned to marry. With some girls rejecting marriage in the 1990s, ethnic differences are probably more important now. In Heidi Mirza's (1992) research, for example, comparing a group of young black African-Caribbean women with young Irish women attending a South London secondary school, she found attitudes to marriage, the family and careers differed from one ethnic group to another. Both groups were the children of immigrants who had moved to England in the 1950s. Whereas Irish girls consistently expressed a desire for marriage and children, which they saw as incompatible with a permanent commitment to the labour market, the young black women were committed to a full-time career, which they did not see as incompatible with children and relationships with men.

It is also likely that for some young Asian women the restrictions placed on them are no less severe than when Amrit Wilson summed up her 1970s investigation into the experience of Asian girls in the following way:

> Once an Asian girl has finished school, whether she is Hindu, Muslim or Sikh, the threat or prospect of marriage begins to brim over her, casting a blight over her chances of further education – or of a worthwhile working career.
>
> (Wilson 1978: 100)

Poor job prospects and rising unemployment among young men are other factors that appear to be influencing girls' attitudes. Prendergast and Forrest (1997) undertook a pilot study of boys and girls at three secondary modern schools in areas of high unemployment and deprivation. All the girls had plans for the future but few spoke about marriage and children. When asked they said 'Perhaps maybe, never, later', 'When I'm 35 if I meet someone, if I can afford it, maybe if I do it on my own'. The young women rejected their male peer group as 'wasters' and predicted that they would 'let you down', 'wouldn't work', and asked questions such as: 'Why should any sensible woman have children with them?' The researchers concluded that the boys appeared to have lost ground compared to the girls and viewed their future pessimistically, speaking with bitterness and frustration about their poor job prospects.

Girls, on the other hand, appear to be gaining confidence and to be far more career-oriented than ten years ago. This is reflected in their improved educational attainment. At a national level young women are now more successful at every level in examinations at 16, although boys still perform better than girls at 'A' level (Arnot *et al.* 1996), especially in Science and Mathematics. Wilkinson (1994) traced the development of 7 million boys and girls between the ages of 18 and 34 and found that school girls now have greater self-esteem, are happier than their male peers, are more ambitious, are more likely to want to continue in education, and are less likely than boys to want to start a family when they leave school. Similar findings are reflected in Norwegian studies. Frones (1995), for example, in a study of school achievement and occupational choice, found girls to be more confident and successful than boys and to be less dependent on relationships with the opposite sex.

Research into young men's attitude to marriage

> I've got a right bird. I've been going with her for eighteen months now. Her's as good as gold. She's fucking done well. She's clean. She loves doing fucking housework. Trousers I brought yesterday. I took 'em up last night, and she turned them up for me. She's as good as gold, and I wanna get married as soon as I can.
>
> (Willis 1977: 45)

This quote from Paul Willis's revealing study of working-class adolescent boys attending a secondary modern school in the Midlands in the 1970s epitomises the servitude that working-class boys expected of their future married partner. The model for the girlfriend was the mother and was based on the assumption that boys would not need to look after themselves.

As Spanksy, one of the boys Willis interviewed explained:

> It shouldn't be done, you shouldn't need to help yer mother in the house. You should put your shoes away tidy and hang your coat up, admittedly, but, you know, you shouldn't vacuum and polish and do the beds for her...her housekeeping and that.
>
> (Willis 1977: 45)

The same attitudes to domesticity were reflected in my study of thirty 16-year-old young men carried out ten years after Paul Willis's study (Lees 1993). Domesticity appeared to be a major consideration of most of the young men I interviewed. Their views of marriage varied. Ten of the young men were from Bangladesh, held traditional views of women's role and did not contemplate marrying out of their ethnic group. Like Willis's lads, many of them saw their future wives primarily as subservient housekeepers. Take, for example, Rajam and Agad's discussion of the kind of girl they would like to marry (they had come to England when they were 6 and 7 respectively):

Rajam   I don't want a girl who will leave you with the washing.
Agad   No one who starts arguing that she doesn't want to do the housework and she doesn't want to care for the child.
Rajam   I want a girl that is nice, gentle and never has contact with boys.

Imtiaz was critical of girls who refused to be subservient and who 'wanted their own way', who'd 'leave you with the washing', and who would 'want to control a man'.

On the one hand, these young men were aware that the world around them was changing and predicted that the high divorce rate would spread to their community. Zebhia and Arman, Bengali young men, recognised that life was different for their mothers in England, where they were not allowed out on their own and therefore suffered from loneliness. Yet their own aspirations regarding marriage appeared to have changed little, if at all.

Some black African-Caribbean and white young men were still committed to getting married but tended to be a little less concerned with subservience. Two of them did express some reservations about the instability of marriage and resulting financial costs. Andy, a middle-class young man who wanted to be an engineer, commented: 'If you get married and you get another girlfriend, you lose money on the divorce' and James commented: 'Marriage costs money. It's stupid getting married as it costs too much'.

Sue Sharpe and Mike O'Donnell conducted a small scale ethnographic study, not yet published, to explore the attitudes, ideas and expectations of marriage and family life of 15- to 16-year-old young men from Ealing in the early 1990s. They found that boys' attitudes to marriage had changed far less than those of girls. In contrast to the girls, three-quarters of the boys uncritically assumed that marriage would be part of their future life. Boys saw marriage as an important way of committing themselves to another person. As Jim said:

For myself I think marriage is pretty important and the father and mother have to be there for the child. I'd live with them and then I'd feel as you get older that marriage is the official statement of your love life, so I'd get married eventually.

Whereas half the boys felt that parents should stay together for the sake of their children, most of the girls believed you could not expect people to stay with the same partner for life. Asked how likely they thought it was they would get divorced one day, few boys thought this likely compared to nearly half the girls.

A significant proportion of the boys did, however, think that men should be more involved with looking after children, and were just as able to look after a home and children as women. As Dan commented:

I think you should have an equal partnership and share (caring for) children and all the chores. Just because you're a man doesn't mean you have to go out and be a breadwinner. If the man feels better at home he could discuss it with his wife. You can't take it for granted that if he's male, then he's going to want to do that and because she's female, she's not going to mind doing it.

One problem here is that boys who adopt non-stereotypical roles are often ridiculed by their male peers. Most boys are not keen on the idea of equality. There is a solid band of resistance, typified in the attitudes of boys like Tony:

I suppose you have to share it (at home), but I'd let the woman do most of the work because I can't really see me doing ironing and hoovering up. I think it's a woman's job. I'd like to put shelves up, fix a car, fix the fridge, washing machine. It might have changed for some people but if you ask the boys around here they say, well let the woman do it. If you asked the girls they'd probably say 'I'll let them do half and let me do half', but I wouldn't do that. I'd just say 'You do that and I'll do something else'. Women always used to stay at home and look after the kids and now it's changed and a lot of men stay home and the women go to work which is a good change. But most men wouldn't do it – I wouldn't like to do it anyway, I'd be bored at home.

There are differing accounts of how far men have adapted to these changes and been prepared to take a more equal role in the home. Connell (1995) in Australia and Morris (1995) in an area of high unemployment in the Midlands in England found that some unemployed men are prepared to undertake child care and housework at least when their wives are working. Yet men who help with the housework, seen as 'women's work', run the risk of being labelled as wimps.

Girls do not necessarily challenge their relegation to housework and still may view men's reluctance to undertake such work as 'natural' male behaviour. Jane Gaskell (1992: 79), for example, found that young working-class women in Canada did little to challenge such views of men, masculinity and the limits of acceptable or natural male behaviour. She concludes:

Girls' construction of masculinity is rooted in an ideology which suggest that what men are like is what men must be like...their perceptions are validated by their experiences of patriarchal family structures. They have not seen men in domestic roles. Their fathers, brothers and boyfriends do housework only as a special favour.

At school few young men are given help in confronting the contradictions in masculine images and roles. The widening discrepancies between young men's own ideas and expectations and those of the young women they hope to marry do not bode well for the future of the two-parent nuclear family. Sam failed to see how the change in girls' attitudes would affect him when he commented:

> Sometimes feminism and women's equality is a load of rubbish, but mostly it's just important for women. It's their choice really, what they do with their lives. Men have got a little bit to do with it but not much.

Overall it appears that the constitution of hegemonic masculinity has changed little (see also Eder 1995; Mac An Ghaill 1996). A few boys I spoke to were aware of issues of equality, but the majority do little to oppose the sexism around them. Most boys saw sexism as a personal rather than a political issue. Sam, for example, saw women's equality as a matter of personal choice. In this way men can distance themselves from any responsibility in the household. Sam fails to see how limited women's choices are and how choice is constrained. Such practices as calling girls 'slags' is a way of objectifying them, not recognising them as people of equal worth. It is also an effective way of controlling female sexuality.

Sexism should not, however, be seen as merely chauvinism. It is deeply ingrained in identity formation, continually endorsed and celebrated by the dominant culture. The influence of the mass media, the daily press, the pornographic magazines and videos all reinforce the objectifying of women's bodies and celebrate a form of macho aggressive masculinity. Violence against women is often condoned, and the fear of violence constricts the lives of women of all social and ethnic groups. Violence is cited as one of the reasons for the increase in divorce (Bradshaw and Miller 1991) and it is significant that the 1990s have seen an unprecedented recognition by governments of domestic violence. The United Nations Declarations on the Elimination of Violence Against Women in 1993 and the declaration by Home Secretary, Jack Straw in February 1998 that he wanted domestic violence to be treated as a crime for which there should be zero tolerance, are but two examples of this.

Implications for government intervention

Almost half of all marriages now end in divorce. This increase in divorce means that one-parent families now comprise one in five families with 2.1 children. These changes raise fundamental issues about the balance between the family, state and individual financial responsibilities. The post-war social security system was based on three important assumptions: full employment, male breadwinners and child benefit. Male wages were the main element of family support and, with the increase in single-parent families, the state has increasingly had to foot the bill. As Smart (1990) pointed out, it was assumed that divorced women would remarry but this has not always happened. This has led to a feminisation of poverty (Ebert 1996). The number of one-parent families with incomes less than half the average rose from 19 to 60 per cent between 1979 and 1990 (Millar 1994).

A high degree of consensus has developed among commentators and politicians in hostility to single parents, and, in particular, to never-married mothers, who are seen as a particular burden on the state and are linked with the threat of an 'underclass', irresponsible and grasping (see Mann and Roseneil, this volume). Margaret Thatcher in a 1988 speech to the National Children's Home, spoke of the 'growing problem of young single girls who deliberately become pregnant in order to jump the housing queue and gain welfare payments' (Macaskill 1993: 44–5). The *Independent on Sunday* (11 November 1993) devoted a whole page to an article entitled 'Single mothers: How many are there? What do they cost the State? Are the children likelier to go astray?' Associations have been drawn between lesbians and feminists as, for example, by Dr Rhodes Boyson, the Conservative local government minister, who in 1986 condemned 'evil' single parents and claimed that the family was under attack 'from extreme feminists, youth cults and homosexual lobbies' (*The Guardian* 10 October 1986).

The increased burden of state financial support for single parents led to the setting up of the Child Support Agency (CSA) in 1991, which introduced a new system of child maintenance aimed at ensuring that absent fathers contributed to the upkeep of their children. Similar schemes were introduced in the USA and Australia with the intention of making men responsible for their children and reducing the benefits bill. Despite cross-party support, it was strongly opposed by a small but vocal group of middle-class fathers who organised into various pressure groups as a network against the Act which led to violent demonstrations and threats to CSA officials. As Mitchell and Goody (1997) point out, the group is an articulate exponent of a virulent backlash against all women who are unattached.

Controversy over single parents came to a head shortly after Labour came to power in May 1997 when cuts in lone-parent benefit were proposed and raised a storm of protest when the motion was carried in parliament, with all but eight women Labour MPs supporting it.[1] Brian Sedgemore MP, who voted against, referred to them as the 'Stepford wives'. This cut was reversed some months later when the Welfare to Work programme was launched, with significant funds allocated to child care.

The solution put forward by the Labour government is to encourage certain groups now on benefit – specifically single parents and unemployed youth – into work, to break what is referred to as the 'dependency culture'. Rather than seeing the problem in relation to changes in the economy, the problem is seen as a result of individual failure, inadequate socialisation or, in relation to single parents, as 'fecklessness'.

Similar psychological inadequacies are posited for youth unemployment which is seen on the one hand as resulting from inadequate socialisation and, on the other hand, as resulting from the competition of girls. *The Times* headline on 5 January 1998, for example, announced that 'Schools minister tackles laddish tendency' and proposed that more male teachers were to be recruited as a drive to stamp out laddish culture that 'had helped girls to win the battle of the sexes at virtually every stage of education'. This is not only untrue, as boys are still excelling in comparison with girls at both 'A' and degree level, but it is not made at all clear how male teachers would 'stamp out laddish culture'!

Two months later, on 26 April 1998 a *Sunday Times* headline dramatically announced that 'Blair tackles men behaving badly'. The article announced that 'cabinet ministers now believe the problems of delinquent single men represent a looming crisis for society' and that the 16–24 age group has been called the 'loaded generation' in Whitehall after the laddish men's magazine. It was announced that an action plan was to be drawn up and it was hoped that the New Deal for 18–24-year-olds would reduce levels of crime. These announcements totally fail to address the implications of a changing economy where well-paid work is simply not available. As Jack Straw said:

> In the past communities were underpinned by the economic structure with large numbers of men working in factories or down the pit providing a clear transition from adolescence to adulthood. The pit village was the obvious example where social organisation was underpinned by the way the local economy was organised. Many of those jobs have gone so we can't rely on the economic structure. The government has got to intervene socially.
>
> (*Sunday Times* 26 April 1998)

What kind of social intervention is envisaged is not clear, but it is clear that men will have to change. Dave Hill (1997a and b), author of *The Future of Men*, argues that men's response to change had frequently been feeble: 'Most have been self-serving, resentful and fearful that women are stealing men's trousers'. He draws parallels between the American Robert Bly's (1991) *Iron John*, the Million Man March on Washington calling for a return to true masculine values, the male campaign against the British Child Support Agency and the rhetoric of Families Need Fathers campaigners, who 'sup long and deep from their foaming mugs of umbrage and speak of feminism as a social disease'.

Conclusion

The research reported in this chapter indicates that young women are becoming less prepared to accept what Pateman has referred to as the 'sexual contract' and take on a subservient role in the family. Although ethnic and class differences are important, there has been a shift in many young women's school achievement and self-confidence, and their prospects of work, albeit low-paid and low-status, have expanded. This appears to be leading many to demand a form of partnership with young men, in which they are no longer prepared to take a subservient role and are less prepared to put up with unsatisfactory, and sometimes violent, relationships. From the evidence of these small-scale studies, and in view of women's greater propensity to seek divorce, it appears that many young men are experiencing difficulty in adjusting to these changing expectations, which often conflict with the model of hegemonic masculinity reflected in the media and in society.

This chapter also indicates that both the Conservative and Labour government have shown little understanding of the impact of changes in the structure of employment and their impact on the family, in particular in enabling young women to find an alternative to the subordination they previously experienced. The approach of the Labour government has been to explain the increased number of lone parents on benefit and the rise in youth unemployment in psychological or moral terms. The welfare to work programme rests on the assumption that the economy can be expanded to employ both groups which, at this stage of capitalist development, is most unlikely. Moreover, the implications of working women questioning the 'sexual contract', and its impact on the raising of children, are not being addressed.

There is a need for schools and youth services to develop relationship and parenthood skills in young men which could lead to a 'transformation of intimacy' along the lines suggested by Giddens (1992) and Arnot *et al.* (1997), but what is also needed is a restructuring of work with increased opportunities for job sharing. No amount of moral pontificating will turn the clock back and reinstate a family system from the 1950s. The causes of the changes in the family need to be addressed realistically in the light of changes in the economy.

Note

1 The 1997 new Labour government saw 101 women elected – over a third of the Labour Party – and expectations for more women-friendly policies had been high. There was however, evidence that a high degree of bullying went on to obtain their vote for the cut in benefit.

Bibliography

Arnot, M., David, M., Weiner, G. (eds.) (1996) Educational Reforms and Gender Equality in Schools, Manchester: *Equal Opportunities Commission.*
Arnot, M., Deliyanni, K. and Tome, A. (1997) 'Changing Femininity, Changing Concepts of Citizenship: Social Representations of Public and Private Spheres in a European Context', Paper presented at the Third European Feminist Research Conference, *Shifting Bonds, Shifting Bounds: Women Mobility and Citizenship in Europe,* Coimbra, Portugal: University of Coimbra, July.
Bly, R. (1991) *Iron John,* Dorset: Element Books.
Bradshaw, J. and Millar J. (1991) *Lone-Parenting in the UK,* London: HMSO.
Brown, G. and Harris, T. (1978) *The Social Origins of Depression,* London: Tavistock.
Campbell, B. (1993) *Goliath: Britain's Dangerous Places,* London: Methuen.
Connell, R. W. (1995) *Masculinities,* Cambridge: Polity.
Ebert, T. (1996) *Ludic Feminism,* Michigan: Michigan University Press.
Eder, D. (1995) *School Talk: Gender And Adolescent School Culture,* New Brunswick, NJ: Rutgers University Press.

Engels, F. (1940) *The Origin of the Family, Private Property and the State*, London: Lawrence and Wishart.

Epstein, D. (1994) *Challenging Lesbian and Gay Inequalities in Education*, Milton Keynes: Open University Press.

Equal Opportunities Commission and OFSTED (1996) *The Gender Divide: Performance Differences Between Boys and Girls at School*, London: HMSO.

Frones, I. (1995) *Gender Revolution: Gender, Generation and Social Change in Norway*, Paper given to ESRC Seminar Series: Childhood and Society, Institute of Education, December.

Gaskell, J. (1992) *Gender Matters from School to Work*, Milton Keynes: Open University Press.

Giddens, A. (1992) *The Transformation of Intimacy*, Cambridge: Polity Press.

Grice, A., Ellis, W. and Norton, C. (1998) 'The Trouble with Boys', *The Sunday Times* 26 April.

Griffin, C. (1997) 'Troubled Teens: Managing Disorders of Transition and Consumption in Consuming Cultures', *Feminist Review* 55 (Spring): 4–21.

Guardian (1986) 'Boyson Condemns "Evil" Single Parents', *The Guardian* 10 October: 32.

Halsey, A. H. (1993) *Panorama*, BBC 1, 20 September.

Haskey, J. (1995) *Trends in Marriage and Cohabitation: the Decline in Marriage and the Changing Pattern of Living in Partnerships*, Population Statistics, OPCS No. 80.

Hill, D. (1997a) 'Men in Crisis', *The Guardian* (Women), 29 December.

—— (1997b) *The Future of Men*, Weidenfeld and Nicolson.

HMSO (1992) *Health of the Nation*, London: Department of Health.

—— (1996) *The Gender Divide: Performance Differences Between Boys and Girls at School*, London: HMSO.

Hudson, F. and Ineichen, B. (1991) *Taking it Lying Down: Sexuality and Teenage Motherhood*, London: Macmillan.

Kiernan, K. and Wicks, M. (1990) *Family Change and Future Policy*, London: Family Policy Studies Centre.

Laws, S. (1994) 'Undervalued Families', *Trouble and Strife* Spring.

Lees, S. (1986) *Losing Out: Sexuality and Adolescent Girls*, London: Unwin Hyman.

—— (1993) *Sugar and Spice: Sexuality and Adolescent Girls*, Harmondsworth: Penguin.

Lesbian and Gay Youth (1988) *Report on High Schools: A Study Prepared For The Coalition For Lesbian And Gay Rights In Toronto*, Toronto: Ottawa Hill.

Mac An Ghaill, M. (ed.) (1996) *Understanding Masculinities*, Buckingham: Open University Press.

Macaskill, H. (1993) *From the Workhouse to the Workplace*, London: NCOPF.

Mann, K. and Roseneil, S. (1994) "Some Mothers Do 'Ave 'Em": Backlash and the Gender Politics of the Underclass Debate', *Journal of Gender Studies* 3: 317–33.

Marriott, D. (1996) 'Reading Masculinities' in M. Mac An Ghaill (ed.) *Understanding Masculinity*, Buckingham: Open University Press: 185–202.

Millar, J. (1994) 'State, Family and Personal Responsibility: The Changing Balance for Lone Mothers in the UK', *Feminist Review* 48: 24–40.

Millar, J. and Whiteford, P. (1993) 'Child Support in Lone-Parent Families: Policies in Australia and the UK', *Policy and Politics* 21(1): 59–72.

Millar, S. (1996) 'Male Attitudes Show "New" Man May Be A Sham', *The Guardian* 12 December.

Mills, H. (1996) 'Breadline Britain', *The Observer* 11 August: 18.

Mirza, H. (1992) *Young Female and Black*, London: Routledge.

Mitchell, J. and Goody, J. (1997) 'Feminism, Fatherhood and the Family in Britain' in A. Oakley and J. Mitchell (eds) *Who's Afraid of Feminism?* London: Hamish Hamilton.

Morris, L. (1995) *Social Divisions: Economic Decline and Social Structural Change*, London: University College London Press.

O'Leary, J. (1998) 'Schools Minister Tackles Laddish Tendency', *The Times* 5 January.

Parsons, T. and Bales, R. (1956) *Family, Socialization and Interaction Process*, London: Routledge and Kegan Paul.

Pateman, C. (1988) *The Sexual Contract*, Cambridge: Polity Press.

Prendergast, S. and Forrest, S. (1997) 'Hieroglyphs of the Heterosexual: Learning about Gender in School' in L. Segal (ed.) *New Sexual Agendas*, London: Macmillan.

Rich, A. (1994) 'Compulsory Heterosexuality and Lesbian Existence', in A. Snitow, C. Stansell, and S. Thompson, (eds.) *Desire: The Politics of Sexuality*, London: Virago: 212–41.

Salisbury, J. and Jackson, D. (1996) *Challenging Macho Values*, London: Falmer Press.

Sharpe, S. (1976/1994) *Just Like a Girl*, Harmondsworth: Penguin.

Smart, C. (1990) 'A Postmodern Woman Meets Atavistic Man', in L. Gelsthorpe, and A. Morris (eds) *Feminist Perspectives in Criminology*, Milton Keynes: Open University Press: 70–85.

Song, M. (1996) 'Changing Conceptualizations of Lone Parenthood in Britain: Lone Parents of Single Mums?', *European Journal of Women's Studies*, 3(4): 377–99.

Stafford, A. (1991) *Trying Work*, Edinburgh: University Press.

Tolson, A. (1977) *The Limits of Masculinity*, London: Tavistock.

Weiss, L. (1990) *Working Class Without Work: High School Students in a Deindustrialised Economy*, London: Routledge.

Westwood, S. (1996) 'Feckless Fathers: Masculinities and the British State' in Mac An Ghaill, M. (ed.) *Understanding Masculinities*, Buckingham: Open University Press.

Wilkinson, H. (1994) *No Turning Back: Generations and the Genderquake*, London: Demos.

Willis, P. (1977) *Learning to Labour: How Working Class Kids Get Working Class Jobs*, Farnborough: Saxon House.

—— (1984) *New Society* 29 March, 5 April, 12 April.

Willott, S. and Griffin, C. (1996) 'Men, Masculinity and the Challenge of Long Term Unemployment' in M. Mac An Ghaill (ed.) *Understanding Masculinities*, Buckingham: Open University Press: 77–95.

Wilson, A. (1978) *Finding a Voice*, London: Virago.

Witz, A. (1993) 'Women at Work' in D. Richardson and V. Robinson (eds) *Introducing Women's Studies*, London: Macmillan.

Wyn, J. (1990) 'Working-Class Girls and Educational Outcomes: Is Self-Esteem an Issue?' in J. Kenway and S. Willis (eds) *Hearts and Minds: Self-Esteem and the Schooling of Girls*, London: Falmer Press.

4 Lesbian and gay families

Legal perspectives

Kath O'Donnell

Contemporary expressions of concern about the perceived decline of the family and urgings to return to 'family values' are firmly based in an ideology of family life which can be described as highly traditional and which revolves around a nuclear unit based in heterosexual marriage. From this traditionalist perspective, the institution of the family is seen to be threatened by the increasing diversity of family structures in society. Although lesbian and gay families form only one part of that diversity, the issues raised by them take on increasing significance and represent a direct challenge to the traditional and privileged orthodoxy of heterosexual family life. How far does increased social acceptance of lesbian and gay relationships extend to recognising them as family relationships – whether the family unit consists only of the adult partners or also includes children? This chapter focuses on the legal construction of family relationships and its exclusion of lesbian and gay families, seeking to offer a critical analysis of a legal perspective which is largely based on traditional ideologies of the family.

Discussion of legal regulation of the family often appears to lag some way behind contemporary family theories identifiable in other disciplines. To write of 'the' family is to imply that there exists one common form of family life, based on a shared set of values: nonetheless, although misleading, it is not an easy term to avoid. Contemporary family theory has however for some time increasingly accepted that the reality of family life experienced in modern society is diverse (e.g. Rapoport *et al.* 1982) and that no one model of family structure is implicitly more ideal than any other – sociologists have seemingly moved beyond the quest to define 'the' family: 'the issue is not whether "the Family" once existed, but how sociologists have ever believed that there existed a single central dominant "type" of family' (Bernardes 1985: 196).

Law, however, seems to require clearly defined boundaries within which legal frameworks may be constructed and operated. In the context of regulating family life this leads to an assumption that a universal truth defining and categorising family structure does exist, despite arguments that such a construction is at least unhelpful (Bernardes 1985: 203) if not positively flawed, given that the process of definition is likely to lead to the exclusion of diversity.

The main criticism to be levelled at the legal construction of the family is its exclusive and restrictive interpretation of what constitutes a valid and legitimate family relationship. It fails to recognise the diversity of family structures experienced by an increasing number of family groups, particularly those based upon homosexual relationships. The law must respond to the changes which are taking place in social structures and must afford some measure of recognition and respect to non-traditional families.

Law regulates the relationships between individuals, and between individuals and the state. Legal status, rights and responsibilities attach to a relationship when it is classified as a family relationship. From this perspective, law is essentially a classificatory and regulatory system, promoting the policies and interests of the state or wider community. By recognising certain relationships as 'family', the state validates the essential worth of those relationships, confirming that they have some positive benefit for wider society (Bradley 1987; Lewis 1988; Ryder 1990). These valuable relationships are therefore worthy of regulation and protection, and the rights and responsibilities of those within them will be recognised and enforced. The status of a legally recognised family relationship confers in most societies rights such as financial support, inheritance, protection of housing rights, welfare benefits, pension entitlements, and the right to regulation of family disputes by the family justice system: particularly disputes concerning children. By contrast, denying legal recognition to non-traditional families denies them validity and self worth, denies the needs of weaker family members (whether adult or child) for protection, and denies those relationships equal access to dispute resolution in the event of the breakdown of the relationship. To deny family status on the basis of sexual orientation alone is blatant discrimination which the law must visibly reject (Lewis 1988; Ryder 1990).

Although the search for a universal definition of family may well be critically flawed, it is clear that the legal construction of family relationships is based on an assumption of uniformity: of common values and shared norms of what constitutes a legitimate form of family life. The law demonstrates a clear preference for one understanding of family, rather than an ability to cope with the diversity which is part of real family lives in modern Western society. The construction which the law promotes is heavily influenced by the traditional ideology of family life and promotes the privileged position of heterosexual relationships within society (Ryder 1990).

In order to regulate family status, the legal system must first be able to categorise relationships as being 'family' or 'non-family' relationships so that status can be attributed; rights and obligations flowing from that status can be known and enforced; and conflict between members of the class 'family' can be regulated and resolved. The law adopts a formalistic approach to this issue of categorisation. Given law's perceived need for clearly defined boundaries, family relationships tend to be constructed from a limited number of formal linking relationships from which status can be seen to flow. The traditional emphasis of family law has been on the concepts of marriage and – to a lesser extent – of parenthood, concepts which have been closely linked throughout the development of the legal regulation of family relationships. These formal linking relationships are interpreted restrictively, as seen below, and exclude non-traditional forms of the family, particularly those based on lesbian and gay relationships.

Denied recognition through the formal links of marriage and (to some extent) parenthood, lesbian and gay families have been compelled to seek other highly artificial means of acquiring formal legal recognition and protection: for example, creating between two adults the legal relationship of parent and child through adult adoption of one partner by the other. Although adult adoption is not permitted in English law, this is a method which has previously been used in some US states which do permit adult adoption (Anderson 1987). This at least confers some family status, although it distorts the reality of the relationship between the partners and highlights the fact that non-traditional families can only gain some measure of legal recognition by denying or rendering invisible to the law an essential feature of the emotional relationship (Ryder 1990; Henson 1993). Although it must be argued that the nature of the sexual relationship between the adult partners should be irrelevant to their recognition as a family, it is an essential part of their human personalities and identities which they should not be forced to deny in order to gain validation (Bradley 1987).

The refusal to recognise homosexual relationships as an equally valid basis for family life is well illustrated by the debate about 'pretended families'. The Local Government Act 1988 contained in Section 28 the prohibition that 'a local authority shall not...promote the teaching in any maintained school of the acceptability of homosexuality as a pretended family relationship'. Seen as a backlash against the growing influence of the lesbian and gay liberation movement during the 1980s (Lind 1996; Edwards 1996) the refusal of central government to allow any modicum of equal respect or legal recognition for lesbian and gay families epitomises the privileged nature of the heterosexual family unit.

Lesbian and gay relationships and marriage

Throughout the history of family law, marriage has been seen as fundamental to any claim of family status. It was of central importance to the family structures of the propertied classes for dynastic planning, and the passing of wealth and property through inheritance to legitimate male heirs (Stone 1979). The primary focus for law was the way in which family status was generated through this formal link.

An emphasis upon the formal relationship of marriage as the main determinant of family status excludes lesbian and gay relationships simply by virtue of the definition of marriage applied by the law. The classic definition of marriage, laid down by Lord Penzance in the case of Hyde v. Hyde and Woodmansee (1866), has acquired 'mythical status in English law' (Bradney 1987: 352):

'Marriage, as understood in Christendom, may for this purpose be defined as the voluntary union of one man and one woman for life to the exclusion of all others' (Hyde v. Hyde 1866: 133). Wherever the nature of marriage has been questioned, courts have reaffirmed its essential nature as a heterosexual relationship.

This understanding of marriage and, by association, the nature of all family relationships, was influenced by religious doctrines and the link between heterosexual intercourse and its consequence – procreation. The sanctified relationship of marriage was seen as the appropriate controlling structure for intercourse and hence for procreation. Legal discussion of the concept of marriage still seems to preserve many of these ideals: the discourse is often one of naturalness and morality which seeks to place the privileged nature of heterosexual relationships beyond rational criticism and analysis (Lewis 1988). Implicit in many judicial decisions are feelings of repugnance and revulsion provoked by 'deviant' and 'abnormal' sexual acts and orientations.

The best illustration of this restrictive interpretation of marriage in English law is the case of Corbett v. Corbett (1970). Corbett concerned April Ashley, a male to female transsexual (or gender dysphoric)[1] who had gone through a ceremony of marriage with a partner who was fully aware of her medical history. The marriage failed and her partner sought a decree of nullity declaring the marriage void on the ground that Ashley was in fact a man. The court was required to rule upon her legal sexual identity and held that sexual identity was determined by biological sex, which was fixed at birth and could not subsequently be altered by surgical intervention. The judge, Ormrod J, adopted a highly restrictive interpretation of sexual identity. In a judgement which has received widespread criticism (see for example Smith 1971; Kennedy 1973; Taitz 1986; Bradney 1987; Armstrong and Walton 1990), he held that sexual identity was to be determined only by biological tests: chromosomal, gonadal and genital. He excluded psychological tests which would show that a transsexual would genuinely possess a gender identity directly opposed to that indicated by biological tests. Ashley had undergone surgery to realign as many of her physical characteristics as possible with her psychological gender identity. At the date of the marriage she had the external appearance and the gender identity of a woman, although her chromosomal structure could not be altered and she could not be provided with the functioning reproductive organs of a woman. However, Ormrod further held that the biological tests were to be applied at the time of birth, thus discounting the subsequent changes in her physical appearance.

Of particular significance is the reasoning which lies behind the judgement. Ormrod J held that:

> sex is clearly an essential determinant of the relationship called marriage, because it is and always has been recognised as the union of man and woman. It is the institution on which the family is built, and in which the capacity for natural heterosexual intercourse is an essential element. It has,

of course, many other characteristics, of which companionship and mutual support is an important one, but the characteristics which distinguish it from all other relationships can only be met by two persons of opposite sex....[E]ven the most extreme degree of transsexualism in a male...cannot reproduce a person who is naturally capable of performing *the essential role of a woman in marriage.*

(Corbett v. Corbett 1970: 48; my emphasis)

The main criticism of this reasoning concerns what Ormrod believes to be the essential role of a woman in marriage. If it is the capacity for heterosexual intercourse then his reasoning is flawed: incapacity does not render a marriage void *ab initio* (although if the marriage has not been consummated as a result then it may be voidable). The judge also ignored the medical evidence to the effect that Ashley was quite capable of engaging in intercourse: he clearly regarded this as 'unnatural' intercourse because her female genitalia had been surgically constructed, despite earlier authority that a woman possessed of a largely constructed vagina was capable of consummation. If the essential role of a woman in marriage is instead related to the capacity to procreate, the judgement is on no stronger ground: infertility is likewise not a ground for declaring a marriage void, or even voidable. The legal reasoning which justifies Ormrod's restrictive tests of sexual identity is weak but it is tempting to infer that his justification was simple: a less restrictive test would have validated the marriage and he was not prepared to validate what he clearly believed to be a homosexual relationship.

The language used in Corbett is particularly revealing. The parties' relationship was clearly judged by reference to some undeclared standard of a 'normal' heterosexual relationship, and found wanting: 'listening to each party describing this strange relationship, my principle impression was that it had little or nothing in common with any heterosexual relationship which I could recall hearing about in a fairly extensive experience of this court' (Corbett v. Corbett 1970: 38). Likewise, some hidden standard of femininity also seemed to be in operation: the judge referred to 'a pastiche of femininity' and added that '[h]er outward appearance, at first sight, was convincingly feminine, but on closer and longer examination in the witness box it was much less so. The voice, manner, gestures and attitude became increasingly reminiscent of the accomplished female impersonator' (Corbett v. Corbett 1970: 47).

The judgement speaks of normality and deviance and displays an ill-disguised abhorrence of homosexuality. The intercourse involved as a result of the construction of an artificial vagina was described as 'the reverse of ordinary, and in no sense natural. When such a cavity has been constructed in a male, the difference between sexual intercourse using it, and anal or intra-crural intercourse is, in my judgement to be measured in centimetres' (Corbett v. Corbett 1970: 49). Despite accepting the medical evidence that the respondent was genuinely transsexual, Ormrod clearly treated her as a male homosexual coincidentally possessed of artificial female genitalia, who could not be permitted to marry because marriage must be exclusively heterosexual.

Corbett illustrates the emphasis placed on marriage as a purely heterosexual relationship, although the issues raised for transsexuals are different from those raised for homosexuals. The question can be treated simply as one of sexual identity. A genuine transsexual will have a gender identity incongruent with her physical appearance. If her gender identity coupled with surgical intervention were accepted as determining her legal sexual identity then she could be legally recognised as a woman. The marriage of such a woman to a man would still therefore be a heterosexual relationship within the essential nature of marriage, and transsexuals are in fact generally heterosexually oriented towards individuals who they perceive to be of the opposite sex to themselves. On this analysis transsexuals pose no challenge to the claims made for the heterosexual nature of marriage.

The reasoning in Corbett appears to be aimed at preventing anything resembling same-sex marriage. The irony is that it does not prevent the transsexual from marrying someone whom they consider to be of the same sexual identity as themselves. Most transsexuals are heterosexually oriented, but it is a startling legal contradiction that however unlikely such an outcome might be, there is at least one recorded marriage between a post-operative male to female transsexual, who was also homosexually oriented, and her female partner (Whittle 1996). This relationship is a valid marriage, despite the fact that it is conceived by both parties to be truly homosexual. As a legally valid marriage, the family relationship of these individuals attracts the full recognition and status afforded by the law. With this rare exception, the emphasis on heterosexual marriage as a formal link from which family status flows, is highly restrictive. The emphasis on marriage also excludes non-traditional families which are based upon heterosexual cohabitation rather than marriage.

The traditional emphasis on marriage has undergone some change: the significance attached to marriage as the central signifier of a family relationship and family status is perceptibly declining. In English law, for example, cohabitants have for some years been able to take advantage of legislation offering protection from domestic violence and protection of housing rights. But this extension of recognition of non-traditional families is piecemeal rather than part of a coherent family policy towards family diversity. This is a limited recognition of non-traditional families, and even this only extends to heterosexual cohabitation which is privileged over homosexual cohabitation. Thus, courts have been prepared to interpret 'family members' so as to include heterosexual cohabitants in the context of succession to tenancies under the Rent Act 1977, but declined to extend the same construction of the term to a homosexual cohabitant. It is clear that for English law, homosexual cohabitation will not receive any recognition or validity as a family relationship. By contrast, some US courts have shown themselves willing to extend recognition to such relationships in similar specific contexts (Anderson 1987).

The law must develop a construction of family that will be of general application to non-traditional families, both heterosexual and homosexual, but how can a more inclusive understanding of the family be structured? As shown, the law takes a formalistic and exclusive approach to the classification of family relationships, particularly those between adults. One alternative is to abandon the emphasis on formalism and instead to adopt a more functional approach to family relationships. Another is to retain an essentially formalistic approach, but instead to widen the category of formal links which will give rise to family status.

A functionalist approach to family relationships

The functionalist approach focuses on whether the relationship shares 'the essential characteristics of a traditionally accepted relationship and fulfils the same human needs' (Note 1991: 1646). This approach has been adopted by courts in the USA in specific contexts such as housing protection (Anderson 1987; Note 1991) and this understanding of the realities of family structure is essentially what underlies the limited degree of recognition afforded to heterosexual cohabitants in English law. Similar ideas about dependence inform the rare example of the recognition of homosexual relationships. Homosexual cohabitants may make a claim for financial provision from the estate of the deceased partner under the Inheritance (Provision for Family and Dependants) Act 1975, if they can show that they were being maintained by the deceased (Section 1(1)(e)). However, this is a general test of dependency that would apply to any claimant who falls outside the classification of family member – by comparison, separate provision is also explicitly made for heterosexual cohabitants. It therefore cannot be seen as in any way reflecting a policy that the relationship should be recognised as possessing the intrinsic nature of a family relationship. There is little evidence that the functionalist approach is being adopted at the heart of English judicial decision making concerning non-traditional forms of family.

The functionalist approach is not unproblematic: it does not dictate what degree of congruence there must be with the traditional model. Each case is therefore approached on an individual basis with wide scope for judicial discretion. This case-by-case approach, coupled with the necessary detailed scrutiny of the quality of the relationship concerned leads to *ad hoc* decision making in an unjustifiably intrusive manner (Note 1991: 1652).

Adopting a different structure of formal links

An alternative way of constructing a more inclusive legal perspective of the family is to retain the current formalistic approach, but to widen the categories of formal links which will be deemed to create family relationships and family status. Two extensions can be suggested. First, to extend the formal relationship of marriage to same-sex relationships. Second, to construct a new formal link –

partnership registration – to which legal status and recognition would attach. These extensions are influenced by the functional approach to family relationships – the main argument for extending legal recognition to lesbian and gay family relationships is that they are in function indistinguishable from traditional heterosexual family relationships. On this analysis, even extending the formal framework of recognised family relationships is justified by reference to a functionalist approach, but in such a way that the perceived flaws of *ad hoc* analysis are avoided: instead, the extension of formal links creates an effective presumption that these relationships are of sufficient value to acquire the recognition and protection of law.

Same-sex marriage

Despite the traditional rhetoric about the essentially heterosexual nature of marriage, the prospect of redefining marriage to include same-sex relationships is very real. The Netherlands is considering – for the second time – passing legislation permitting same-sex marriage, giving full legal status to the relationship except for the ability to adopt children jointly. There has also been discussion of some similar moves in South Africa. In the USA the gay rights movement has a long history of challenge to the heterosexual status of marriage (Dupuis 1995), through the avenue of judicial constitutional challenge rather than legislative intervention. The state of Hawaii is currently facing a challenge to the prohibition of same-sex marriage by three gay couples (Baehr v. Lewin 852 P 2d 44). The case, evocative of the anti-miscegenation cases in the 1960s, has passed the early constitutional hurdles: the Hawaiian Supreme Court held that the state must show a 'compelling reason' to discriminate against same-sex couples. The lower court's decision in 1996 that the state cannot show such a compelling interest will now be re-examined by the Supreme Court but Dupuis (among others) predicts that the court will find against the state. Couples in several other states have apparently also filed similar constitutional suits. One of these cases was recently heard in Alaska, where the Supreme Court followed the same line of reasoning as in Baehr v. Lewin (Brause and Dugan v. Bureau of National Statistics 1998).

In theory, if this challenge to the exclusivity of heterosexual marriage were successful then a same-sex marriage contracted in Hawaii would have to be recognised by other states throughout America under the 'full faith and credit' provisions of the Constitution. This perceived threat has prompted Congress to pass the Defense of Marriage Act, which would allow other states to refuse to recognise the validity of such a marriage performed in Hawaii: an Act which arguably contravenes the Constitution (Griffin: 1997). The very title of the legislation highlights the ideological debate aroused by the claims of homosexual couples to equal recognition and respect for their relationships. It presumes that marriage is not just sacred but also fragile; that it will be destroyed by any acceptance of marriage between homosexuals. This immediate response to a perceived threat (which bears comparison with the UK Conservative government's prohibition of 'pretended families') simply highlights the privileged ideological position occupied by traditional constructions of the family.

It should however be noted that there is vigorous debate amongst the gay and lesbian movements over whether the extension of the formal concept of marriage is the most appropriate route for recognition of gay and lesbian family relationships. For some, marriage is an essential part of the patriarchal ideology which they choose to reject and it is not clear whether similar objections would apply to the alternative suggested means of extending the formal framework of legally recognised family relationships.

Registered partnerships

Although several US states have domestic partnership ordinances (Anderson 1987; Note 1991), these are currently of very limited practical effect. The most comprehensive registered partnership schemes are found in Denmark, Norway and Sweden (a similar scheme is now in place in the Netherlands and has been proposed in France). In all three countries the system is almost identical to marriage in terms of the rights and duties which flow from formal registration (Neilsen 1990; Henson 1993; Dupuis 1995). However, these relationships are explicitly stated not to be marriage. Marriage retains its central place in family ideology: the privileged status of marriage is still reserved for heterosexuals and linked to procreation. The main distinction in practice is that there is no right to adopt jointly in a registered partnership. These partnerships, although given considerable legal recognition, still acquire lesser status than heterosexual marriage and are regulated in a more intrusive manner than marriage: the formal framework for recognition still discriminates against homosexual relationships. Another criticism of this type of formal recognition is that even these measures discriminate against and exclude other more diverse forms of family life, such as group families (Ryder 1990): the privilege of legal recognition formerly confined to heterosexual relationships is now simply extended to include a relationship which in function closely resembles the traditional heterosexual nuclear family.

English law, by comparison, clearly shows no willingness to abandon its traditional construction of heterosexual marriage, but some change has occurred in the legal construction of the family. There has been a lessening of emphasis on the adult relationship (dependent on marriage in the traditionalist perspective) as the determinant of family status (Dewar 1992). The limited degree of recognition afforded to heterosexual cohabitation is one reflection of this, but more significantly, increasing focus is being placed upon the status of parenthood and the recognition of relationships between adults and children. Does this changing understanding of parent–child relationships offer hope for a more inclusive construction of families and for recognition of lesbian and gay family relationships?

Lesbian and gay families: children

Recognition of parenthood has always been a vital constituent element of the legal construction of the family but law's emphasis on the formal link and status of parenthood was essentially secondary to and derived from the formal relationship of marriage. Marriage still provides the basic framework for the allocation of the legal status of parenthood, but the legal perspective of the family has shifted to place more emphasis on recognising the nature and quality of a given relationship between adult and child: emphasis is placed not only on the legal status of parenthood but also on functional parenthood. The functionalist approach has influenced English law on family relationship between adults only piecemeal and restrictively; it can be seen as informing the changing focus of family law on relationships between parents (or other adults) and children. The criticism that this approach is too intrusive in the context of adult relationships is thought to be less problematic in analysing parent–child relationships, where the degree of intrusiveness is seen to be justified by reference to the child's welfare (Note 1991).

Parenthood is primarily acquired through the fact of biological parenthood (although it can alternatively be acquired through the legal mechanism of adoption). Legal parenthood is located in the birth mother and where she is married, paternity is presumed to be located in her husband. The legal construction of the relationship between parent and child has undergone some change. Increasing recognition has been afforded to the relationship between unmarried father and child: he now acquires the status of parent, but does not automatically acquire all the responsibilities and rights associated with parenthood and known as parental responsibility. Additionally, given modern techniques of assisted reproduction, new rules have been required to locate legal parenthood in individuals not biologically related to the child, for example in cases of gametes or embryo donation. This is in itself a recognition of the reality of the relationships which the adults involved (donors and recipients) will have with the child, rather than an emphasis on purely genetic criteria, but in general the status of parenthood is one acquired purely by procreation (for a more comprehensive treatment of the area see Barton and Douglas 1995).

This changed focus is clearly displayed in the overhaul of child law in the Children Act 1989. Previously the rights and duties of parenthood were confined to legal parents. Under the Act, these have become 'parental responsibility' and can be acquired independently of the status of legal parenthood. For example, the unmarried father has the legal status of parent but does not at present automatically acquire parental responsibility (in contrast to the mother and married father). However, recent proposals for reform are likely to result in the unmarried father also automatically acquiring parental responsibility. Another consequence follows from the separation of parenthood and parental responsibility: individuals who are legally regarded as non-parents may also seek legal recognition of the reality of their relationship with a child and acquire parental responsibility in relation to a child. Although only an unmarried father can specifically apply for parental responsibility, non-parents may apply for residence orders settling with whom the child is to live or for orders that they may have contact with the child. Only a residence order also confers parental responsibility for the child, but the very fact that non-parents may obtain these orders offers some legal recognition that they have a valuable relationship with the child, outside the normative framework of blood ties and marriage.

These changes are based on an increased understanding within law of social or functional parenthood and of different family structures. They admit that models of family life exist where a child has significant relationships with adults who have no other legal status or responsibility for it. The emphasis placed by modern family law upon the welfare of the child leads to an understanding that the child's needs require legal recognition of its relationships with adults. The law will not confer the status of parent upon the adult carer, short of an application for the formal link provided by adoption, but it will afford some status and recognition of the relationship between adult and child, based on a more functional or affective approach to the nature of the relationship. In dealing with issues concerning children the law is clearly adopting a less formally restricted approach and is instead moving towards a recognition of individual circumstances and emotional attachments. For non-traditional families such as lesbian and gay families the crucial question is whether this offers any potential for a new and more inclusive understanding of the family.

Lesbian and gay families present more of a challenge for this new approach to relationships with children than other forms of family diversity, because they are so clearly removed from the norm of the heterosexual ideal. The traditional legal construction emphasises marriage and procreation and excludes homosexual relationships from these concepts. This emphasis upon the heterosexual and procreative nature of family life is still preserved when addressing which functional relationships between adults and children can be included in the legal construction of family.

The main factor which is relevant in determining whether the relationship should receive legal recognition is the child's welfare, which has been of increasing significance in family law throughout this century (Bainham 1993). The traditional perspective of parent–child relationships was of children as possessions belonging to their parents, who had exclusive rights in relation to them, justified by virtue of their procreative role (Page 1984). Gradually this has given way to an increasing concern with the rights of the child and an understanding that parental rights are in fact responsibilities which exist for the benefit or welfare of the child.

Statutes and judicial decision making have long included references to the welfare of the child as being the court's guiding principle when dealing with children and the review of child law in the Children Act sought to clarify earlier confusion over the weight of the child's welfare by stating that in disputes concerning the upbringing of a child, the child's welfare is the court's paramount consideration (Section 1(1)).

In a climate of increasing child centredness, this welfare principle acquires an unchallengeable rhetoric, but its broad scope is problematic (Mnookin 1975). Decisions about the welfare of children are normally left in the hands of their parents (Dewar 1992), but where the parents are in dispute then the child's welfare is determined by the courts. The welfare principle implies that there is an objective standard of welfare, the content of which can be precisely determined by neutral arbiters but 'the law's ability actually to recognise and serve the welfare of children is necessarily limited'. (Barton and Douglas 1995: 173). Although the Children Act provides a statutory list of factors which must be taken into account when deciding what the welfare of the child requires, it is unclear how much weight should be attached to specific factors. The exercise is entirely one of judicial discretion and despite the presence of a 'welfare checklist', the exercise of that discretion will be influenced by the judge's own values and his perception of societal norms. There is a danger that the checklist is simply used to give legitimacy to the judge's subjective preferences or perception of public policy on issues such as what constitutes good parenting: for example, good mothering (Smart 1989; Brophy 1989). In the context of lesbian and gay families, welfare concerns can easily become a means of controlling the 'deviant' behaviour of the parent and ensuring conformity with the assumed shared norms of family values.

Thus judges decide what issues are relevant as part of the process of ascertaining the child's welfare, and it is clear that they regard the sexual orientation of an adult as relevant to whether their relationship with the child should be recognised; or if the relationship already has legal status such as parenthood, how it should be regulated. There is a clear preference for the traditional ideal of two parents of heterosexual orientation, preferably married to each other:

> I regard it as axiomatic that the ideal environment for the upbringing of a child is the home of loving caring and sensible parents, her father and mother. When the marriage between father and mother is at an end, that ideal cannot be attained. When the court is called upon to decide which of two possible alternatives is then preferable for the child's welfare, its task is to choose the alternative which comes closest to that ideal....A court may well decide that a sensitive loving lesbian relationship is a more satisfactory environment for a child than a less sensitive or loving alternative. But that the nature of the relationship is an important factor to be put into the balance seems to me to be clear.
>
> (C v. C (No 2) 1992)

Adults in all non-traditional families must overcome this preference, but less recognition is afforded to lesbian and gay families simply because their homosexuality is a more obvious deviation from the judicially perceived norms. Lesbian and gay parenting is seen as a threat to the traditional ideology of the family and is therefore penalised (Richardson 1978). Since the welfare of the child is treated as the only relevant test in conferring recognition on the adults, then the exclusion of lesbian and gay parents must be justified by reference to welfare considerations. The role of prejudice or policy towards homosexual family units is therefore disguised by presenting justifications that lesbian and gay parenting is intrinsically harmful and contrary to the interests of children (Lewin 1981; Steel 1990). The agenda becomes the promotion of the traditional family form through the guise of concern about children's welfare and, given the discretionary nature of the welfare exercise, it becomes difficult to challenge decisions made in disputes concerning children.

In fact, the evidence is that lesbian and gay parenting is no more harmful than heterosexual parenting (e.g. Green 1978; Golombok *et al.* 1983; Tasker and Golombok 1991). Yet even where this evidence is presented, it tends to be disregarded or is outweighed by a judicial preference for other factors involved in the child's welfare. In the face of this prejudice, lesbian and gay parents are forced to render themselves and their sexuality invisible in the legal process. It must be argued that sexual orientation between adults is not a relevant factor when determining whether to recognise the adult's relationship with a child, but the legal construction of families at once insists on its relevance and then forces lesbian and gay parents to deny an essential element of their family relationships in order to meet the legal norms of family structure.

Three main areas can be identified where the law is required to classify a set of relationships as being worthy of recognition as family relationships: the regulation of existing rights and responsibilities of lesbian and gay parents; the creation by lesbian and gay couples of family units including children; and dealing with the consequences of the breakdown of a lesbian or gay family unit.

Regulating existing parent–child relationships

An assumption that lesbians and gays are completely excluded from the legal classification of parents is clearly flawed: they will have the status of being parents of their biological children in exactly the same way as a heterosexual parent. Sexual orientation is irrelevant in the allocation of parenthood to biological parents. Where biological parents engage in dispute about arrangements for the children, then the law, having already allocated family status to those involved, must regulate the consequences of the status flowing from that allocation. It is here that the sexual orientation of the parents is treated as a relevant factor in deciding whether they should continue to exercise any or all of the responsibilities and rights which flow from their legal status as parents.

Despite the fact that the body of case law concerning these issues is relatively small, it is clear that judges are reluctant to accept that the relationship between a homosexual parent and her child is worthy of the respect afforded to heterosexual parents. The few reported cases provide illuminating examples of judicial attitudes.

It is interesting in itself to note that the body of available case law is small, and the few recorded decisions available largely concern lesbian mothers (Bradley 1987). Lesbian mothers clearly suffer humiliation and distress in their dealings with the courts. Equal respect is not afforded to them and in general a presumption has operated that a lesbian mother is implicitly an unfit mother. It is therefore likely that many disputes between heterosexual fathers and lesbian mothers over the care of children do not even come before the courts. Lesbian mothers at least benefit from another (although weakening) judicial assumption: the maternal preference principle, or the assumption that the needs of children, particularly young children, are best served by being cared for by the mother. Gay fathers do not even have that residual advantage and this helps to explain the lack of cases dealing with the claims of the gay father to care for his children or to have contact with them. The gay father thus suffers from a double burden of invisibility. His relevance as a parent is diminished both by his being a father and by his sexual orientation.

Furthermore, decision making in these cases is not routinely recorded. The family is seen to be located at the heart of the private sphere (O'Donovan 1985), and disputes between parents about the future upbringing of children are seen as being intrinsically private and individual. Decision making is on an *ad hoc* basis: residence and contact disputes are rarely seen as raising issues of principle. Instead, each case is seen as raising similar issues which must be considered on an isolated and individualistic basis because the precise facts of each case are perceived to be unique (Fricker 1995). Because these disputes are rarely thought to give rise to issues of wider principle, and to preserve the privacy of the family members (particularly the children), these hearings take place in private and are rarely reported. Even where disputes reach the higher courts and are reported, and are treated as laying down statements of principle, the lack of accessibility to judgements at the lowest levels means that it is impossible to clarify whether these principles are being followed in practice.

This area illustrates well the claim that law seeks to make the parent's sexual orientation relevant to the decision, while at the same time declaring it to be irrelevant (Beresford 1994). The reported case law often contains statements that the fact of the mother's lesbianism is not an automatic disqualification of her claims to care for her children, but this apparent neutrality is always qualified by a clear preference expressed for placing the child in a 'normal' environment. Homosexuality may no longer be deemed to be an automatic disqualification, but heterosexuality is implicitly deemed to be better (Boyd 1992).

The emphasis on welfare requires that homosexuality be related in some way to the child's welfare and thus assumptions are promoted that the mother's lesbianism is in some way harmful (Lewin 1981; Falk 1989): for example it has been assumed that homosexual relationships are inherently less stable than heterosexual ones, with consequent harm to the child. There are also implicit fears that the child will be 'corrupted' or will grow up homosexual, occasionally coupled with the offensive implication that homosexuality exposes the child to the risk of sexual abuse by the parent or their partner.

Other objections based upon the child's welfare are that even if the quality of parenting is as good as that available with a heterosexual parent, the child will inherently suffer from living in a household which deviates from the perceived norm, an argument which ignores the diversity of many different forms of family structure experienced in modern society. It is assumed that the child will suffer stigma in its relationships with peers as a result of its family structure. Again, there is no evidence that this is a significant issue adversely affecting children in lesbian and gay households (Lewis 1980). Even learning about the parent's homosexuality has been held to create a potential risk to the child's welfare: in the case of Re G (Minors) (1983) the homosexual father was denied contact after a gap of several years because the children 'may get to know their father but they may be disturbed by this. They may start to ask questions about his life and they may wish to stay with him. Such a wish would raise many disturbing questions'.

Treating sexual orientation as a relevant factor results in highly intrusive enquiries into the nature of the parent's sexual relationship with a partner. In an unreported case discussed by Edwards (1996), the court made highly detailed enquiries into the mother's sexual life and similar enquiries can be seen in most of the reported cases. Lesbian mothers whose sexual orientation is deemed to be too visible are penalised:

> What is so important in cases is to distinguish between militant lesbians who try to convert others to their way of life...and lesbians in private....I am dealing with two lesbians who are private persons who do not believe in advertising their lesbianism and acting in the public field in favour of pro-moting lesbianism....So it is a wholly different kind of case from that of the militant lesbian where the risk...may be so much greater.
>
> (B v. B (Minors) (Custody, Care and Control) 1991)

In this way the court exercises control over the 'deviant' parent: where contact and residence orders have been obtained by the homosexual parent, they are frequently subject to conditions imposed upon their sexual lives, in the interests of the child's welfare, or are subjected to regular scrutiny by state agencies. Homosexual parents are forced to conceal and render invisible a central part of their lives and personalities (and in the process present their children with falsehoods rather than truth), but when they do so, they may still be penalised:

> It would be an odd arrangement at mother's and one which could not be explained. It would be an odd arrangement at father's, but could be ex-plained. Mother and Miss H [the mother's partner] are going to be sly and employ a certain falsity about the things to be explained to the child.
>
> (Eveson v. Eveson 1980)

It is made clear that the heterosexual alternative will be preferred in almost any situation: the lesbian mother becomes an acceptable carer of the child only when there is no heterosexual alternative available; for example, where the alternative was a care order for the child:

> I accept that it is not right to say that a child should in no circumstances live with a mother who is carrying on a lesbian relationship with a woman who is living with her, but I venture to suggest that it can only be countenanced by the courts when it is driven to the inevitable conclusion that there is in the interests of the child no acceptable form of custody.
>
> (Re P (A Minor) (Custody) 1982)

This brief analysis of the case law in this area (more comprehensively discussed in Bradley 1987; Edwards 1996), serves to illustrate with some force the policies which the judiciary clearly believe to inform the recognition and validation of lesbian and gay parenting. If this is the approach taken to regulating the existing rights and responsibilities of parents who happen to be homosexual, then the law is likely to afford even less recognition where gay and lesbian couples seek to augment their existing family relationships by introducing children.

Attempting to bring children into the family unit

Lesbian and gay couples are increasingly seeking to bring up children together as an integral part of their family unit, but the law seeks to exercise strict control over such attempts, claiming this is justified by the need to protect the interests of the child. Clearly homosexual couples cannot procreate through using genetic material of both parties, but various alternatives exist.

One partner might bear or father a child with someone outside the couple, through intercourse or through artificial insemination. Such informal arrangements will result in the allocation of legal parenthood in accordance with biological parenthood. As long as the parents agree on the arrangements for the child – such as with whom it will live – then there will be no further involvement by the law, but this approach is not free from problems. Legal parenthood is located in an individual outside the family unit, while the law fails to allocate any recognition to the functional co-parent within the family unit. The emotional relationship of the co-parent with the child receives no recognition or protection, and essentially there is no recognition of the family unit as a whole. The other biological parent, however, has legal status which might receive further support from the court if that parent subsequently wished to establish an emotional relationship with the child. A court faced with such a dispute between the biological parents is likely to assume that the welfare of the child is best served by promoting an emotional relationship with both biological parents. In this dispute the co-parent is essentially regarded as a legal stranger to the child. Furthermore, even where the other biological parent does not wish to establish any relationship with the child, he may be compelled to live up to the responsibilities imposed on a legal parent: for example the duty to maintain the child under the Child Support Act 1991.

An alternative approach for a lesbian couple is to seek to avoid the potential complications presented by the legal presence of the biological father and instead turn to formal artificial insemination or other reproductive technology. The Human Fertilisation and Embryology Act 1990 provides that parenthood will not be allocated to the donors of genetic material, but will instead be located in the couple seeking treatment together. However, the formulation of the Act was strongly influenced by policy concerns aimed at preventing 'single' women, i.e. women without a male partner, from obtaining fertility treatment. Section 13(5) of the Act stipulates as a condition of a licence for such treatments that 'a woman shall not be treated…unless account has been taken of the welfare of any child who may be born as a result of the treatment (including the need of that child for a father)'. This arguably means not that the child should have a father, but that the mother should have a man (Morgan and Lee 1991: 155). The legal preference is clearly for the child to have two parents and the law is not prepared to see the two parenting roles filled by parents who happen to be of the same sex. One policy concern is that where the donor is an anonymous donor he will not be treated as the father of the child, and if the mother has no heterosexual partner, there will be no one in law who is the father of the child. This is seen as a grave shortcoming, and the policy clearly has the effect of limiting the availability of such treatments to lesbians.

The simplest option for a lesbian or gay couple would therefore seem to be for both to seek adoption, either of a child unrelated to both, or of the biological child of one party. Adoption confers the full legal status of parenthood, but the law's preference for heterosexual parenting through marriage is again clear: joint adoption is only permitted for married couples (Section 14 Adoption Act 1976). Even in the event of an application by only one party, they must still overcome the judicial prejudice about homosexual parenting. A familiar policy can be detected: that two parents are better than one and that allocating parenthood to a homosexual parent is only acceptable when there is no other available alternative.

The co-parent is therefore in an ambiguous position. She has a very real emotional relationship with the child, but finds herself excluded from the law's conception of parenthood. The only means by which both parties may acquire some recognition of their parenting relationship with the child would be for one to acquire the legal status of parenthood (by adoption or through procreation) and for the co-parent to seek to harness the potential of the Children Act. The stronger emphasis in the Act on the functional quality of the adult's relationship with the child means that the co-parent could seek a residence order for the child, which would bring with it legal recognition in the form of parental responsibility, albeit not legal parenthood. In view of the policy of not permitting joint adoption in such circumstances and the clear statements of judicial prejudice in the context of residence or contact disputes, it is a surprising, but promising, development that at least one such residence application has been granted by a court. However, it should be stressed that this is simply legal recognition of the co-parent's relationship with the child. Although it indirectly recognises that all three individuals constitute a family unit, it confers no legal status upon the unit as a whole. It still does not provide directly for recognition of the relationship which exists between the adult partners.

Dealing with the breakdown of the lesbian or gay family

Similar issues can be identified here. The child of the lesbian or gay family will not be the biological child of both parties: one adult will have parenthood but unless legal recognition of the co-parent's relationship with the child had already been sought and obtained through a residence order, then the co-parent has no status at all in the family unit which is comprised, for the purposes of law, of the biological parents and their child. However, when lesbian and gay family units which involve children separate, the same issues will need to be resolved as arise in the context of heterosexual relationship breakdowns. The co-parent may desire to keep a relationship with the children with whom she has built up a caring relationship. There may be disputes not just about contact between child and co-parent but also about where the child should reside.

Again, the framework of the Children Act potentially allows such a co-parent to seek permission from the court to apply for an order for residence or contact, and in deciding whether to grant permission and whether to make the order requested the court will consider the emotional reality of the relationship between co-parent and child. If an order were made, the co-parent would have achieved some legal recognition of her relationship with the child.

The co-parent is however disadvantaged by the very fact that she or he is not regarded as a parent. As between a heterosexual and a homosexual parent the heterosexual parent is likely to be preferred. As between a legal parent and a non-parent in the eyes of the law, the parent is likely to be preferred, because the legal construction of the family still allocates more weight to biological links than to purely functional ones. Where both adults are homosexual, then the biological parent will be preferred by a combination of their biological link and the fact that no heterosexual alternative is available. Against this background, it is unlikely that the more functional approach of the Children Act would result in a court making a residence order in favour of the co-parent. The most that would be likely is that a contact order might be made. While this would not confer parental responsibility upon the co-parent, let alone confer the status of parent, it would at least provide some recognition of the quality and value of the relationship between adult and child, a recognition which would not have been available to the co-parent before the changes in approach encapsulated in the Children Act.

Conclusion

Legal perspectives of the family are ill-equipped to cope with the modern diversity of family lives and structures. The traditional legal construction of family life refuses to award recognition and status and to validate models of family organisation unless specific linking relationships are present. Although some changes in the legal perspective can be identified, such as an increased willingness to recognise parenting existing outside marriage, the law still tends to emphasise traditional concepts in its construction of the family and thus adopts

an exclusive approach to its construction of the family, denying recognition and validity to what are perceived to be 'abnormal' forms. The emphasis placed upon marriage as the source of family status excludes homosexuals (and transsexuals) who cannot validly marry and whose relationships with each other are devalued. The increasing emphasis which modern family law places on children and recognition of relationships with children may provide limited recognition for those whose lesbian and gay family units include children, but still denies the adults recognition of their relationship with each other and is still exclusive of those whose family units do not also include children.

Note

1   A transsexual is a person possessing a psychological gender identity directly opposed to the sexual identity indicated by their physical characteristics. This medical condition is more accurately described as gender dysphoria and it is generally accepted that the most effective form of treatment is surgery to align as many of the physical characteristics as possible with the patient's psychological gender identity.

Bibliography

Anderson, L. (1987) 'Property Rights of Same-Sex Couples: Towards a New Definition of Family', *Journal of Family Law*, 26: 35–372.

Armstrong, C. N. and Walton, T. (1990) 'Transsexuals and the Law', *New Law Journal* 140: 1384–90.

Bailey, R. (1979) 'Recent Cases' *Australian Law Journal* 5: 659–60.

Bainham, A. (1993) *Children – the Modern Law*, London: Family Law.

Barton, C. and Douglas, G. (1995) *Law and Parenthood*, London: Butterworths.

Beresford, S. (1994) 'Lesbians in Residence and Parental Responsibility Cases', *Family Law* 643–45.

Bernardes, J. (1985) 'Do We Really Know What "The Family" Is?' in P. Close and R. Collins (eds) *Family and Economy in Modern Society*, London: Macmillan.

Boyd, S. B. (1992) 'What is a "Normal" Family', *Modern Law Review* 55: 269–78.

Bradley, D. (1987) 'Homosexuality and Child Custody in English Law', *International Journal of Law and the Family* 1: 155–205.

Bradney, A. (1987) 'Transsexuals and the Law', *Family Law*, 350–53.

Brophy, J. (1989) 'Custody Law, Child Care and Inequality in Britain' in C. Smart and S. Sevenhuijsen *Child Custody and the Politics of Gender*, Routledge: London.

Dewar, J. (1992) *Law and the Family*, London: Butterworths.

Dupuis, M. D. (1995) 'The Impact of Culture, Society and History on the Legal Process: An Analysis of the Legal Status of Same-Sex Relationships in the United States and Denmark', *International Journal of Law and the Family* 9: 86–118.

Edwards, S. (1996) *Sex and Gender in the Legal Process*, London: Blackstone Press.

Falk, P. J. (1989) 'Lesbian Mothers: Psycho-Social Assumptions in Family Law', *American Psychologist*, 44, 6: 941–7.

Finlay, H. A. (1980) 'Sexual Identity and the Law of Nullity', *Australian Law Journal* 54: 115.

Fricker, N. (1995) 'Family Law is Different', *Family Law* 306.

Golombok, S., Spencer, A. and Rutter, M. (1983) 'Children in Lesbian and Single-Parent Households: Psychosexual and Psychiatric Appraisal', *Journal of Child Psychology and Psychiatry*, 24, 4: 551–72.

Green, R. (1978) 'Sexual Identity of 37 Children Raised by Homosexual or Transsexual Parents', *American Journal of Psychiatry* 135(6): 692–97.

Griffin, A. (1997) 'Another Case, Another Clause – Same Sex Marriage, Full Faith and Credit and the US Supreme Court's Evolving Gay Rights Agenda', *Public Law* 315–27.

Henson, D. (1993) 'A Comparative Analysis of Same-Sex Partnership Protections: Recommendations for American Reform', *International Journal of Law and the Family* 7: 282–313.

Kennedy, I. McC. (1973), 'Transsexualism and Single Sex Marriage' *Anglo American Law Review* 2: 112.

Lewin, E. (1981) 'Lesbianism and Motherhood: Implications for Child Custody', *Human Organization* 40: 6–13.

Lewis, C. A. (1988) 'From This Day Forward: A Feminine Moral Discourse on Homosexual Marriage', *Yale Law Journal* 97: 1783–803.

Lewis, K. G. (1980) 'Children of Lesbians: Their Point of View', *Social Work*, May: 198–203.

Lind, C. (1996) ' "Pretended Families" and the Local State in Britain and the USA', *International Journal of Law, Policy and the Family* 10(2): 134–58.

Mnookin, R. (1975) 'Child Custody Adjudication: Judicial Functions in the Face of Indeterminacy', *Law and Contemporary Problems* 39: 226.

Morgan, D. and Lee, R. (1991) *The Human Fertilisation and Embryology Act 1990: Abortion and Embryo Research, the New Law*, London: Blackstone Press.

Nielsen, L. (1990) 'Family Rights and the Registered Partnership in Denmark', *International Journal of Law and the Family* 4: 297–307.

Note (1991) 'Looking for a Family Resemblance: the Limits of the Functionalist Approach to the Legal Definition of Family', *Harvard Law Review* 104: 1640–59.

O'Donovan, K. (1985) *Sexual Divisions in Law*, London: Weidenfeld & Nicolson.

Page, E. (1984) 'Parental Rights', *Journal of Applied Philosophy* 1: 187.

Rapoport, R. N., Fogarty, P. and Rapoport, R. (1982) *Families in Britain*, London: Routledge & Kegan Paul.

Richardson, D. (1978) 'Do Lesbians Make Good Mothers?', *Community Care* 2 August: 16–17.

Ryder, B. (1990) 'Equality Rights and Sexual Orientation: Confronting Heterosexual Family Privilege', *Revue Canadienne de Droit Familial* 9: 40–97.

Smart, C. (1989) 'Power and the Politics of Child Custody' in C. Smart and S. Sevenhuijsen *Child Custody and the Politics of Gender*, Routledge: London.

Smith, D. K. (1971) 'Transsexualism, Sex Reassignment Surgery and the Law', *Cornell Law Review* 56: 963.

Steel, M. (1990) *Lesbian Mothers, Custody Disputes and Court Welfare Reports*, Norwich: Social Work Monographs.

Stone, L. (1979) *The Family, Sex and Marriage in England 1500–1800*, London: Penguin.

Taitz, J. (1986) 'The Law Relating to The Consummation of Marriage Where One of the Spouses is a Post-Operative Transsexual', *Anglo-American Law Review* 15(2): 141–48.

Tasker, F. L. and Golombok, S. (1991) 'Children Raised by Lesbian Mothers: the Empirical Evidence', *Family Law*: 184–87.

Whittle, S. (1996) 'An association for as noble a purpose as any', *New Law Journal* March: 366–68.

Case references

References used are the standard citations for law reports.

B v. B (Minors) (Custody, Care and Control) [1991] FLR 402.

Baehr v. Lewin 852 P 2d 44 (Hawaii 1993).

Brause and Dugan v. Bureau of National Statistics and Others (unreported) Case No. 3 AN–95–6562 CI 1998–0207 (Alaska Supreme Court).

C v. C (No. 2) [1992] 1 FCR 206.

Corbett v. Corbett [1970] 2 All ER 333.

Eveson v. Eveson 27 November 1980, Lexis.

Hyde v. Hyde and Woodmansee (1866) LR 1 P&D 130.

Re G (Minors) 23 March 1983, Lexis.

Re P (A Minor) (Custody) [1982] 4 FLR 401.

5   Poor choices?

Gender, agency and the underclass debate

Kirk Mann and Sasha Roseneil

Recent years have seen a growth in the number of women having children outside marriage and bringing them up alone. This trend has been accompanied by extensive public debate about lone motherhood. This chapter explores these developments and reflects on the implications of this debate. Our particular focus is on the powerful and widespread discourse which gripped the media and policy circles in the early 1990s; this discourse links lone motherhood with the creation and reproduction of an 'underclass' in contemporary society. Whilst this period is certainly not unique in its concern about the breakdown of 'the family' and the rise in the number of never married mothers, this specific discursive construction of lone motherhood is particularly interesting. The role of the media, leading politicians and academics in promoting the idea of a dangerous and growing underclass is considered. Commentators on both sides of the Atlantic have spoken of 'the demoralization of society' (Himmelfarb 1995), a process in which the lone mother has been seen as playing a catalytic role.

In this chapter we explore why this discourse about lone mothers, absent fathers and the underclass has achieved such widespread currency. Our focus is primarily on its expression in Britain, though we identify its origins in the United States, and we pass comment on the differing courses it has taken on each side of the Atlantic. We attempt to unravel some of the complex threads of moral concerns about the decline of the family, fiscal concerns about welfare benefits and 'the costs' of dependency, and a largely unspoken, but lurking, anti-feminism. We suggest that this discourse is located within the framework of a welfare state which is in the process of restructuring, and within a wider project of 'patriarchal reconstruction' (Smart 1989), that it constitutes a 'backlash' against long term changes in gender relations and against feminism. However, and in contrast to other feminist and critical commentators, we accept that there are some interesting social changes in train that merit more attention. Consequently we conclude the chapter with a discussion of agency which we suggest is at the heart of the discourse.

1993: the year of the lone mother

Our initial interest was prompted by the widespread moral outrage which followed the murder of a 2-year-old boy, James Bulger, in February 1993. In the period that followed the murder, the media homed in on lone mothers and their fatherless, supposedly criminally inclined children, identifying them as the core of the underclass and the source of many contemporary social problems. Although the intensity of this 'moral panic' ebbed in the months that followed, 1993 was, in many respects, 'the year of the lone mother' in Britain. The press, tabloid and broadsheet alike, was full of articles about the 'problem' of never married mothers, and television and radio documentaries and discussion programmes were devoted to the topic. For the second year running the Conservative Party Conference in the autumn of 1993 rang to denunciations of single mothers, and an ill-fated 'back to basics' programme to restore the nation's morality was launched.[1]

The discourse about the underclass which developed in 1993 dichotomised women along age old lines – good women who do the right thing, get married and then have children, versus bad women, who have children, don't get married and depend on state benefits. By the second half of the year, attention was not just on the social costs of fatherless families which fail properly to socialise their children, but included the financial costs as well.

As Smart (1992; 1996) and many other writers have documented, the problematisation of unmarried mothers (who are consistently condemned more than mothers who are single through divorce, abandonment or widowhood) has a long history and has at different times emphasised variously the economic, the moral and the psychological problems caused by lone mothers.[2] Moral outrage about lone mothers, particularly young mothers, existed throughout the 1980s (McRobbie 1989; Phoenix 1991), and it had been escalating from 1987 (Fox Harding 1993a). In 1991 the media erupted in a brief furore about 'virgin births', as evidence that growing numbers of women, particularly lesbians, were becoming 'lone mothers by choice', and doing so even without sexual contact with men (Radford 1991). Despite this history, there are good reasons for seeing developments in 1993 as novel.

First, the level of political vitriol against lone mothers, particularly never married mothers, reached a new intensity by 1993; the speeches of Conservative Ministers Lilley and Redwood seized the headlines on numerous occasions and whipped the Tory faithful into ecstatic applause. Second, the context within which the discourse was produced was different from that pertaining during previous outbreaks of outrage about lone mothers. Throughout the 1980s there was a significant increase in the proportion of families headed by never married mothers; by the beginning of the 1990s, 27 per cent of births were to unmarried mothers, with especially high rates in some areas (for example, 54 per cent in North Manchester) (Muncie *et al.* 1995). Of course, many of these mothers will get married, may be in a heterosexual relationship already, or will not be intending to rely on single-parent benefits. Nevertheless, we would suggest that a significant minority of lone mothers do not intend to marry and see no place in their families for a 'father figure' (see, for example, Renvoize 1985; Morris 1992; Gordon 1990, 1994). Whilst this may have been true of a very small proportion of lone mothers in the past, there appears to be a new confidence and assertiveness amongst many women. For many, despite the difficulties associated with lone motherhood, there seems to be a pragmatic feeling that they can manage, albeit with state support, and that the father is an obstacle to a stable life for themselves and their children. These women are not necessarily 'abandoned' by the fathers, nor should their pregnancies be assumed to be 'accidents'; in this respect, they are not victims.

The final reason why the 1993 discourse about lone mothers is significant is that it was disseminated extremely widely throughout the media. It dominated the political agenda to an unprecedented extent and elicited a considerable degree of consensus across the left/right political divide. With its differing strands, emphasising morality or economics, the discourse united Tory traditionalists concerned with 'family values' and morality, Christian socialists and liberals with similar interests, and Thatcherite hard-liners keen to continue 'rolling back the welfare state'. Moreover, and in contrast to earlier panics about the morality of young women, events in 1993 enabled these groups to engage with each other. Above all, the authority of the discourse rested on the status of two of its leading exponents – the American, Charles Murray (1990), and the Briton, A. H. Halsey (1992).

Moral panic: juvenile crime and the problem children of problem mothers

As Hall *et al.* (1978) point out, a widespread 'moral panic' about the 'steadily rising rate of violent crime' has been simmering away in British society since the 1960s. The most recent outbreak of moral indignation began with a focus on car crime committed by young men, and the racing of stolen cars around council estates drew widespread media coverage in 1991.

However, media attention to juvenile crime reached unprecedented heights in February 1993 following the murder of James Bulger. Still photographs from security video cameras in the mall showed the child with two figures, who appeared to be in their early teens. A hunt began for the murderers, during which several teenage boys were arrested and then eventually released uncharged. When two 10-year-old boys finally appeared in court, a crowd of about 250 people gathered outside, many hurling missiles and abuse at the accused (*Guardian* 23 February 1993).

The concern about juvenile crime which crystallised around the Bulger case can be labelled a 'moral panic', given the unanimity with which police, politicians, journalists and sections of the public reacted 'out of all proportion to the actual threat' (Hall *et al.* 1978: 16). Initially the panic concerned juvenile crime, but later it transpired that the 'real', underlying problem was lone mothers. From the breaking of the news about the murder of James Bulger until several weeks after the charging of suspects, the issue of juvenile crime dominated the media. The commentary of 'experts' and the 'vox pop' of the general public saturated the press, television and radio, all discussing the 'new' phenomenon of serious juvenile crime. From one murder, within the background context of rising car crime, was extrapolated a major new social scourge.

Condemnation of juvenile crime was not limited to those traditionally vocal on issues of law and order; indeed, the Labour Party made much of the running in the aftermath of the Bulger murder, with Tony Blair, soon-to-be Labour Party leader, declaring Labour policy to be 'tough on crime, and tough on the causes of crime' (*Guardian* 22 February 1993).

The gender politics of this moral panic about juvenile crime emerge in the analyses proffered by the media and by those 'experts' asked to explain the phenomenon. Despite Prime Minister John Major's declaration that society should 'condemn a little more and understand a little less', a veritable industry of pop sociology emerged during the lifetime of the panic. Both Murray and Halsey, appearing in the *Sunday Times* and the *Guardian*, respectively, along with editorials in almost every newspaper, linked the phenomenon of juvenile crime with the emergence of an underclass in British society, and this with the breakdown of the nuclear family and the increase in births outside marriage. Rising juvenile crime was presented as both the evidence and the result of a growing underclass composed primarily of never married mothers and their children. The solution to the problem therefore (sometimes implicit, other times explicit) was simple: the reconstitution of the nuclear family and the reassertion of the power and role of the father within it (e.g. Halsey 1992; Murray 1990).

Choosing the inadequate families

Although Murray does not reflect the views of any sizeable academic constituency in Britain, he is an important and influential figure. In 1987 he had meetings with Department of Health and Social Security and Treasury officials and members of the then Prime Minister's Policy Unit, and two years later he addressed the then Prime Minister Thatcher (Dean and Taylor-Gooby 1992: 5). The press are not generally noted for their keen interest in the work of social scientists but the views of Murray have been invoked to provide academic credibility for various leader writers and social commentators. The *Sunday Times* has persistently cited Murray, with Andrew Neil, the paper's then editor, pointing out that it was his newspaper which introduced Murray to the British public and sponsored his 'research' in Britain in 1989. Murray's ideas have also been disseminated by News International Group newspapers in other countries. In Britain, the Institute of Economic Affairs, and in Australia, the Centre for Industrial Studies (right-wing think tanks), have been quick to adopt Murray's arguments, both publishing his work (1990), and imprinting their other publications with the mark of his theories (e.g. Dennis and Erdos 1992; Davies 1993). Thus, and in spite of the fact that he has done little primary research, Murray has found a receptive international audience and a number of followers amongst journalists and politicians. As an American, Murray is considered to be well placed to tell Britain what the future may hold if unmarried mothers are allowed to continue reproducing the underclass unchecked. Comparisons with the US are commonplace within the British discourse, with the spectre of American inner city social dislocation and violence given prominence (MacGregor 1990).[3]

According to Murray there are three types of behaviour associated with membership of the underclass: illegitimacy, violent crime and drop out from the labour force. He does not make clear whether these forms of behaviour are cause or consequence of underclass membership. What is clear, however, is that the underclass, to put it in the 'common sense' language Murray is so fond of, is composed of 'idle, thieving bastards' (Bagguley and Mann 1992).

Like many right-wing observers Murray presents the issue in terms of rational choices. Whereas choice is usually portrayed by the right as a tremendous benefit to society and the economy, it is seen as inappropriate for women who want to have children without the support of an economically active man. Thus David Green of the Institute of Economic Affairs (in the Institute's series entitled 'Choice in Welfare') laments the fact that, 'The traditional family of "mum, dad and the kids" has become just another lifestyle choice'. He goes on to ask, 'Is every moral value just another lifestyle option? Or is there a minimum stock of values which we ignore at our peril?' (Green 1993: vi).

Never married mothers are deemed to have made the wrong choices, albeit, according to Murray, rational ones. Murray argues that lone mothers choose dependence on the state in preference to marriage because the benefit system privileges the lone mother over the two-parent family. This combines with the fact that there is no longer a stigma to illegitimacy, to mean that many young women no longer see the need to marry in order to have children. Murray goes on to suggest that these women are denying their children suitable masculine role models and denying young men a respectable role as father figures. There is a moral vacuum, it is claimed, which has its roots in the 'permissive society' of the 1960s, the period when Murray detects a shift in social values. The stigma which Murray feels is so important in deterring illegitimacy was eroded by the 'sexual revolution of the 1960s' (Murray 1990: 28). As he says:

> There is an obvious explanation for why single young women get pregnant: sex is fun and babies endearing. Nothing could be more natural than for young men and women to have sex, and nothing could be more natural than for a young woman to want to have a baby.
>
> (Murray 1990: 28)

Only the financial restraints of subsistence benefits and social opprobrium can restrain such biologically determined natural inclinations. In Murray's world view both men and women are driven by essential impulses – men to reckless barbarian behaviour and promiscuous sex, women to reproduction and motherhood. In order for society to function smoothly, this Hobbesian state of nature must be tamed by moral codes and economic sanctions. However, he does not suggest that all 'fatherless families' are part of the underclass: widows and divorcees are generally exempt, as are affluent women with careers who choose to be unmarried sole parents. The focus is squarely on working-class women.

According to Murray, 'illegitimacy' is bad for both men and boys, and as a consequence is bad for society as a whole; whether or not it is good or bad for women does not enter his discussion. First of all, boys brought up without a male role model in female-headed households do not receive adequate socialisation into manhood:

> Little boys don't naturally grow up to be responsible fathers and husbands. They don't naturally grow up knowing how to get up every morning at the same time and go to work. They don't naturally grow up thinking that work is not just a way to make money, but a way to hold one's head high in the world.
>
> (Murray 1990: 10–11)

Without a father, adolescent boys are unruly and criminal; 'in communities without fathers the kids tend to run wild. The fewer the fathers, the greater the tendency' (Murray 1990: 12).

Not being a real father, a father who works to provide for his wife and family, is also bad for adult men themselves. Paid work must be 'the centre of life' for young men.

> Supporting a family is a central means for a man to prove to himself that he is a 'mensch'. Men who do not support families find other ways to prove that they are men....[Y]oung males are essentially barbarians for whom marriage – meaning not just the wedding vows but the act of taking responsibility for a wife and children – is an indispensable civilizing force.
>
> (ibid.: 23)

In 1994 Murray reiterated his concerns and claimed that the empirical evidence during the intervening period confirmed his worst fears. Britain is, he claimed, heading towards a moral precipice with the survival of free institutions and a civil society at stake (1994: 32). Although it is men, particularly young men, who are threatening society, responsibility for the future rests with women.

> The welfare of society requires that women actively avoid getting pregnant if they have no husband, and that women once again demand marriage from a man who would bear them a child. The only way the active avoidance and the demands are going to occur is if child bearing entails economic penalties for a single woman. It is all horribly sexist. I know. It also happens to be true.
>
> (Murray 1994: 32)

These views about the vital importance of fathers to social stability have since been echoed by Halsey, speaking from an 'ethical socialist' perspective:

> The very, very important ingredient of a role model of a working man, a person who goes to work and comes back and does all sorts of DIY and is a responsible adult person, is missing. And that seems to be a way of making sure you don't have barbarism. Because young men, grown men have got nothing to do with anything that really matters and they just faff (sic) around satisfying their own desires, tastes.
>
> (*Panorama*, BBC1 20 September 1993)

Following the Bulger murder the *Sunday Times* solicited Murray's views from the United States about the problem of juvenile crime and resurrected his earlier commentary. The marks of his theories are clearly visible in an editorial entitled 'Return of the Family':

> It is becoming increasingly clear to all but the most blinkered of social scientists that the disintegration of the nuclear family is the principal source of so much social unrest and misery. The creation of an urban underclass, on the margins of society, but doing great damage to itself and the rest of us is directly linked to the rapid rise in illegitimacy.
>
> The past two decades have witnessed the growth of whole communities in which the dominant family structure is the single-parent mother on welfare, whose male offspring are already immersed in a criminal culture by the time they are teenagers and whose daughters are destined to follow the family tradition of unmarried mothers....[F]or communities to function successfully they need families with fathers.
>
> (*Sunday Times* 28 February 1993)

Startlingly similar opinions have also been expressed in the British liberal press. Melanie Phillips in the *Guardian* had already been writing about the problem of the underclass before the juvenile crime panic erupted; the Bulger murder provided the moment for a full scale campaign to 'rediscover the values of the family' (*Guardian* 26 February 1993). Phillips hangs her polemic on the work of Halsey, whom she interviewed for the *Guardian* (23 February 1993). Halsey 'feels passionately that the decline of the nuclear family is not merely at the root of many social ills but is the cancer in the lungs of the modern left'. He laments the disappearance of the specificity of the 'family contract', and the absence of male role models in contemporary families. 'We're talking about a situation where the man never arrives, never mind leaves. There is a growing proportion of children born into single parent families where the father has never participated as a father but only as a genital' (*Guardian* 23 February 1993).

Apparently Halsey feels that without a father, the child (implicitly male), grows up unable to see women 'as anything other than objects of sexual manipulation and gratification'. (Presumably when mothers also perform domestic labour for their husbands, fathers disavow boys of the idea that women only provide sexual servicing!)

Using Halsey's ideas as academic legitimation for her own, and citing the work of the Institute for Public Policy Research, Phillips argues that being brought up by a lone mother is bad for children's psychological development. Public policy should explicitly support two-parent families, and enforce paternal responsibility. Like Murray, Halsey, and the editor of the *Sunday Times*, Phillips is convinced of the self-evident truth of her argument and feels that the state can do very little to change people's behaviour. Unlike Murray she is deeply concerned that divorce and middle-class behaviour be addressed since these set the tone that filters down to the working class.[4]

> It is impossible to shake off Murray's analysis of Britain's underclass because it has exposed a decay at the core of our society that most of us would prefer to ignore....Like Murray, I believe that the progressive collapse of the intact family is bringing about a set of social changes which is taking us into uncharted and terrifying waters. Like Murray I recognise that there are now whole communities, framed by structural unemployment, in which fatherlessness has become the norm. These communities are truly alarming because children are being brought up with dysfunctional and often anti-social attitudes as a direct result of the fragmentation and emotional chaos of households in which sexual libertarianism provides a stream of transient and unattached men servicing their mothers. But unlike Murray I do not believe that the collapse of the intact family is confined to the lower social classes.
>
> (Phillips 1994: 59)

And a little later:

> Intellectuals and politicians therefore bear an enormous responsibility to stop peddling the silly lie that the dismembered family is no worse than the intact family. And the middle classes bear a heavy responsibility too to reaffirm *by their own behaviour* the desirability of bringing up children inside a stable marriage (emphasis in original).
>
> (Phillips 1994: 63)

In contrast to Murray, Phillips wants to offer: 'more carrot than stick to make marriage the attractive option. At the same time, the declaratory route should mean that divorce should not be made easier and assisted fertility should only be provided for married couples' (Phillips 1994: 63).

So, the views of the conservative Murray, the liberal Phillips, and the socialist Halsey, are remarkably close. The most obvious difference between them is that Halsey places considerable emphasis on the need for real men to be keen on DIY and Phillips favours the carrot rather than the stick. All three paint a peculiarly romantic picture of patriarchal masculinity which seems to be locked into the 1950s. But with the decline of the sort of 'respectable working-class' employment in manufacturing industry which Murray's 'mensch' would have taken, the rise in the service sector, women's employment and part-time working, their ideal family structure confronts head-on the reality of the free market in the 1990s.

Fiscal crisis and the welfare state

By mid-1993 the lone mother was being assessed in terms of her economic as well as her moral and social costs to the nation. The *Sunday Times* (11 July 1993) again led the way for the media with a special pull-out with the following headlines across four pages: 'Wedded to Welfare'; 'Do they want to marry a man or the state?'; 'Once illegitimacy was punished – now it is rewarded'. Murray was once again provided with space to argue that there is, 'no point fiddling with welfare at the margin', and that 'only marriage and the "principle of legitimacy" will preserve a liberal society'. The cartoon which accompanied this special pull-out – a faceless male social security officer with a pregnant bride on his arm and three children emerging from beneath her dress, a beer-swilling man/father just in the background – hardly corresponded with any liberal values of tolerance. Likewise leader comments in the *Daily Telegraph*, *The Mail* and *The Express* (15 July 1993) echoed Welsh Secretary John Redwood's (2 July 1993) condemnation of women who had children 'with no apparent intention of even trying marriage or a stable relationship with the father of the child' (quoted in Blackie 1994: 18).

The simple equation that was propagated was as follows: public spending is out of control, a major reason for the increase in public spending is the number of mothers on benefit, they reproduce the values of welfare dependency in their children, an underclass of such people is forming, therefore a downward spiral of moral decline and an upward spiral of welfare costs is the future Britain faces.

Lone mothers were not the only group relying on public welfare to be the target of critical comments, but they were seen as one of the 'softer' political targets.[5] As the debate within the Conservative Party over how to tackle the public debt intensified, attention which had already that year been focused on lone mothers as the producers of the underclass was harnessed in their direction once more. Speeches in July 1993 about the economic burden of never married mothers occurred shortly after a seminar organised by the Institute of Economic Affairs, which attracted some of those who were subsequently so vocal on the topic.

Apart from the work of Murray, whose research consisted of little more than a trawl through some existing secondary sources and a few conversations with interesting 'characters', the media was not interested in existing research. Whilst Murray was held up as a beacon of academic integrity and Halsey as someone who had seen the light, and Phillips lambasted social scientists for failing to research the problems, there was no interest in work which contradicted

Murray. No one quoted MacNicol (1987) who has pointed out that in the past it was common for observers to discuss 'the dangerous classes', the 'residuum' and their 'culture of poverty', but that these notions have been discredited in recent years. Likewise, and despite the fact that the US was so often the 'nightmare' haunting Britain, no one thought it worth quoting William Prosser, Senior Policy Advisor to President Bush, who dismissed the underclass idea as little more than a reworking of older discredited concepts like the culture of poverty (Prosser 1991; Mann 1992). Recent empirical work, such as that of Dean and Taylor-Gooby (1992), which shows that lone parents hold views which 'adhere to the mainstream values of work and family ethics' (1992: 5) were never mentioned. Rather, the press used 'common sense' to ride rough-shod over complex social issues and changes. The fact that the average duration of lone parenthood for never married mothers is only 35 months (Ermisch 1986), that many lone mothers may live in fear of the child's father, and that the majority of lone mothers are not 'single' but divorced or separated (Brown 1989), was rarely reflected in the press.

Anti-lone mother discourse in Britain and the United States

Although much of the preceding discussion is unique to Britain in the early 1990s, there are many parallels with the United States. In both countries there has been a concerted ideological offensive against the welfare state by radical conservatives, and in both countries lone mothers have been highlighted as a serious financial burden on the taxpayer. Murray's analysis, which he developed in the 1980s, was exported from the USA pretty much wholesale to Britain, and with this came suggestions that Britain adopt policies such as the New Jersey scheme which refuses benefit to women who have a second child whilst they are still dependent on welfare.

However, there are two substantial differences between anti-lone mother rhetoric in Britain and the United States. First, in the US the discourse has long been racialised in a more forthright manner than in Britain. Solinger argues that there are 'two histories of single pregnancy in the post-World War II era, one for Black women and one for white' (1994: 287). Whereas white women who gave birth outside marriage increasingly became subject to a psychological discourse, which constructed them as maladjusted and in need of help, black women who did the same were seen as merely expressing their 'natural', 'unrestrained sexuality' (Solinger 1994: 299). Illegitimate white babies could therefore be removed from their mothers and adopted by 'stable' couples (thereby fulfilling the demand for white babies for adoption) on the grounds that this would provide their mothers with the best chance of overcoming their neuroses, and at the same time offer the best future to the child. Illegitimate black babies, on the other hand, were left with their mothers, perhaps because adoption demand was less than for white babies, and because it was thought that their mothers were not in need of a 'cure'. Public discourse about lone motherhood in this period focused on black women. Southern Dixiecrats and Northern racists united to condemn the social liability of black illegitimate children, and opinion polls suggested that the American people wanted to withdraw Aid to Dependent Children from these children (Solinger 1994: 301). Black women thus became, often unwillingly, the first group in the US to receive publicly subsidised birth control, sterilisation and abortion (Ward 1986).

In the 1980s and 1990s the American discourse continued to highlight the special 'problem' of black lone motherhood. With the conservatives to the fore, liberal commentators increasingly acquiesced to the growing consensus that 'something did have to be done about the offspring of the (mainly black) underclass, who, raised by teen moms, grow into gun-wielding, benefit-draining, drug-dealing hoodlums' (*Guardian* 31 January 1995: and see Mann 1994).

'Race' has been a less significant feature of the recent discourse in Britain. In the 1970s sociologists concerned with social exclusion and racial discrimination referred to a 'racially' specific underclass, but they did not focus on lone mothers (Rex 1973; Giddens 1973). In the 1980s there was also some discussion of whether a correspondence of class and race might mean a black underclass would, through social disorder, challenge racism in Britain (Gilroy 1980; Sivanandan 1982). Although there has been no widespread discussion of race and the supposed British underclass, in the 1990s Murray was given the opportunity on BBC television of elaborating on his ideas about a link between intelligence, race and the formation of an underclass (*The Battle of Ideas*, BBC 1995). Nevertheless, to date, black women have not been specifically targeted in Britain in the same way as in the US (Phoenix 1996).

The second difference between the discourse in the United States and Britain is that it has achieved far greater hegemony in the US. Both countries have seen the highest increases in lone motherhood in the developed world (Chandler 1991), but rates, particularly for lone mothers under 20, remain higher in the US (Phoenix 1991). This, combined with the far greater political and cultural strength of the right in the US, has meant that the discourse has been pushed further there than in Britain. In 1994 the Republicans regained control of Congress on the basis of their 'Contract with America', which promised to eradicate 'the culture of welfare dependency'. Two major planks in the programme of the Republican speaker of the House, Newt Gingrich, both constituted attacks on lone motherhood: the 'American Dream Restoration Act', which promised tax credits for two-parent families, and the proposal to remove children from their unmarried mothers and place them in orphanages, in order to break the cycle by which the underclass is reproduced (*Guardian* 26 November 1994, 31 January 1995). So widely accepted have such ideas become that the 1996 presidential contest has witnessed Republicans and Democrats seeking to cap each others' antagonism towards lone motherhood.

In Britain, in contrast, although 'discrimination' against couples with children and in favour of lone parents in the allocation of council (state subsidised) housing has been condemned by government ministers, the policy response has been to remove the obligation on local authorities to give priority to the statutory homeless in the allocation of housing. This move will disproportionately affect lone mothers, but is not aimed exclusively at them. This suggests that it has been more difficult to translate political rhetoric into policy proposals in Britain than it has been, and probably will be, in the US.

Anti-feminist backlash

Thus far our analysis of why the 1990s has seen such widespread concern about lone mothers has focused on the moral panic which erupted over the issue of juvenile crime and the targeting of lone mothers as part of the ideologically and fiscally motivated restructuring of the British welfare state. Both of these elements are crucial to understanding the form taken by the anti-lone mother discourse in Britain. However, there is another strand to this discourse, one which applies equally in Britain and the United States: that of anti-feminism.

The notion of 'backlash' has achieved some popular and academic credibility recently, with the publication of Faludi's work about anti-feminism in the US and Britain (1992) and an article by Walby (1993), which add to the literature about the gender politics of the new right and Thatcherism (e.g. ten-Tusscher 1986; McNeil 1991; Somerville 1992). Both Franklin *et al.* (1991) and Walby (1993) have problematised the concept of 'backlash'. We agree with Franklin *et al.* (1991: 42) that to conceive of the gender politics of Thatcherism, or indeed any recent conservative government in Britain or the US, as a straightforward 'backlash' against feminism is problematic, as it implies too simplistic a model of social and cultural change. Walby's (1993) critique of Faludi's analysis of the 1980s as a period of concerted effort to push women back into the home is also apposite; such a project gained less ground in Britain than in the US. Indeed, even in the US women's participation in paid work continued to increase, and divorce and unmarried motherhood rates continued to climb. This said, an 'anti-feminist backlash' can be observed in discourses about lone mothers and the underclass in Britain in 1993, and in the anti-lone mother discourse of the early 1990s in the United States; they can be seen as part of a project of 'patriarchal reconstruction' (Smart 1989).

In general this backlash is directed against feminism and against many of the social changes of the past two decades which have reduced women's economic and social dependence on men. Walby (1990) suggests that women's increased involvement in paid work and the increase in divorce and births outside marriage are part of a shift from a private to a more public form of patriarchy, in which women are less likely to be wholly financially dependent on a husband, and more likely to be dependent on paid work or the state. In the discourse of the backlash, however, the specificities of these social and economic changes are rarely discussed; rather, blame is laid at the door of 'trendy theories' propagated by the likes of the authors and the readers of this book. For example a *Sunday Times* leader stated: 'Over the past 20 years, an assorted collection of sociologists, feminists, left wing idealogues and agony aunties have made the abnormal family into the norm' (*Sunday Times* 11 July 1993).

A 'focus special' identified a group of American and British intellectuals – Alvin Toffler, Gloria Steinem, Germaine Greer, Harriet Harman, Neil Kinnock, Jenni Murray and Susie Orbach – as 'the pundits who made [families without men] politically correct' (*Sunday Times* 11 July 1993).[6]

An article entitled 'The Price of Feminism' in *The Mail on Sunday* (7 March 1993) implicitly linked the murder of James Bulger with the women's liberation movement. A photograph of a 1970s march showing women carrying placards reading 'women demand equality' was placed next to a photograph of a young boy, wearing a balaclava helmet, pointing threateningly at the camera in 1993. The headline above them read 'Did this…lead to this?' In the article Kathy Gyngell argues that feminism, by encouraging women to take paid employment, is responsible for juvenile crime and moral and social decline. Echoing theories of maternal deprivation from the 1950s (e.g. Bowlby 1951, 1953), she claims that children are being neglected by their absent mothers, and draws upon essentialist notions of maternal instinct:

> Feminists may complain that it is unfair that mothers are primarily responsible for the upbringing of their children. But it is an unavoidable fact of life. Nature provides women not only with the body to bear children, but the instinct to foster their emerging sense of morality.
>
> (*The Mail on Sunday* 7 March 1993)

Social policies to encourage women to stay at home with their children was the suggested solution.

We have identified four aspects of anti-feminist backlash within recent discourses surrounding the underclass and lone motherhood.

First, there is the (re-)promotion of the heterosexual nuclear family, which Chafetz and Dworkin (1987) argue is the key feature of anti-feminist backlash. As we have shown, this is a unifying feature of recent discourses about juvenile crime, lone mothers and the underclass. Increasing rates of birth outside marriage must be halted, and fathers must return to their rightful role within the family. The degree of patriarchal power and form of paternal responsibility differs slightly between Murray's right-wing and Halsey's and Phillips' liberal versions of the argument, but the message is the same: families need fathers. This position has been especially strong in the United States where advocates of the importance of fathers from the new right, the fathers' rights movement and the liberal legal tradition have together created a powerful cultural force (see Fineman 1989; Brophy 1989; Smart 1989).

Second, public debates about juvenile crime and the underclass operate by reversal, in a similar way to the wider backlash (Faludi 1992; Walby 1993; Franklin *et al.* 1991). Thus, instead of the poverty and material deprivation suffered by many lone mothers and their children being regarded as a social problem demanding policy attention, lone mothers themselves become 'the problem'. Rather than considering conditions to facilitate lone mothers being able to support their families by entering paid employment, for instance through state provision of child care, the question is, how can women, and men, be powerfully dissuaded from conceiving children outside marriage (Murray 1990). Proposed solutions actually involve making life harder for lone mothers, with workfare, enforced sterilisation, cuts in benefits and the removal of rights to social housing all being suggested.[7]

Similarly, McNeil's (1991) concept of 'the new oppressed' illustrates the way discourses over juvenile crime and the underclass operate by reversal. McNeil argues that under Thatcher a number of social groups were constructed as 'oppressed': these include parents, fathers, burdened taxpayers and foetuses. The rights of these groups were seen as under attack from 'female and feminist bogeys' (McNeil 1991: 229), above all, the lone mother. Thus Murray (1990), for instance, describes how difficult life is made for two-parent families who are unfortunate enough to have to try to raise their children in neighbourhoods full of single mothers and their illegitimate offspring. The decent honest, respectable, hardworking father, the only father to attend his little girl's Christmas play, is undermined, indeed oppressed, by single mothers whose existence makes a mockery of his attempts to be a proper father.

Likewise Frank Field, a Labour MP, Chair of the Parliamentary Committee on Social Services, and a noted anti-poverty campaigner, enthusiastically endorsed comments by Peter Lilley, then Secretary of State for Social Security and a renowned critic of the welfare state, about the necessity of supporting 'the normal family'. Lilley and Field agreed that social policy should do more to support the 'traditional nurturing unit, the two parent family', and that there was a need to reassert 'family values'. The discussion between these eminent politicians of opposite party political affiliations ended with Frank Field agreeing with Peter Lilley that previously they had 'all been too frightened to raise the issue of family values' (*Newsnight*, BBC2 8 July 1993). Of whom these powerful men were afraid was not made explicit, but the implication was that 'political correctness' had previously prevented them speaking their minds. This instance shows again how a myth of oppression, a reversal of actual dominant power relations, is constructed.

The third way in which discourses about juvenile crime and the underclass parallel other elements of the backlash is in their 'one gender fixation' (Faludi 1992). Like much of the new right, these discourses are concerned primarily with the fate of young men; their attention is on the deleterious effects of unemployment for men, and of the lack of a male role model for boys. The well-being of girls and women does not enter the agenda. It could be suggested that this concern with men is an appropriate recognition that it is overwhelmingly men and boys who commit crime. However, the attention to problems of men is not the same as attention to the problem of masculinity or any sort of problematisation of masculinity. On the contrary, a return to traditionally hegemonic forms of masculinity (economically dominant husband and socially dominant father) is seen as the solution to the problem. In this sense feminist analysis and political campaigning which draw attention to the feminisation of poverty and to the problems of hegemonic masculinity are implicitly attacked.

Finally, mention must be made of the essentialist constructions of masculinity and femininity that characterise much of the discourse on juvenile crime, lone mothers, and the underclass. As has been pointed out earlier, Murray conceives of men and women as propelled by innate biological urges, in the case of men towards sex, and in the case of women towards procreation. These natural instincts, he argues, must be harnessed and used in a socially appropriate manner. Leaving aside the implications of social engineering, and the question of how this might be achieved, such essentialism is clearly anti-feminist.

The question of agency

Lurking in the shadows of this discourse about lone mothers and the underclass is an issue which we believe must be addressed head on: the issue of human agency, or in this instance, specifically, women's agency. Right-wing ideologues, conservative politicians and anti-feminists lay much of the blame for the perpetuation of the underclass through lone motherhood on the agency exercised by women; they have no trouble suggesting that women make *choices* to have children outside marriage, and without the support of a man. Defenders of lone mothers in recent debates, however, particularly the poverty lobby and feminists, have found it much harder to acknowledge women's agency.[8] In challenging the individualising of the problems associated with lone motherhood, their focus has been on the material, structural constraints which operate on poor, working-class women. In order to refute the claims of writers such as Murray and Halsey, they seem to have thought it necessary to emphasise the lack of choices open to women with few educational qualifications in run-down inner cities. They implicitly suggest that agency is something reserved for the well-off and educated, and that whilst small numbers of women may be *choosing* to become lone mothers, most lone mothers are the 'victims' of their social circumstances.

This position is made explicit by Lash (1994) in his discussion of the processes of individualisation and reflexive modernisation which can be discerned in contemporary Western societies. He criticises the thesis advanced by Beck (1994) and Giddens (1994) that agency is progressively being freed from structure and that individuals are increasingly engaging in the reflexive construction of their own life narratives, less hindered by tradition and structure than at previous moments in history. His challenge to Beck and Giddens takes the 'single mother in the urban ghetto' as the prime exemplar of the limits of reflexive modernisation:

> [J]ust how 'reflexive' is it possible for a single mother in an urban ghetto to be? Ulrich Beck and Anthony Giddens write with insight on the self-construction of life narratives. But just how much freedom from the 'necessity' of 'structure' and structural poverty does this ghetto mother have to construct her own 'life narratives'?
>
> (Lash 1994: 120)

Whilst we would not wish to suggest that women living in inner city 'ghettos' can choose to escape 'structural poverty' (but nor, probably, would Beck or Giddens), we do believe that there are women living in situations of structural poverty who are exercising agency, and consciously deciding to have children without depending on a male partner. In this sense they are undoubt-edly reflexively constructing their own 'life narratives', and are not just the victims of their social circumstances. Moreover, they are not behaving very differently from middle-class unmarried women who are choosing to have children; the main difference is their poorer material circumstance. Working-class women with few educational qualifications who choose to have children outside marriage clearly make use of the meagre resources available to them to facilitate their decision: these resources include social housing and welfare benefits.

Thus we are in agreement with Beck and Beck-Gernsheim (1995) who argue that a 'new type of unmarried mother' is emerging, for whom a traditional partnership with a man is unnecessary. They cite Burkart, Fietze and Kohli (1989), writing about Germany, where the rate of births outside marriage is considerably lower than in Britain or the US:

> An illegitimate child is less and less the unwanted pregnancy of earlier years, and ever more frequently the planned pregnancy of women over 25. Extra-marital fertility, then, is less and less a 'misfortune' of young women and rather an obviously planned or at least consciously accepted decision of older women.
>
> (Burkart, Fietze and Kohli 1989: 34, cited in Beck and Beck-Gernsheim 1995: 205)

Beck and Beck-Gernsheim acknowledge that this does not apply to a majority of women, but point to the striking change in attitudes of young women to unmarried motherhood; in 1962 89.4 per cent considered it important for a woman with a child to be married, whereas in 1983 only 40 per cent did (Allerbeck and Hoag 1985, cited in Beck and Beck-Gernsheim 1995: 205). They also point to the explosion of articles in women's magazines about lone motherhood, which not only proclaim that single mothers can be good and happy mothers, but often offer advice on getting pregnant. There is also, they suggest, a significant theme in recent women's writing, both fiction and autobiography, which sees love for a child replacing love for a man, with the mother/child dyad replacing the co-habiting heterosexual couple as the primary source of intimacy and fulfilment in women's lives. In an individualis-ing society, where marriages and heterosexual partnerships are increasingly prone to failure, and where women are seeking identities for themselves, many women place trust in the permanence and stability of a relationship with a child.

We would add to Beck and Beck-Gernsheim's analysis mention of the role of feminism in this process. It is surely a measure of the success of feminism over the past century that some women have the confidence to exercise a decision to rely on the state rather than an individual man in raising their children. Probably only a small proportion of 'lone-mothers-by-choice' would identify themselves as feminists (Gordon 1990), but the creation of a cultural climate in which women are more able to live autonomous lives, is, in part, the product of the slow but deep rooted social change which feminism has promoted.

Conclusion

In this chapter we have explored the creation of a discourse which links lone mothers with the reproduction of an underclass. We have highlighted the role of the moral panic about juvenile crime in Britain in calling forth this discourse, and suggested that the perceived fiscal crisis of the welfare state and the conservative desire to reduce welfare spending have been harnessed to this discourse in both Britain and the United States. Conservative politicians in both countries, together with many liberal commentators, have reached a degree of consensus which consists of seeing the lone mother as the source of juvenile crime, welfare dependence, and ultimately, societal disintegration. The resultant call for social policy to go 'back to basics' (in Britain), or to 'restore the American dream' (in the US) encapsulated the forlorn hope that a 'golden age' of moral turpitude, economic self-reliance and family values could be recovered. Murray's and Halsey's identification of the failure of a generation of fathers could appear to be merely a benign, if outdated, paternalism. We are less generous and it is our contention that the discourse that has developed around their work is firmly anti-feminist. Certainly in contrast to other attempts by Christian fundamentalists and moral crusaders to attach their anti-feminist campaigns to economic individualism, making use of the underclass concept has proved very successful.

This emergent consensus needs to be confronted because it constitutes an attack on feminism and, most importantly, on millions of women living in poverty. If the anti-feminism expressed by the discourse that we have analysed is to be addressed and understood effectively, we must not collude in the eradication of the agency of those who are most attacked by it. We must recognise that lone mothers are actors in their own right and that many make active choices to be mothers.

Thus we wish to jolt the debate between right and left, anti-feminists and feminists, out of its dualisms of blame/exoneration, guilt/innocence, agent/victim. The reluctance of the poverty lobby and those sympathetic to lone mothers to address the role of agency is understandable, given the onslaught against them, but ironically it has created space for their critics. We believe that it is time to shift the agenda of the debate towards consideration of ways of enhancing the choices available to lone mothers, rather than seeking to deny them choices or to deny that they have ever exercised choice.

Notes

1 For a more detailed discussion of the events of 1993, see Mann and Roseneil (1994).
2 See for example, Fox Harding (1993a, 1993b); Abbott and Wallace (1992); Solinger (1994); Spensky (1989).
3 For example, *Guardian* 27 February 1993; *Sunday Times* 28 February 1993; *Independent* 27 February 1993.
4 Phillips also elaborated her views in a BBC2 television programme *Who Killed the Family?* with Janet Daly and Roger Scruton (BBC2, 31 October 1995). The programme pointed to the collapse of moral leadership by the middle classes, suggested that the women's movement had undermined the family, and that the church and intellectuals had failed to provide moral leadership as moral relativism took hold in the 1960s and 1970s.
5 As Sinclair (1994) argues, drawing on the work of Wilensky (1975) and Sen (1981), benefits which are considered to have been 'earned', such as pensions and sickness benefit, receive far more widespread public support than those which accrue to 'the undeserving', of whom prime exemplars are non-working lone mothers.
6 For a discussion of the demonisation of feminism and other liberatory movements within the academy through the construction of 'political correctness' as all powerful, see Roseneil (1995).
7 For example, Michael Jones and Charles Murray *Sunday Times* 11 July 1993; Tom Sackville (Junior Health Minister), in a speech in Liverpool, 7 July 1993; and Michael Howard at the 1993 Conservative Party Conference. See also *Guardian* 9 November 1993 for a discussion of leaked policy documents.
8 For a discussion of the poverty lobby and sociologists of poverty's lack of attention to agency, see Mann (1986); for a discussion of feminism's lack of attention to women's agency see Roseneil (1995).

Bibliography

Abbott, P. and Wallace, C. (1992) *The Family and the New Right*, London: Pluto Press.
Allerbeck, K. and Hoag, W. (1985) *Jugend ohne Zukunft*, Munich.
Bagguley, P. and Mann, K. (1992) ' "Idle thieving bastards": scholarly representations of the underclass', *Work, Employment and Society* 6(1): 113–26.
Beck, U. (1994) 'The reinvention of politics: towards a theory of reflexive modernization' in U. Beck, A. Giddens and S. Lash *Reflexive Modernization: Politics, Tradition and Aesthetics in the Modern Social Order*, Cambridge: Polity.
Beck, U. and Beck-Gernsheim, E. (1995) *The Normal Chaos of Love*, Cambridge: Polity.
Blackie, A. (1994) 'Family fall-out', *Times Higher Education Supplement*, 4 March: 18.
Bowlby, J. (1951) *Maternal Care and Mental Health*, Geneva: WHO.
—— (1953) *Child Care and the Growth of Love*, London: Penguin.
Brophy, J. (1989) 'Custody law, child care and inequality in Britain' in C. Smart and S. Sevenhuijsen (eds) *Child Custody and the Politics of Gender*, London: Routledge.
Brown, J. (1989) *Why Don't They Go to Work? Mothers on Benefit*, London: HMSO.
Burkart, G., Fietze, B. and Kohli, M. (1989) *Liebe, Ehe, Elternschaft*, Materialen zur Bevolkerungswissenschaft, No. 60, Wiesbaden: Bundesinstitut fur Bevolkerungsfor-schung.
Chafetz, J. S. and Dworkin, A. G. (1987) 'In the face of threat: organised anti-feminism in comparative perspective', *Gender and Society* 1(1): 33–60.
Chandler, J. (1991) *Women Without Husbands: An Exploration of the Margins of Marriage*, London: Macmillan.

Dahrendorf, R. (1987) 'The erosion of citizenship and its consequences for us all', *New Statesman* 12 June: 12–15.

Davies, J. (ed.) (1993) *The Family: Is it Just Another Lifestyle Choice?*, London: IEA Health and Welfare Unit.

Dean H. and Taylor-Gooby, P. (1992) *Dependency Culture*, Hemel Hempstead: Harvester Wheatsheaf.

Dennis, N. and Erdos, G. (1992) *Families without Fatherhood*, London: Institute of Economic Affairs.

Ermisch, J. (1986) *The Economics of the Family: Applications to Divorce and Re-Marriage*, London: CEPR.

Faludi, S. (1992) *Backlash: The Undeclared War against Women*, London: Chatto and Windus.

Fineman, M. (1989) 'The politics of custody and gender: child advocacy and the transformation of custody decision making in the USA', in C. Smart and S. Sevenhuijsen (eds) *Child Custody and the Politics of Gender*, London: Routledge.

Fox Harding, L. (1993a) ' "Alarm" versus "Liberation"? responses to the increase in lone parents – Part 1', *The Journal of Social Welfare and Family Law* 2: 101–12.

—— (1993b) ' "Alarm" versus "Liberation"? responses to the increase in lone parents – Part 2', *The Journal of Social Welfare and Family Law* 3: 174–84.

Franklin, S., Lury, C. and Stacey, J. (eds) (1991) *Off-Centre: Feminism and Cultural Studies*, London: HarperCollins.

Giddens, A. (1973) *The Class Structure of the Advanced Societies*, London: Hutchinson.

—— (1994) 'Living in a post-traditional society' in U. Beck, A. Giddens and S. Lash *Reflexive Modernization: Politics, Tradition and Aesthetics in the Modern Social Order*, Cambridge: Polity.

Gilroy, P. (1980) 'Managing the underclass: a further note on the sociology of race relations in Britain', *Race and Class* 22(1): 47–62.

Gordon, T. (1990) *Feminist Mothers*, London: Macmillan.

—— (1994) *Single Women*, London: Macmillan.

Green, D. (1993) 'Foreword', in J. Davies (ed.) *The Family: Is it Just Another Lifestyle Choice?*, London: IEA Health and Welfare Unit.

Hall, S., Critcher, C., Jefferson, T., Clarke, J. and Roberts, B. (1978) *Policing the Crisis: Mugging, the State and Law and Order*, Basingstoke: Macmillan.

Halsey, A. H. (1992) 'Foreword' in N. Dennis and G. Erdos (eds) *Families without Fatherhood*, London: IEA Health and Welfare Unit Choice in Welfare No. 12.

Himmelfarb, G. (1995) *The De-moralization of Society; From Victorian Virtues to Modern Values*, London: IEA. Choice in Welfare Series No. 22.

Lash, S. (1994) 'Reflexivity and its doubles: structure, aesthetics, community' in U. Beck, A. Giddens and S. Lash *Reflexive Modernization: Politics, Tradition and Aesthetics in the Modern Social Order*, Cambridge: Polity.

MacGregor, S. (1990) 'Could Britain inherit the American nightmare?', *British Journal of Addiction* 85(7): 863–72.

MacNicol, J. (1987) 'In pursuit of the underclass', *Journal of Social Policy* 16(3): 293–318.

McLananhan, S. and Garfinkel, I. (1989) 'Single mothers, the underclass and social policy', *Annals of American Academy of Political and Social Science* 501: 92–104.

McNeil, M. (1991) 'Making and not making the difference: the gender politics of Thatcherism' in S. Franklin, C. Lury and J. Stacey (eds) *Off-Centre: Feminism and Cultural Studies*, London: HarperCollins.

McRobbie, A. (1989) *From Jackie to Just Seventeen*, London: Macmillan.

Mann, K. (1986) 'The making of a claiming class: the neglect of agency in analyses of the welfare state', *Critical Social Policy* 15(Spring): 62–74.

—— (1992) *The Making of an English "Underclass"? The Social Divisions of Welfare and Labour*, Buckingham: Open University Press.

—— (1994) 'Watching the defectives; observers of the underclass in Britain, Australia and the USA', in *Critical Social Policy* 41(Autumn): 79–98.

Mann, K. and Roseneil, S. (1994) ' "Some Mothers Do 'Ave 'Em": backlash and the gender politics of the underclass debate', *Journal of Gender Studies* 3(3): 317–31.

Morris, J. (ed.) (1992) *Alone Together: Voices of Single Mothers*, London: Women's Press.

Morris, L. (1994) *Dangerous Classes: The Underclass and Social Citizenship*, London: Routledge.

Muncie, J., Wetherell, M., Dallos, R. and Cochrane, A. (eds) (1995) *Understanding the Family*, London: Sage.

Murray, C. (1984) *Losing Ground*, New York: Basic Books.

—— (1990) *The Emerging British Underclass*, London: IEA Health and Welfare Unit.

—— (1994) *Underclass: The Crisis Deepens*, London: IEA Choice in Welfare Series No. 20.

Phillips, M. (1994) 'Where are the new Victorians?' in C. Murray *Underclass: The Crisis Deepens*, London: IEA Choice in Welfare Series No. 20.

Phoenix, A. (1991) *Young Mothers?*, Cambridge: Polity.

—— (1996) 'Social constructions of lone motherhood, a case of competing discourses' in E. Silva (ed.) *Good Enough Mothering: Feminist Perspectives on Lone Motherhood*, London: Routledge.

Prosser, W. R. (1991) 'The underclass: assessing what we have learned', *Focus* 13(2): 1–18.

Radford, J. (1991) 'Immaculate conceptions', *Trouble and Strife*, 21: 8–12.

Renvoize, J. (1985) *Going Solo: Single Mothers by Choice*, London: Routledge and Kegan Paul.

Rex, J. (1973) *Race Colonialism and the City*, London: Routledge and Kegan Paul.

Roseneil, S. (1995) 'The coming of age of feminist sociology: some issues of practice and theory for the next twenty years', *British Journal of Sociology* 46(2): 191–205.

Saffron, L. (1994) *Challenging Conceptions: Planning a Family by Self-Insemination*, London: Cassell.

Sen, A. K. (1981) *Poverty and Famines: An Essay on Entitlement and Deprivation*, Oxford: Clarendon Press.

Sinclair, S. P. (1994) 'Public hostility towards lone mothers', Paper presented at the Social Policy Association Annual Conference *Families in Question*, University of Liverpool.

Sivanandan, A. (1982) *A Different Hunger: Writings on Black Resistance*, London: Pluto Press.

Smart, C. (1989) 'Power and the politics of child custody' in C. Smart and S. Sevenhuijsen (eds) *Child Custody and the Politics of Gender*, London: Routledge.

—— (1992) (ed.) *Regulating Womanhood*, London: Routledge.

—— (1996) 'Deconstructing motherhood' in E. Silva (ed.) *Good Enough Mothering: Perspectives on Lone Motherhood*, London: Routledge.

Solinger, R. (1994) 'Race and "value": black and white illegitimate babies, 1945–65' in E. Nakano Glenn, G. Chang and L. Rennie Forcey (eds) *Mothering: Ideology, Experience and Agency*, New York: Routledge.

Somerville, J. (1992) 'The new right and family politics', *Economy and Society* 21(2): 93–128.

Spensky, M. (1989) 'From the workhouse to the home for unmarried mothers: a feminist perspective', Paper presented at the British Sociological Association Annual Conference, Plymouth Polytechnic.

ten-Tusscher, T. (1986) 'Patriarchy, capitalism and the new right' in J. Evans, J. Hills, K. Hunt, E. Meehan, T. ten-Tusscher, U. Vogel and G. Waylen (eds) *Feminism and Political Theory*, London: Sage.

Walby, S. (1990) *Theorising Patriarchy*, Oxford: Blackwell.

—— (1993) ' "Backlash" in historical context' in M. Kennedy, C. Lubelska and V. Walsh (eds) *Making Connections: Women's Studies, Women's Movements, Women's Lives*, London: Taylor and Francis.

Ward, M. (1986) *Poor Women, Powerful Men: America's Great Experiment in Family Planning*, Boulder: Westview Press.

Wilensky, H. L. (1975) *The Welfare State and Equality: Structural and Ideological Roots of Public Expenditure*, Berkeley: University of California Press.

6 'Family values' and Conservative government policy: 1979–97

Lorraine Fox Harding

Introduction

This chapter begins by outlining the development of the 'family values' position, its main arguments and aims for government policy. The movement developed over the late 1970s, 1980s and 1990s, comprising a variety of groups in the US and Britain. Its main concerns are usually stable marriage and child-rearing, a gender division of roles, the confinement of sexuality to the permanent married heterosexual unit, and the support of these patterns through government policy. There are, however, some ambiguities in the view of the role governments should play. This consideration leads to the question of how far 'family values' are necessarily 'right-wing'. It is concluded that while such arguments have sometimes been convenient to governments of the right, the 'family values' lobby and the 'new right' should not necessarily be identified. The chapter concludes by summarising the 'successes' and 'failures' of the family lobby in influencing Conservative government policy in the 1980s and 1990s up to 1997, and therefore the extent to which the Conservative party in office may be considered to have been a friend of 'family values' and traditional family forms.

The development of 'family values'

Berger and Berger (1983) used the term 'neo-traditionalist' to describe a type of family lobby which they observed in the US in the late 1970s and early 1980s. This movement was seen as a 'backlash' phenomenon reacting against developments in the late 1960s/early 1970s – sexual 'permissiveness', liberal legislation (for example, on divorce, abortion), the changes in women's position and feminist ideas, and so on. Family change away from the model apparently current in the 1950s, of male breadwinner, economically dependent female home-maker, with low divorce and 'illegitimacy' levels, was blamed as the root cause of many social problems. In the British context, Parton (1981) identified a 'moral fundamentalism', and Fitzgerald (1983) referred to a report by a group of Conservative lawyers appearing in the late 1970s, which strongly implied that if lifelong marriage were the foundation of each home, then certain problems would disappear – truancy, delinquency, and violence in the family, for example. Fitzgerald saw this type of 'familialism' as firmly located within the Thatcherite economic strategy and political doctrines of the early 1980s, and in fact, towards the end of the first Thatcher administration (1982–83) a Cabinet Family Policy Group was ordered to produce ideas for policy which would strengthen 'the family'. Proposals included encouragement of mothers with young children to stay at home; encouragement of the family to take more responsibility for the disabled, the elderly, and unemployed 16-year-olds; a reconsideration of benefits for single mothers; and encouragement of parents to take more responsibility for their children, including their anti-social behaviour.

In the early 1980s also, new groups of the moral, traditionalist and 'family values' type emerged in Britain – for example, the Responsible Society, which became Family and Youth Concern; and the Festival of Light, which became Christian Action, Research and Education (CARE) (see Durham 1991). In the mid-1980s others appeared. They included a group within the Parliamentary Conservative Party, the Conservative Family Campaign (critical of its own party in government), formed in 1986; and the National Campaign for the Family, appearing the following year. The Conservative Family Campaign said in its publicity material: 'The time-honoured family unit, where father provides and mother cares, is the most fulfilling and effective way of maintaining a stable society'. The same leaflet talked about: 'the acceptance of abnormal relationships, in particular the concept of single parenthood as an equal and viable alternative to the two parent family'. Its platform resembled that of the National Campaign for the Family, which was concerned about the undermining of stable family life and about national moral decay (seen as linked). The campaign defended traditional marriage and parental responsibility; it supported education for marriage and family life. Its publication *Families Matter* (Whitfield 1987) argued: 'Through our neglect of "home defence" we have sown the seeds of social collapse and allowed the deep personal alienation of, and loneliness among, a significant proportion of our young people' (p. 2). The welfare state was blamed for causing a loss of functions for the family. The importance of parents of both sexes was stressed, and there was criticism of right, left and centre of the political spectrum for their attitudes to children and the family. The Social Affairs Unit, a right-wing think tank, produced 'Family Portraits' around the same time (Anderson and Dawson 1986). This spoke of the 'normal family', seen as composed of husband, wife and children, the parents seriously intending to stay together, the husband the principal if not the only breadwinner. This, it was claimed, had been overlooked in the face of attention paid to newer and more deviant family forms. The publication was critical of Conservative government policies, but among its other targets were the Church of England, feminists, and reproductive technology.

Partly in response to these criticisms, by the late 1980s and 1990s the issue of lone parents and their cost to the Exchequer was being explicitly taken up by Conservative government ministers. Social security changes introduced in 1988 (after the Social Security Act of 1986) had not specifically tackled this 'problem' head on, and indeed a 'Single Parent Premium', an extra amount of weekly benefit, had been included in Income Support, although the 'family values' position would generally be that single parents already received too favourable treatment and should not be 'privileged' further. In 1990 speeches by Thatcher and Baker focused on lone parenthood and prepared the ground for change. These speeches made reference to grave social problems arising from the loss of the father's presence in the family (Family Policy Studies Centre 1990, 1991). Parental responsibility was emphasised, in particular that of fatherhood. The turn of the decade saw the development of something of a 'moral panic' about lone parenthood, now focused mainly on the rising public expenditure costs (see Fox Harding 1993). The Conservative government turned its attention to the possibilities for reducing social security expenditure on mothers who were not in paid work and had no child support payments from 'absent fathers'. Hence the White Paper appearing late in 1990, *Children Come First* (Lord Chancellor 1990), which proposed a new and more rigorous system for assessing and collecting such payments from non-resident parents, and subsequently the Child Support Act 1991 (preceded by some prior 'tightening up', under the Social Security Act 1990 and the Maintenance Enforcement Act 1991).

Unmarried mothers were also periodically attacked by politicians for 'jumping the [Council] housing queue', indeed deliberately becoming pregnant in order to do so; and there was criticism of the general benefits and housing systems for being too generous to them. Influential with Conservative government thinking from the late 1980s was the writing of the American right-wing author Murray (1984, 1990, 1994), who argued that the structure of welfare provision had made it rational to have children out of wedlock and avoid marriage, as well as to engage in drug use and crime. Lone parent provisions were placed under review again in 1993, when, as Lister (1996) notes: ' "the breakdown of the family" hit the top of the political agenda' (1996: 15) (see also Burghes and Roberts 1995). At this time Prime Minister Major announced a 'Back to Basics' campaign, and anti-lone mother statements were made by government ministers such as Redwood, Lilley, Portillo and Howard (Durham 1994b). Soon restrictive changes were threatened to homelessness legislation, which were subsequently adopted. The implicit target seemed to be lone parents, who were disproportionately likely to reach local authority housing through the homelessness route (Lister 1996). In 1995 cuts to lone parents' benefits were announced, in the shape of freezing and (later) phasing out the extra child benefit received since the 1970s, and the Single Parent Premium in place since 1988. Also in 1996 the law on divorce was changed, to give greater emphasis to mediation and counselling. Meanwhile a spate of publications on family values themes emerged from the Institute of Economic Affairs (IEA) in the early 1990s (Dennis and Erdos 1992, 1993; Davies 1993; Dennis 1993; Quest 1992, 1994; Morgan 1995). Themes included the dangers of absent fathers and excessive individualism, the stabilising influence of the conventional nuclear family, the failings of feminism – for women as well as for society in general – and the failure of government policy to support the married two-parent family. One author (Morgan 1995) focused on the relation between the state and the family and argued that government policies on taxes and benefits had favoured lone-mother over two-parent (one male earner) units, worsening the position of couples over time, while also creating a 'warrior class' of men outside the family.

The lobby's main concerns

By the mid-1990s, the 'family values' lobby was still an active force. Its main concerns can be identified as stable marriage and child-rearing, a gender division of roles, and the confinement of sexuality to the permanent married heterosexual unit. Broadly speaking, this viewpoint regards recent family changes, such as more divorce, cohabitation, lone parenthood and employed motherhood, as negative, and would seek to reverse such changes if possible. It aims to reinstate what is perceived as a 'traditional' family form – the stable married family held together by a breadwinning male head who is also a source of authority, the family form characteristic of the 1950s, which is idealised in this viewpoint. Abortion and contraception may be opposed, as indeed may sex education, because of the freedom they allegedly give to express sexuality outside marriage. Another element is intolerance of the expression of gay and lesbian sexuality (by definition – in Britain anyway – extra-marital). A critical view is taken of feminism and its demands. Children are seen as best cared for and socialised within a permanent two-parent unit which should not be disrupted during their childhood. Obligations in families are stressed rather than individual interests or rights. However, 'the family' is thought to be of positive emotional significance and what most people actually want. There is sometimes both a critical acknowledgement of change *and* a denial of it – the 'normal' family is seen as both established *and* threatened.

The state, it is thought, should take steps (exactly what may be left vague or not be the subject of complete consensus) to reverse recent change, and reinstate and reward traditional forms of sexual morality and child rearing. Possible ways forward – or rather backward – might be to adjust the tax and benefits systems to reward (or to reward to a greater extent) traditional patterns of behaviour, especially marriage, to make it more difficult to obtain a divorce and to restore a stronger notion of 'fault' to divorce, to make abortion and contraception less accessible and to do the same for sex education, to discourage women, or certainly mothers, from being in the labour market, to penalise – or remove perceived rewards for – lone parenthood while actively promoting the two-parent family, and to enforce parental and other types of family responsibility. That is, governments should defend or where necessary re-establish a 'traditional' pattern of family life. There are, however, some ambiguities in the view of the role governments should play towards families.

Ambiguities on the role of the state in this viewpoint

Ambiguities in the view of the state in relation to families arise from the apparent – yet discomfiting – need for the state to influence and control personal behaviour in order to reinstate the kind of traditional, stable, fixed-role family form that this lobby wants to see and believes is socially beneficial. How should the state proceed? Does it even need to *do* anything at all? Uncertainty in this area, often combined with a preference for a *laissez-faire* state and economy and a belief that it is state intervention, among other factors, which has hastened the family's demise, can produce a situation in which the family values position veers uncertainly between extreme authoritarianism and extreme *laissez-faire* in its prescription for the role of the state.

A basic paradox here relates to how families are formed and maintained. If a position of biological essentialism is adopted, then a 'hands-off' approach by the state would make sense, because the belief is basically that letting nature take its course without interference will produce the desired shape of the family. If most of the diverse forms of family life are essentially a distortion, it is logical to argue that state or any other organised interference in families should withdraw, because the family will then revert to its 'natural' shape. This position is compatible with the 'new right' view on minimal state intervention in general. A minimal state would provide for internal and external security, uphold laws governing the general rules of conduct, and mostly leave the family as a private arena providing welfare, care and some control for its members. Arguments about the 'free society' and 'free market' (for example, Quest 1992) suggest that people should be free to run their families as they wish.

Problems arise, however, if left to themselves people do *not* in fact form the 'traditional' type of family preferred by the family values lobby but exercise a variety of choices. It may be argued that the evidence on family change suggests that, to a degree at least, individuals have chosen changed and diverse family forms rather than merely been forced or pressured into these by circumstances. The 'choice' factor is a difficult one, and it has been argued, for example, that most lone mothers have found themselves in their situation due to circumstances outside their own control, while for only a minority is unmarried motherhood a matter of personal choice (see, for example, Hardey and Crow 1991). But it may also be that the 'liberal' legislation of the late 1960s on divorce enabled many more people to choose divorce as an alternative to continuing with an unhappy marriage; that as social controls surrounding extra-marital sexuality and child bearing diminished, more people came to consciously embrace these options; that as it became easier both legally and socially for men not to maintain their biological children from an earlier relationship (prior to the Child Support Act 1991), more men actively chose not to do so (perhaps in order to concentrate on a subsequent family). And as Roseneil and Mann (1996) comment, there are women (even in poverty) who are: 'consciously deciding to have children without depending on a male partner' (1996: 208). Accessible abortion and contraception have been specifically argued for in terms of women's choice. When family change is described or argued for positively, this may be done in terms of a desirable expansion of individual choice. Lesbian and gay sexuality may also be argued for as a matter of choice.

Yet there is a wish on the part of the family values lobby for state policies to limit choice – to support their preferred family form by punishing or preventing alternatives, and to give clear signals about what is approved or disapproved family behaviour. The attempt to revive earlier forms of family life can surely become and feel coercive. For example, under the Child Support Act men are compelled by means of various sanctions to make (higher) child maintenance payments and lone mothers are compelled to apply for them. Family members may be directly or indirectly pressured, regardless of their wishes, to take on larger roles of maintenance and support towards each other by the withdrawal of the state in the fields of social security, student maintenance, and community care. And various issues on which the moral lobby have campaigned (see Durham 1991) illustrate how they aim to restrict choices by means of changing legislation, for example on abortion or divorce. The field of sexuality in particular provides an example of the more authoritarian strand of the lobby where it is desired to limit choice. This is in head-on collision with the libertarian argument that the family and the personal are private areas which should be left alone.

Are 'family values' right-wing?

It may now be useful to consider both congruences and conflicts between 'family values' and right-wing ideology. There are different views here. Abbott and Wallace (1992), for example, see a clear reinforcement of social and economic ideologies in the 'moral' new right, firmly identifying 'pro-family' and traditionalist views with the new right. They comment:

> the New Right are arguing for a return to what they see as the traditional family form....They perceive this 'natural' family as having been under-mined by feminism and the welfare state. The family is seen to be the foundation of a strong, moral society and to be essential for the mainte-nance of capitalism. This view of family and family life is central to New Right thought.
>
> (Abbott and Wallace 1992: 16)

Two other feminist authors quoted by Durham (1991), David (1984) and ten-Tusscher (1986), also argue for the identification of the new right and the neo-traditionalist/anti-feminist perspective. In their view, Thatcherism was centrally concerned with sexual counter-revolution and/or the restoration of patriarchy. Durham also refers to Hall (1986), who suggested that discourses on abortion, sex education and women's position were key bastions of Thatcherite ideology.

For Durham, however, the situation is more complex than this and these analyses collapse together different elements. Having reviewed a number of moral crusades, he claimed that they could not simply be identified with Thatcherism, and that there was no simple equation between the moral lobby, anti-feminism, and Thatcherism or even the new right (broader than Thatcherism). In fact, as he notes, the moral lobby in the 1980s was very critical of the Thatcher government at times. The anti-abortion movement is not necessarily right-wing (bills in the 1970s and 1980s to restrict abortion have been private members', not government, bills, with the exception of the Human Fertilisation and Embryology Act 1990), and abortion has not been a party political issue in the House of Commons. The government's proposals for divorce reform in the 1990s, eventually resulting in the Family Law Act 1996, provide another example of a moral issue which in a sense was not party political and divided the Conservative Party. Writing at the turn of the decade, Durham (1991) commented:

> what we have not seen in the eighties, and are not likely to see in the nineties, is the coming together of the political right and the moral lobby and a shift from a rarely implemented government rhetoric to a sustained 'moral majority' stance.
>
> (Durham 1991: 179)

Earlier he said: 'the New Right does not speak with one voice on family and sexual issues but is divided' (ibid.: 140). In a later article (1994a) Durham argued similarly, saying: 'the Thatcher years do not present a picture of a Conservatism centrally concerned with the family and "traditional" values' (1994a: 67), and that the picture under the Major governments was even more mixed.

This brings us more directly to the question of conflict between the ideology of the right and the family values viewpoint. The clash between family values and a minimum state, *laissez-faire* type of ideology has already been commented on. This relates to a deeper conflict within right-wing ideology itself, also discussed by Abbott and Wallace (1992). While economic liberalism advocates *laissez-faire*, traditional authoritarian Conservatives want the maintenance of a strong state, with a commitment to nationhood and law and order to ensure good behaviour. Such a divide militates against any clear consensus on family issues and policies. For example, the new right's emphasis on the family is clearly tied to Conservatism, while liberal theory emphasises more the (male?) individual. Abbott and Wallace contrast: 'the conservative emphasis on tradition and hierarchy', with 'the liberal emphasis on autonomy and the fundamental equality of autonomous individuals...explicitly constructing *men* (as opposed to all adults) as autonomous individuals' (1992: 18).

In practice, these two conflicting ideologies on the right have accommodated each other (Abbott and Wallace, citing King 1987). A combination 'Libertarian Conservatism' ('the articulation of conservative political thought with *laissez-faire* economic principles' – Abbott and Wallace 1992: 20), adopted by the new right in Britain and the US, supports *laissez-faire* economics, *but* a strong state to maintain traditional and family values. Even so, it may be argued, this accommodation of the two ideological strands might be an uneasy one when faced with some family issues. Examples might be whether mothers of young children should be in paid work, whether individuals should be free to leave one partner and find another, leave one family and found another (perhaps in the service of maximising their economic gain), and whether employers should be made to pay a 'family wage' or give any regard to workers' family commitments. Additionally, a government influenced by right-wing ideology has other priorities than the straightforward promulgation of 'family values' objectives, most obviously (in the case of Conservative governments of the 1980s and 1990s) control of public expenditure, reduction of inflation and taxation, deregulation of the labour market, and general improvement (in their terms) of the state of the economy. These objectives are sometimes, but not always, consonant with family values concerns. For example, the arguments of the family values lobby were convenient to Conservative governments when rhetoric about family responsibility could be harnessed in the drive to reduce the welfare state and public spending. Specifically, arguments about parental responsibility could be deployed in defence of the Child Support Act (Fox Harding 1994). However, Conservative economic objectives were not so easy to align with family values arguments in other cases. For example, lone mothers moving into employment may have been desirable for government because of likely benefit savings, yet for the family traditionalists mothers of young children should be full-time at home (although, yes, sometimes a haze of ambiguity surrounds their prescriptions for what *lone* mothers should do). Conservative governments, seeking to make the economy more competitive, promulgated a low wage policy, yet the family values lobby would wish to see a 'family' (and therefore not so low) wage paid to households with children, in encouragement of the one-breadwinner model (see, for example, Morgan 1995), while the mobility of labour issue provides another example of a conflict between economic objectives and the maintenance of family ties and responsibilities.

'Family values' in Conservative government policy

It will be clear from some of the preceding argument that a right-wing consensus on family policies might be difficult to achieve and that a 'family values' agenda is not necessarily right-wing. This chapter concludes by summarising some of the 'successes' and 'failures' of the family lobby in influencing Conservative government policy in the period 1979–97, and therefore the extent to which the Conservative Party in office may be considered to have been a friend of family values/traditional family forms. Three broad themes in Conservative policy will be considered – relating to parenthood; to heterosexual couplehood (marriage, divorce and cohabitation); and to sexuality specifically.

Parenthood

With regard to parenthood, the most obvious Conservative measure which springs to mind is the Child Support Act 1991; this piece of legislation connects with a new debate about, and preoccupation with, 'parental responsibility', which has also been reflected in the Children Act 1989, the Criminal Justice Act 1991 (see Fox Harding 1994, 1996a), and the Criminal Justice and Public Order Act 1994. The Acts in their differing ways emphasise parental responsibility as binding (it cannot simply be relinquished), as determined by biology (with some assistance from the law in the case of unmarried fathers), and as carrying serious liabilities – for example, an increased liability to be punished for a child's offences. There is an underlying concern here that parental – and in particular paternal – responsibility and commitment have been declining over time, and, in the case of the Criminal Justice Act, a belief that firmer parental *control* of children can be reinstated (by, in effect, more coercive action by the state towards parents themselves). The Child Support Act embodies an emphasis on financial responsibility, but is also ambiguous in terms of a family values agenda. It is controlling, but for men as well as women – and its most vociferous opponents have been men coerced into paying larger amounts of child support. It cannot be seen as defending patriarchy in a sense that necessarily benefits men (see, for example, Fox Harding 1996b). And it has emphasised lone mothers moving into paid work, not merely their being more financially dependent on individual men rather than the state.

Another aspect concerns young people's increased economic dependence on their parents, and therefore extended parental responsibility for young adults. This occurred in the late 1980s and 1990s because of reduction or removal of various benefits for the young and a reduction in student maintenance grants. Parental financial responsibility was expanded *de facto* – it was not legally enforceable. But with this goes the possibility of greater control – there is a financial leverage which parents may use to influence young people's behaviour. This possibility of enhanced control might be welcomed from a family values point of view. In reality, however, parents might give up because of financial and other difficulties, and young people become the responsibility of *neither* parents *nor* the state.

Another aspect of policy concerns leave from employment for reasons of maternity, paternity, or parental responsibilities generally, for example when a child is ill. The Conservative government's lack of support for EU directives on such leave is notorious. In a sense this may be seen as indicating a lack of a family values ethic, a lack of support for parenthood, but the waters are muddied. If, in the ideal family of the family traditionalists, one parent (the mother) is always at home, then presumably maternity and parental leaves from work are not necessary. If, further, the extended family is active and available to help at times of childbirth, perhaps paternity leave is not necessary either. However, Conservative arguments in this area were rather put in terms of making it more expensive for employers to employ workers (for example, Portillo, reported in the *Guardian* 7 November 1995).

Another area is publicly-provided child day care (pre-school and out-of-school). Here the Conservative record was inconsistent. Despite the increase in working mothers of very young children, state provision did not expand significantly during the 1980s and 1990s; it was care in the private and voluntary sectors (including childminders) that grew to meet the demand (Department of Health 1988, 1995), as did the employment of private nannies (Gregson and Lowe 1994). In other words, the growing need for care of young children outside the *family* was also being met outside the *state*. However, a tax concession on employer-provided child care, having been removed by government (1984), was reinstated (1990), and then extended to employers' payments as well as their actual provision (1992), so here there was some (indirect) state assistance. A 'disregard' (or effective benefit increase) for child-care costs for part-time workers on Income Support was abolished in 1988, yet in the mid-1990s a disregard for such costs was introduced for some claimants of the means-tested Family Credit (although arguably not of a sufficient amount to cover the costs involved). In 1996 an experimental scheme of nursery vouchers for 4-year-olds began to be phased in, with a similar scheme for 3-year-olds planned. However, there was disagreement about what the effects of the policy would be (see, for example, *Poverty* 1995: 3–4; *Guardian* 17 April 1996) and scepticism about its helpfulness to working mothers. Overall, with a degree of ambiguity, and some differences between the 1980s and 1990s, Conservative governments were not supportive of child day care in a way which would facilitate mothers undertaking paid work. The family values lobby might approve.

Also relevant to parenthood is the only universal state benefit payment for children, Child Benefit, usually claimed by mothers whether working or not. This was allowed to decline in real value in the 1980s, but was then uprated and pegged to price inflation under the Major governments from the early 1990s. In this area at least there was a distinct difference between the approaches of the Thatcher and Major governments. Interpretations in terms of support for a family values agenda are not clear-cut. One type of family values argument might be that motherhood should indeed be financially supported by the state, as a recognition of its importance as well as meeting some of the costs of children and perhaps helping mothers to stay out of the labour market (although from this point of view the amount paid may be deemed insufficient). Another argument, however, connects with family values views of parental responsibility – that is, the principle that parents should be *entirely* responsible for their children, and that this should usually mean both women's and children's financial dependence on a male breadwinner. From this perspective Child Benefit is presumably a bad idea. Another idea, in fairness not commonly aired by the family values lobby, might be that Child Benefit should be restricted to the married unit. This would support motherhood/parenthood in the approved context, emphasising that *both* parents should undertake responsibility before gaining recognition and assistance from the state.

On the issue of government policy and *lone* parenthood specifically, the Child Support Act has already been considered briefly above. Its significance for lone parents (usually mothers) was an increased dependence, in place of social security benefits, on a more problematic source of income – unpredictable and irregular payments from a former partner, sometimes carrying the risk of harassment and violence, sometimes involving the loss of other forms of support from him (see, for example, Clarke *et al.* 1994, 1996). Making life more difficult for lone mothers (and their erstwhile partners) may be seen, from a more extreme family values viewpoint, as having a desirable deterrent effect: the argument would be that individuals will avoid undertaking or creating separated parenthood if that position is made very tough. The most well-known and extreme exponent of this view is the American, Murray, who has said, for example: 'I favour eliminating benefits for unmarried women altogether (for potential new entrants....)....The state should stop intervening, and let the natural economic penalties occur' (Murray 1994: 30–31). Government statements and proposals specifically hostile to lone mothers/parents appeared in the 1990s (see above; see Durham 1994a, 1994b; Burghes and Roberts 1995). Two new moves already mentioned were to freeze and phase out the extra Child Benefit paid to lone parents since the mid-1970s, and the Single Parent Premium paid with Income Support since 1988, thus reversing the earlier recognition of lone parents' special needs and costs, and, particularly in the case of the Single Parent Premium, reducing further their already low level of income.

What might be said of Conservative policy on parenthood in general? (See the section on sexuality for the question of parental control of young people's sexual activity.) There was a preparedness to expand parents' responsibilities for children and young people by depriving and coercive means, but not to offer these responsibilities much positive support in the form of day care, parental leave, or better benefits. What may be identified in the 1990s was an intensifying antagonism to lone mothers and a preparedness to express this in harsher policies. With some qualifications, then, Conservative government policy followed a family values line.

Marriage, etc.

In the complex area of family law Conservative governments might be deemed to have failed to support the idea of permanent marriage, by enabling divorce to become easier and by reducing the disadvantages of 'illegitimacy' or birth out of marriage. Under the Matrimonial and Family Proceedings Act 1984, it became possible to petition for divorce after one year of marriage rather than waiting three years. This effectively made divorce easier, and the Act was indeed followed by an upwards 'blip' in the divorce rate the following year (Fox Harding 1996a, citing Elliott 1991). The Act also favoured 'clean break' patterns where ex-wives did not receive maintenance in their own right (as opposed to receiving it for children), thus making the post-divorce situation of women who had adopted a 'traditional' (not in paid work) pattern more difficult. This would not be in line with the family values preference for home-maker wives who presumably should be protected, rather than penalised for, or deterred from, being full-time housewives.

In 1990 other changes to divorce law were considered in a document from the Law Commission (Law Commission 1990) which was at first endorsed by the Lord Chancellor. These proposals would have moved further in the direction of 'no fault' divorce (that is, divorce without specific grounds related to conduct), and could have been perceived as making divorce 'easier', albeit accompanied by a conciliation process. The proposals were shelved, but reappeared in 1993 in a Lord Chancellor's Green Paper (Lord Chancellor 1993), followed by a White Paper in 1995 (Lord Chancellor 1995), and subsequently a Bill in 1995 which (after much debate and amendment) passed through parliament as the Family Law Act in 1996. The changes removed the 'fault' basis from divorce altogether; the one ground for divorce would now be the passage of time – usually twelve months, this time being to reflect, consider and settle issues, with couples having to attend an information session, and then being offered mediation or counselling.

Such steps are not altogether in the direction that a family values position would favour, although the precise impact of the Family Law Act is unclear. One perception has been that the Act would make divorce 'easier' (although in some cases it would certainly make it slower), and that the notion of fault or specific ground should not be removed as this would undermine marriage as an institution. The contrary argument is that the current system allows divorces to go through very rapidly and easily indeed (see, for example, Booth 1996), and that the new delay and emphasis on information-giving and counselling would act as a brake – which may or may not be welcomed. The proposals and the Bill met with resistance from those who saw them making divorce easier and less moralistic, some of which came from the Conservative benches, most notably from Baroness Young who headed the opposition in the House of Lords. Prior to the proposals reaching parliament, the family values writer Quest (1994), noted that: 'Lord Mackay's proposals seem bound to reduce people's incentives to get married, stay married, and behave properly within the marriage' (1994: 4).

In another field of family law Conservative government action was again at variance with family values preferences. The Family Law Reform Act of 1987 removed virtually all the remaining legal disadvantages attached to birth out of marriage, thus continuing a long-term twentieth century trend towards amelioration of the formerly highly disadvantaged status of the 'illegitimate', and indeed removing the very word from legal documents (see, for example, Dewar 1992). Unmarried fathers also acquired more rights under this Act and the Children Act 1989. The social stigma attached to 'illegitimacy' had been in decline since, arguably, the 1960s, and the reduction of its legal disadvantages may be seen as a public statement of the need to reduce difference between those born into different types of family situation. This has long been thought a laudable aim in many quarters, where discrimination against the 'illegitimate' is seen as unjustifiable denial of their rights; but for some of the family values lobby it is socially important to *maintain* a distinction between those born in and out of wedlock. This is thought to help shore up the institution of marriage by encouraging the restriction of sexuality and procreation to that context. For example, the jacket of Morgan's (1995) book *Farewell to the Family?* states: 'The stigma attached to illegitimacy represented the fear that the culture could not survive if biological parents were not formally bound to care for their children'.

Lastly on marriage, it is worth mentioning the treatment of married couples by the tax system under the Conservatives. The third Thatcher government in 1988 removed a policy which had (unintentionally no doubt) favoured the cohabiting over the married. This was an extra tax concession on mortgage interest for joint home purchasers not married to each other (which had in fact favoured *any* non-married jointly purchasing unit, whether heterosexual cohabitants or not). From 1988 the tax relief related to the property rather than the purchaser, thus removing this advantage. This would be welcomed from a family values perspective, which is in general anxious not to penalise marriage in any way, preferring positively to reward it. The long-standing married tax allowance continued – this had traditionally been paid in almost all cases to the husband rather than the wife. But it declined in value, and two developments in the 1990s are notable – the freezing of the allowance from 1990 and therefore its effective phasing out, and the possibility, after 1993, of couples deciding for themselves which partner should receive it or whether it should be split between them. Payment continued to be restricted to the legally married, however. Married women were increasingly treated as separate entities by the Inland Revenue, and all their income could be treated separately from their husband's for tax purposes from 1990. These trends are ambiguous from a family values position. If marriage is to be regarded as a socially desirable institution then it should receive the privilege of a tax allowance, as it does – but perhaps a much larger one? And if wives are ideally the economic dependants of their husbands, then treating them as separate individuals for tax purposes, or paying the married tax allowance to them, would presumably not make much sense.

On family law, then, Conservative government moves may be seen to have been broadly in contradiction of family values objectives, while in taxation policy the picture has been mixed. The family values lobby might find much to criticise in the Conservative government's record on marriage.

Sexuality

The third area is sexuality, and here the Conservative government was on some issues, but not on others, susceptible to the family values lobby's desire to limit legitimate sexuality to the married, heterosexual unit. The greatest 'success' of the lobby may be seen as the inclusion within the Local Government Act of 1988 of the notorious Section 28 (see Durham 1991), which prohibited local authorities from intentionally promoting homosexuality as a 'pretended family relationship'. This affected any service that local authorities might provide and might have been construed broadly, but no prosecutions followed. A quite different measure was the reduction of the age of homosexual consent in 1994, from 21 – not to the age for heterosexual consent, 16, as some campaigners wished, but to 18. This seems like a compromise; the family values lobby would presumably want the age to remain at 21, or would not want consenting homosexual acts to be legal at all.

A policy area where the family values viewpoint had some effect was sex education, although here it has to be said that the Conservatives' position fluctuated. Under an Education Act in 1986 it was specified that sex education where taught should be placed in a moral and family framework – although parents had no right to withdraw their children (see Durham 1991). This was reinforced by later guidelines in 1994 which advised that sex education should be taught in the context of moral and family values (Durham 1994a; Lister 1996). However, sex education also became a compulsory part of the curriculum in secondary schools at this time, although with parents having the right to withdraw their children where it was not part of the national curriculum. Sex education was voluntary in primary schools (it being a governors' decision whether to provide it). Education circulars in the late 1980s and the 1990s cautioned teachers against giving contraceptive advice to under-16s without parental knowledge or consent (Pilcher 1996). Something of a compromise position had been reached, perhaps. It is not altogether clear where a 'family values' position might point in this area – would the desired pattern of sexual behaviour be better produced by educating children and adolescents about sex within a marital framework only, or by not educating them (that is in school) about sex at all? Supporters of family values have sometimes argued that sex education should ideally be carried out by parents rather than the educational system (see Durham 1991) yet surveys show that this is a difficult area for many parents (see, for example, Moss 1996).

A notorious failure of family values campaigns may be seen in the so-called Gillick judgements of 1985 and 1986. Here the government was in collision with the family values movement as represented by Victoria Gillick, a parent who wished for an assurance that her children under 16 could not be given contraceptive treatment or advice without her consent. As this assurance could not be given by the (then) Department of Health and Social Security, since much depended on medical discretion, a series of court cases began between the Department and Gillick. The Conservative government fought Gillick's campaign all the way up to the House of Lords. While Gillick was successful at the Court of Appeal stage, where the judgement was that contraception or abortion were *not* to be provided by the NHS to under-16s without parental consent, this judgement was reversed by the House of Lords. Here the view was that young people under 16 *should* be able to receive advice and treatment at the doctor's discretion, although subject to their own age and understanding being sufficient – this became known as 'Gillick competence', a standard which has now become quite widely applied. In the eventual judgement, then, the arguments in favour of medical discretion held sway. In undertaking this battle the Conservative government clearly placed itself in an opposing position to the family values lobby whose concerns here were under-age sex (which is by definition also extra-marital sex) and parental control of adolescent behaviour. While Conservative government policy aimed to reduce the number of teenage pregnancies, this was presumably not thought to be helped by doctors denying access to birth control.

There was, then, only a partial success for family values in the field of sexuality, and in general it may be concluded that Conservative policies over the 1980s and up to 1997 were conflicting. It is important to look at actual measures in depth, not merely at Conservative government rhetoric, in assessing 'family values' influence. The influence may not be as widespread as may appear or as has sometimes been believed, and indeed the criticisms which the traditionalist lobby themselves make of Conservative governments indicate this. There have also been some differences between the Thatcher and Major governments, notably on Child Benefit, also on child day care, although if anything government hostility to lone mothers intensified under the Major governments.

Conclusion

This chapter has shown that the family values movement of the 1980s and 1990s has embraced a variety of groups and issues, but has been centrally concerned with the promotion of stable marriage, embodying gender-differentiated roles, as the only acceptable site for sexuality and procreation; that views of the role of the state in promoting the desired family form are ambiguous; that a family values position is not necessarily right-wing; and that the record of the Conservative governments in the three areas of parenthood, marriage and sexuality was mixed and sometimes in contradiction to family values concerns. The author broadly agrees with Durham's (1994a) conclusion that: 'We find...neither within the Conservative tradition in general nor its most recent incarnations in office, the devotion to the "traditional" family that we might expect' (1994a: 70). Nevertheless, the arguments of the family values lobby, along with family change itself, remain insistently present on the political scene, and these arguments – which are not exclusively associated with the right – continue to be influential under a Labour government.

Bibliography

Abbott, P. and Wallace, C. (1992) *The Family and the New Right*, London: Pluto Press.
Anderson, D. and Dawson, G. (eds) (1986) *Family Portraits*, London: Social Affairs Unit.
Berger, P. and Berger, B. (1983) *The War over the Family*, London: Hutchinson.

Booth, M. (1996) 'Divorced from reality', *Guardian* 5 March, Guardian Law: 13.

Burghes, L. and Roberts, C. (1995) 'Part Three: lone parents', *Community Care* 6–12 July: ii–viii.

Clarke, K., Craig, G. and Glendinning, C. (1994) *Losing Support: Children and the Child Support Act*, London: Children's Society.

—— (1996) *Small Change: the Impact of the Child Support Act on Lone Mothers and Children*, London: Family Policy Studies Centre.

David, M. (1984) 'Teaching and preaching sexual morality', *Journal of Education* 166(1).

Davies, J. (ed.) (1993) *The Family: Is It Just Another Lifestyle Choice?*, London: IEA.

Dennis, N. (1993) *Rising Crime and the Dismembered Family*, London: IEA.

Dennis, N. and Erdos, G. (1992/1993) *Families without Fatherhood*, London: IEA.

Department of Health (1988/1995) *Personal Social Services Local Authority Statistics Children's Day Care Facilities at 31 March, England*, London: Government Statistical Service.

Dewar, J. (1992) *Law and the Family*, London: Butterworths.

Durham, M. (1991) *Sex and Politics: The Family and Morality in the Thatcher Years*, Basingstoke: Macmillan.

—— (1994a) 'The Conservative Party and the family', *Talking Politics* 6(2): 66–70.

—— (1994b) 'Major and morals: back to basics and the crisis of Conservatism', *Talking Politics* 7(1): 12–16.

Elliott, B. J. (1991) 'Demographic trends in domestic life 1945–87' in D. Clark (ed.) *Marriage, Domestic Life and Social Change: Writings for Jacqueline Burgoyne 1944–88*, London: Routledge.

Family Policy Studies Centre (1990) *Family Policy Bulletin*, No. 8 Spring, London: Family Policy Studies Centre.

—— (1991) *Supporting our Children: The Family Impact of Child Maintenance*, London: Family Policy Studies Centre.

Fitzgerald, A. (1983) 'The new right and the family' in M. Loney, D. Boswell and J. Clarke (eds) *Social Policy and Social Welfare: a Reader*, Milton Keynes: Open University Press.

Fox Harding, L. (1993) ' "Alarm" versus "Liberation"? responses to the increase in lone parents – Parts 1 and 2', *Journal of Social Welfare and Family Law* 2 and 3: 101–12 and 174–84.

—— (1994) ' "Parental responsibility" – a dominant theme in British child and family policy for the 1990s', *International Journal of Sociology and Social Policy* 14 (1/2): 84–108.

—— (1996a) *Family, State and Social Policy*, Basingstoke: Macmillan.

—— (1996b) ' "Parental responsibility": the reassertion of private patriarchy?' in E. Silva (ed.) *Good Enough Mothering? Feminist Perspectives on Lone Motherhood*, London: Routledge: 130–47.

Gregson, N. and Lowe, M. (1994) *Servicing the Middle Classes: Class, Gender and Waged Domestic Labour in Contemporary Britain*, London: Routledge.

Guardian (1995) 7 November.

—— (1996) 17 April.

Hall, S. (1986) 'No light at the end of the tunnel', *Marxism Today* December: 16.

Hardey, M. and Crow, G. (1991) 'Introduction' in M. Hardey and G. Crow (eds) *Lone Parenthood: Coping with Constraints and Making Opportunities*, Hemel Hempstead: Harvester Wheatsheaf.

King, D. S. (1987) *The New Right: Politics, Markets and Citizenship*, London: Macmillan.

Law Commission (1990) *The Grounds for Divorce* No. 192, London: HMSO.

Lister, R. (1996) 'Back to the family: family policies and politics under the Major government' in H. Jones and J. Millar (eds) *The Politics of the Family*, Aldershot: Avebury.

Lord Chancellor (1990) *Children Come First: The Government's Proposals on Child Maintenance*, Cm 1264, London: HMSO.

—— (1993) *Looking to the Future: Mediation and the Ground for Divorce*, London: Lord Chancellor's Department.

—— (1995) *Looking to the Future: Mediation and the Ground for Divorce: The Government's Proposals*, London: HMSO.

Morgan, P. (1995) *Farewell to the Family? Public Policy and Family Breakdown in Britain and the USA*, London: Institute of Economic Affairs.

Moss, S. (1996) 'Daddy, how do you do sex?', *Guardian* 22 May.

Murray, C. (1984) *Losing Ground: American Social Policy 1950–1980*, New York: Basic Books.

—— (1990) *The Emerging British Underclass*, London: Institute of Economic Affairs.

—— (1994) *Underclass: the Crisis Deepens*, London: Institute of Economic Affairs.

Parton, N. (1981) 'Child abuse, social anxiety and welfare', *British Journal of Social Work* 16(5): 511–31.

Pilcher J. (1996) 'Gillick and after: children and sex in the 1980s and 1990s' in J. Pilcher and S. Wagg (eds) *Thatcher's Children: Politics, Childhood and Society in the 1980s and 1990s*, London: Falmer.

Poverty (1995) 92 (Winter): 3–4.

Quest, C. (ed.) (1992) *Equal Opportunities: A Feminist Fallacy*, London: Institute of Economic Affairs.

—— (ed.) (1994) *Liberating Women…From Modern Feminism*, London: Institute of Economic Affairs.

Roseneil, S. and Mann, K. (1996) 'Unpalatable choices and inadequate families. Lone mothers and the underclass debate' in E. Silva (ed.) *Good Enough Mothering? Feminist Perspectives on Lone Motherhood*, London: Routledge.

ten-Tusscher, T. (1986) 'Patriarchy, capitalism and the new right' in J. Evans, J. Hills, K. Hunt, E. Meehan, T. ten-Tusscher, U. Vogel and G. Waylen (eds) *Feminism and Political Theory*, London: Sage.

Whitfield, R. (ed.) (1987) *Families Matter: Towards a Programme of Action*, Basingstoke: Marshall Pickering.

7 Family values and the nation-state

Paul Gilbert

Family and nation

It is a cliché that much nationalism draws, to a greater or lesser extent, on metaphors of the family (see Parekh 1995: 33–5), which is seen as exemplifying the relationships of members of the nation in miniature. Yet it is seldom enquired what specific conception of the family is drawn upon to furnish the image of the nation that a particular nationalist politics wants to project; nor how that conception of the family must, in consequence, suffuse the social policy which such a politics involves. What I wish to do here is to investigate a particularly interesting case of the functional relationships between nationalism and family policy, namely that provided by the New Right.[1] After a critique of New Right thinking in these areas I shall briefly sketch an alternative, socialist conception of the family and then go on to investigate how, and to what degree, this figures in current New Labour thought about the nation.

'The most natural state'

'The family', wrote Herder in 1783, 'is a product of Nature. The most natural state is, therefore, a state composed of a single people with a single national character....For a people is a natural growth, like a family, only spread more widely' (reprinted in Zimmern 1939: 165). The New Right espouses, I suggest, this romantic conception of the nation. It is an ethnic conception, in the sense that it makes membership of the nation, in normal circumstances, an ascriptive characteristic deriving from pre-political facts as to one's identity. In so far as these facts are taken to be biological facts of genetic relatedness like those that hold between members of the family, or rather between members of a supposedly *natural* family, then this ethnic conception can be described as a racist one. This, as we shall see, is a slight over-simplification, but the tendency to racism is inherent in the ethnic conception of the nation. For the attempt to demarcate a single people on the basis of a 'single national character', regarded as explicable naturalistically, is almost bound to lead to racial exclusiveness.

The use of the family as a model for the nation emphasises, of course, quite other considerations. It emphasises ties of loyalty founded on supposedly natural sentiments and the security such ties bring. The unity of the nation is thought of, like the unity of the family, as founded on such ties – ties which extend so far and no further. Thus a life in common with one's compatriots is thought of as made possible by such ties, just as family life is thought to be made possible. The 'natural state' is, therefore, the one that corresponds to and regulates a people leading such a common life. The family model that shapes such thinking is, of course, a commonplace in the claims to statehood of ethnic nationalists.

Why should the New Right need such a conception of the nation? The answer, I believe, is that it needs it principally to resolve the problem of legitimising a *minimal* state – that is to say, a state which interferes as little as is deemed possible with the freedom of the individual to enter contractual relationships and to retain the benefits of them.[2] Thus, in theory, the minimal state restricts itself to the maintenance of internal order and external security, together with whatever is needed, by way of minimal welfare provision, to conduce to them. The New Right does not just believe that the state should ideally be a minimal one, but that no other kind of state is legitimate.

The liberal state is, of course, legitimised through the presumed consent[3] of its members to an organisation which safeguards their interest in order and security while maximising their scope for individual freedom. Yet what is to determine the limitations on their freedom to which members might consent? Might not the members of a particular state be presumed to consent not only to a minimal political organisation, but to one which provided, for example, considerable welfare? Indeed, might they not *withdraw* their consent to one that did not? The Libertarian Right[4] replies that welfare would be purchased at a cost in the freedom to dispose of one's income as one wished that one could not, on reflection, regard as just. But this is at least contestable, so that a liberal state need not be minimal. There is, however, a problem for any liberal state. If a tax haven provided someone with an acceptable level of security at an agreeable cost then, under liberal or libertarian principles, nothing need prevent them from transferring their national loyalties there. Another way of putting essentially the same point is to say that the motives for entering such contractual agreements with the state may be inadequate to secure continuing loyalty to an existing one (cf. Fukuyama 1992: Chapter 30). For, to the extent to which a state offers only minimal cover to its citizens, then, like an insurance company, it can command no special loyalty. To the extent to which it does command loyalty, then, like an old fashioned friendly society, it risks becoming more than minimal, since then it draws on motivations other than those prudential ones which drive the minimal state. So, there is a problem for the New Right in justifying existing states as both essentially minimal political organisations and worthy foci of national loyalty – a loyalty that must be sufficiently motivated to ensure state security (often through personal self-sacrifice) but also limited in its manifestations to such acts.

The New Right's solution to this problem is to regard membership of the state as, in some sense, *naturally*, rather than voluntarily determined, and thus evoking spontaneous, rather than calculated, loyalty for a political organisation whose proper scope is, as we shall see, fixed by the same facts of nature. The sense of 'nature' involved here is undoubtedly vague. On the one hand there is the pre-scientific notion of a naturally arising national character, partly in the 'blood', partly environmentally acquired, and transmitted partly by inheritance, partly by natural acculturative processes.[5]

National character can therefore be lost by miscegenation[6] or bad education – by bad breeding in both senses of the phrase. What is crucial, of course, is that national character is pre-political – not shaped by the state, which would be going beyond its role of giving maximum scope for individual inclinations if it tried to *change* them (rather than preserve them from processes which might), and which would thereby be depriving itself of its natural basis of legitimacy into the bargain. The national way of life which the state safeguards – through exercising its minimal roles of law enforcement and national security provision – is not, then, something which it creates but something which derives naturally from its people's shared character – a character that leads them to share a common loyalty and, what is more, gives them a reason for allegiance to a state so organised as not to change that character. It is worth mentioning that the point is an entirely general one (pace Parekh 1994). Though in the rhetoric of Thatcherism the British state is justified by reference to the rugged individualism of the English character, a minimal French state, for example, would be one which did not interfere with the French way of life. It would not, let us suppose, sweep away its supposedly rational framework, if this were indeed rooted in the French national character.

This is one way of regarding the nation as natural. At the other extreme a scientistic conception of nationhood might locate it in ethological or sociobiological notions[7] such as kin altruism, whereby loyalty, even self-sacrificial loyalty, is shown to groups of those to whom we are genetically related, or with whom we share a way of life, because they have, in evolutionary history, usually been genetically related to us. Notice that by incorporating this alternative the sociobiological account is capable of regarding a 'racially mixed' society, such as the USA, as a *nation*, because held together by naturalistically explicable loyalties. The pre-scientific account in terms of shared 'blood' cannot do so. However, the sociobiological account is as committed as the pre-scientific one to regarding immigration as imperilling established bonds, for immigrants will not normally evoke naturally altruistic responses from residents because they do not share a common way of life with them. The New Right philosophy is founded on such alleged facts of human capacity as these, rather than on claims about what human beings *ought* to do. Thus, it is argued, groups as large as nations can be regarded as *natural* groups evoking spontaneous loyalty as a result of their members' genetic and cultural relatedness. To be legitimate a state must represent people as *capable* of a common loyalty. But an existing state organised on minimalist lines cannot rely on doing this on the basis of its members' shared interests alone. There must therefore be a basis in deep biological affinities.

The point common to all naturalistic nationalism of the New Right is that part of one's individual identity consists in one's national identity because it consists in natural facts about one which, in normal circumstances, determine one's national identity. Not only is one's national identity not chosen, it is something *given*, and given not by finding oneself in a certain community, for example, and sharing its common concerns, but by being born into a certain group, held together by common kinship and common attitudes.

The family, or rather the family under a particular naturalistic conception, acts as a model, but more than a model – a mechanism – for the New Right account of the nation. It acts as a model because the family is thought of as essentially a social group held together by kin relations, and the relations between the members of the nation as extended kin relations. The family acts as a mechanism too: national identity is reproduced in and through the acculturation of the young to national membership. The family thus performs the educative role that the truly minimal state cannot. We must turn, then, to look in more detail at the New Right conception of the family.

'Naturall lust'

For the New Right the nuclear family is the natural unit of human social organisation.[8] Whereas on liberal principles[9] the nuclear family arises as a result of a contractual relation between husband and wife judged to be in their mutual interest, the New Right sees it, like Hobbes,[10] as founded on 'naturall lust' – a bond that is essentially non-contractual and instinctual or sentimental. Hobbes was careful to point out, however, that

> the right of Dominion by Generation...which the Parent hath over his Children; and is called PATERNALL...is not so derived from the Generation, as if therefore the Parent had Dominion over his Child because he begat him; but from the Childs Consent, either expresse, or by other sufficient arguments declared....And whereas some have attributed the Dominion to the Man onely, as being of the more excellent Sex; they misreckon in it. For there is not always the difference of strength or prudence between the man and the woman, as that the right can be determined without War.

The patriarchal thinking of the New Right, by contrast, betrays both the naturalistic assumptions that Hobbes criticises. The natural family is a patriarchal one because the father is, by nature, a provider and, as Hobbes would agree, 'the Dominion is in him that nourisheth'.

As in nature, pair bonding creates an environment for parenting. In particular, the father's economic support is required for the child rearing undertaken by the mother. Any invasion of the nuclear family by the provision of welfare represents a threat to the natural order, a temptation to break the bond or not even to enter it. In this important area of life the minimalism of the state can be justified by the nature of the family itself. It follows that national obligations are limited to those that more narrowly familial obligations cannot cover, most notably defence, which is nonetheless modelled on the protection that adult males provide, supposedly naturally, for their families.

Just as the existing state is legitimised by an allegedly natural grouping – the nation – so its proper functions are thus determined by the natural group which serves as the nation's model and mechanism – the family. In this respect the minimalism of the New Right has a quite different grounding from that of the Libertarian Right with its liberal underpinnings. The former rests on alleged facts about what natural groups there are, the latter on the freedom of individuals to construct what groups they choose. The minimalism of the New Right is, therefore, a qualified one, restricting the state to what cannot be achieved by the family – law and order, and defence. But the law and order function is not simply the enforcement of contracts and the prevention of infringements to rights in property and the person, as under Libertarianism. It extends to protecting the way of life which the nation, through its constituent families, enjoys – so long as this does not interfere with the economic relationships which the family supposedly requires.[11]

The family is 'a haven in a heartless world'[12] just because it escapes the scope of merely contractual relations and offers values of love and loyalty which, supposedly, are rooted in our natural needs and affections. The responsibility of care for one's family is their natural counterpart, not the consequence of contract, and hence not dissoluble along with it.[13] Indeed the family is the location of one's real, because natural and original, identity. In it and because of it I am a *particular* person,[14] the child of such and such parents, so and so's father, etc. – not just the interchangeable holder of a role I find myself occupying in civil society. It is only because the treatment of people as members of the family is treatment of them as having a particular identity that we can treat others similarly and not simply as bearers of rights and obligations. But this way of treating people is what marks out a sphere of *private* life as that wherein the value of relationships can be enjoyed. The family provides the natural centre and the inevitable source of it. (Paradoxically it is relationships of this sort, by contrast with the intrinsically worthless market relationships which typify the public sphere, that characterise our associations with compatriots, according to nationalism which exploits this family model).[15]

The politics of the New Right family

This picture of the family clearly has its apparent attractions as well as its obvious dangers. It may be countered, however, that it is not a picture of a timeless natural state but of a particular historically located social phenomenon. As Michael Walzer puts it, 'the sentimental family is the first form the distribution of kinship and love takes…once household and economy are pulled apart' (Walzer 1983: 234). The distinction between familial and civic, between private and public roles is only possible when this happens, which is not, of course, to deny that the distinction distorts and exaggerates the nature of this happening. We can put these points together by observing that the family as described by the New Right is not a natural fact but a *social construction*.[16] The actual relationships that constitute it are contingent upon historical processes, not given prior to them: they are shaped for specific reasons by social agents, and the vehicle for their formation is the production of a discourse wherein they are described and valorised.

On a social constructionist view of the family, the New Right's emphasis on biological relationships is part of an attempt to control ties that do actually exist within society through shaping people's discourse about, and evaluation of, them. If the account I have given of the way the family and nation play crucially related roles in New Right thinking is correct, then the reasons why families and nations so structured and conceived should exist is reasonably clear. The existence of the nuclear family with its private sphere of responsibility justifies a minimal state that allows maximum scope for the accumulation and application of private capital. But it also reproduces and legitimises the nation-state, which otherwise either lacks a long term basis or threatens to become more than minimal. The social agents responsible for the family's discursive formation are those who hold political power – the power to control government in their own interests, which, in this instance, are supposedly secured by nation-states of a minimalist tendency. In that case, though, the family's attractions look decidedly suspect, the values it offers questionable.

It is the naturalism, and more especially the biologism, of the New Right's conception of the family that is unacceptable, and in any case, nothing follows from merely biological facts about our drives and their outcomes as to what it is good or right to do.[17] Yet it is on such foundations that the New Right constructs a conception of paternal responsibility that derives wholly from biology and owes nothing to a mother's *claim* on behalf of her child, a claim arising from the presumption of a supportive relationship surrounding the act of conception.[18] Notice how crucial for the New Right is the ascription of responsibility for child support to biological fathers. The male line must be maintained, even when the traditional families that sustained it have been irredeemably shattered. For if the male line is undermined then *women* alone become definitive of membership of society. In that case their needs threaten to reshape it along inescapably collectivist lines, since society's entire future will be a collective, not an individual, responsibility.

The social and economic inequalities between the sexes that patriarchy generates are not accidental features of the New Right state. They are necessary to its functioning as a 'natural state'. For the presence of these inequalities serves to confirm their presumed basis in the natural order which legitimises the state and its social arrangements. There is a parallel here between the existence of sexism and of racism. Though New Right legislation may seek to mitigate their 'excesses', both are viewed as reflecting, perhaps distortedly, inescapable natural facts about relations between the sexes and between national groups. While the former supposed facts are primarily invoked to justify social arrangements within the state, the latter, as we have seen, determine the shape of the state itself.

The New Right family is indeed an objectionably patriarchal one in which the discharge of a father's duty of support gives him a right to the obedience of his children. This enables him to fulfil his specific acculturative role of preparing them for the public world of the nation into which, as his children, they are born. And in this world the father has a pre-eminent place precisely because he must gain the means to discharge his duty of support by contracting his labour or accumulating capital. Apart from these duties being natural ones the story is structurally similar to that of the typical family under liberalism. But its point is different under the New Right; for without patriarchy the minimal state would be impossible and the fear of exotic miscegenation would undermine the basis of its claimed legitimacy. The question to be asked is whether the family can survive the extirpation of such patriarchal elements.

'Reconstructing family values'

What we need to ask now is whether the family can be rescued from the New Right. They did not, after all, invent it. Indeed, to suppose that the family should be abandoned to the Right may be to take an oversimplified view of the ideological role of such notions as 'the family'. These are not simply instruments of mystification employed by a dominant group, but sites of contest for a share in power between different groups. To abandon the family is, it may be argued, to retreat from a politically important battleground (see Harding, this volume). The question to be asked, then, is whether the family can survive the extirpation of its unacceptable patriarchal elements.

One answer, which draws on a communitarianism incorporating traditional socialist values, is that the family can survive, so long as we see it as an essentially *communal* institution, shaped in response to need rather than in pursuit of power. The features of communal living involved here are the pursuit of a common purpose as determined collectively and as valued partly for the relationships which that involves. We can call the family so formed a communal family. Any actual family, of course, will involve a mix of communal and other elements. But insofar as it is a communal one, then to that extent it is worthwhile (pace Frazer, this volume).

Here we must pause to ask what, more precisely, is a family. 'The family' it has been suggested 'is a group of persons united by ties of marriage, blood or adoption; constituting a single household, interacting and communicating with each other in their respective social roles of husband and wife, mother and father, brother and sisters; creating a common culture' (Burgess and Locke cited in Mitchell 1968: 76). The advantage of this definition, questionable in its details as it is, is that it characterises the paradigmatic family in terms of its members' social roles rather than their biological relationships. Blood is but one basis for the relevant roles, just, one might add, as is marriage. What is crucial to occupancy of the roles is recognition of certain needs in others and a preparedness to pursue a collective project aimed at meeting them. The needs in question are of certain kinds of support, in particular of children for the support of adults who can play a parenting role.[19] To rescue the family from the New Right would be to show that there was a value in a parenting project undertaken by a domestic group committed to it, and, perhaps, a value not to be achieved by socialised parenting or other non-familial arrangements. The claim is not an empirical one, though empirical findings are relevant to it. Rather it concerns what sort of values are in principle available in different kinds of relationship. Just as 'free love' is not, for better or worse, a kind of sexual *love*, as we understand it, so socialised parenting does not offer parental love. But to reject socialised parenting leaves open a wide range of possible family types, for parental love is possible across a much wider range of relationships than are envisaged by the New Right.

To unpack the possible value of the family would be a major task. I can float only two suggestions here. First, the value that the family offers lies in a response to what is *given*, to the circumstances we find ourselves in rather than those we choose, which is not to say that we cannot choose to reject these circumstances, to respond differently. But it is the givenness[20] of the situation in which we have a possible role to play which elicits a collective response that is worthwhile. In so far as one's identity is tied closely to the family, this is not because one's identity is fixed by nature. It is that relationships within the family are of particular importance in determining it. These people, their projects, have an inescapable significance in my life, though so do others. Second, and relatedly, the response to need is the *particularised* response of love, rather than the generalised response of benevolence. Yet the particularity of the loved one has no necessary connection with any biological stimulus that they provide. Rather it marks out the *kind* of collective project in which one plays a role within the family,[21] as against many others one plays in society at large.

These features of the family are, it may be suggested, among those we take for granted and which the New Right relies upon for the appeal of its distorted picture. Arguably, the communal family, conceived as realising socialist values, makes better sense of them. What is more, the values such a family offers are values of a sort that can be realised, in different forms, in the wider social world[22] – in particular in one consciously shaped by a socialist apprehension of these values. They do not close this world off from providing a communally motivated welfare nor militate against its welcoming into its ranks ethnically diverse compatriots so that the communal family relates to the wider society within which it is embedded quite differently from the patriarchal family of the New Right.

New Labour and the nation

The conception of the family which I have sketched is in some respects – though not, as we shall see, in all – that which has been adopted under the growing influence of communitarianism, by the ideologues of the present Labour government in Britain. I do not have time here to assess it critically (but see Frazer, this volume). What I want to do, though, is to raise the question of how a New Labour conception of the family bears on its approach to nationhood. To this end I shall look at the role the family plays in the Oxford philosopher David Miller's thinking on nationality – a body of work over the last ten years which has evidently had a significant influence upon New Labour.

Just as the New Right agenda requires a conception of nationhood which will legitimise the state and demarcate the scope of market relationships within it, so too these are, in different ways, demands upon a conception which opposes the New Right without relinquishing its nationalism and free market philosophy. Specifically what New Labour needs are a defence of the current nation-state against more local – or more global – challenges for the loyalty to which the state lays claim, and a justification for some version of the welfare state. The first can be provided, according to David Miller, via the second. In brief, a welfare state is the expression of the fact that its citizens make up a worthwhile ethical community whose members display a special concern for the needs of their compatriots. But the nation is just such a community. No smaller, or larger, grouping could provide a welfare system as fairly, or as effectively. The nation is thus the best sort of group for having a state which is a welfare state. I shall now look in more detail at how the two requirements – of justifying the nation-state and the welfare state – are met.

The first requirement arises directly from a rejection of naturalistic ways of demarcating the nation in favour of viewing it, along social constructionist lines, as a certain type of group constituted by its members recognising each other as compatriots and acknowledging the mutual obligations which membership brings. Miller maintains that such a group is a community, as that is understood and valued by socialists.[23] He explicitly treats the family as operating in an analogous way: someone who is recognised as a member of a group displaying the right familial relationships *is* thereby a member even if there has been 'some dreadful mix up at the hospital' (Miller 1988a: 655). The difficulty in satisfying the first requirement is now apparent. If communities are groups of self-recognising mutually obligated people then why should communities of just the scope of the nation be privileged as *political* communities and accorded separate statehood, when there are other communities of which we are members?

In order to answer this question we must look, as noted above, at the second requirement on a New Labour conception of the nation, namely that it should provide a justification for the welfare state. The following quotation indicates how Miller sees the welfare state and the role of the nation in safeguarding it.

We see at present how the European welfare states, which for half a century have provided their members with some degree of protection against losing out in market competition, are having to be cut back radically in order that the economies in those countries should remain internationally competitive. If people's economic position depends increasingly on whether they have the skills and talents (and good luck) to be able to compete in the world market, then we may expect to see progressive polarisation between an elite of highly skilled professionals able to pay for their own welfare needs and to enjoy the benefits of high culture, and a non-elite of low-paid unskilled workers who will have to put up with cut-price state welfare and a lowest-common-denominator mass culture provided by the international corporations. In the absence of national solidarity political leaders will have neither the means nor the incentive to counteract this polarisation.

(Miller 1997 : 70)

The *scope* of the political community is set as that at which a welfare system which helps those left worst off by the operation of the market can function best. This, Miller argues, is coextensive with the scope of the nation. To set it at a sub-national level, at the level of the ethnic community, say, is undesirable, for if a state were just a combination of ethnic communities then it would be riven by conflicts about the distribution of resources in which dominant groups would win out and members of subordinate ones fail to obtain a fair share of welfare.[24] To the state there needs to correspond a nation which transcends ethnic and other differences.

Why, though, should we stop at the level of nationality? Why should we not see ourselves as members of a wider community still, with obligations outside our own country which would lead us to expect the same for disadvantaged nations beyond as we demand for groups within? Why, that is to say, should we be nationalists rather than internationalists so far as political organisation goes? Miller is clearly a nationalist, for all his uneasiness with the *word* (1995: 10), and his answer to the question is uncompromising. It is the Humean one, 'that the generosity of man is very limited, and that it seldom extends beyond their friends and family, or, at most, beyond their native country' (quoted Miller 1995: 58). These are *natural* sentiments which, unless they can be shown to be objectionable, must be acknowledged and built upon in devising social and political institutions. Given the limits of these sentiments the nation provides a basis for the widest scheme of welfare that is practicable.

The model for the operation of such sentiments is, of course, the family, thought of as that which confers on me my identity as an individual embedded willy-nilly in a network of ethical relationships.[25] And thus it is to the family that Miller turns to justify his ethical particularism – his view that I can have commitments to others in virtue of the particular people they are, my children, for example, not in virtue of general facts about them. It is because I identify with my family, he maintains, that I feel loyalty to those who are its members and acknowledge special obligations towards them – loyalty and obligations that do not stand in need of further justification. Given that 'nations...tend to think of themselves as extended families' (Miller 1995: 121), then his supposition that national membership generates the same sort of loyalties and special obligations may be explained.

It is precisely the loyalties and obligations of national membership that are needed to justify the welfare state. For this expresses the concern that members have for their compatriots, a concern without which a welfare system would not commend itself to citizens, so that 'we would expect states that lacked a communitarian background such as nationality provides to be little more than minimal states' (Miller 1995: 72). Here Miller draws a very different conclusion from the analogy between family and nation than does the New Right, and he does so precisely because he sees the communal character of the family as valuable, and as therefore replicated in a worthwhile way at the level of the state.

Yet Miller's conception of the family is in other respects at variance with the communal one sketched above, and it is perhaps in part his departures from it which vitiate his view of nationhood. To start with, Miller does not justify the existence of certain social relationships like the family by reference to the value of the co-operation they bring to a situation which is given. Rather he takes such relationships themselves as given, and as naturally producing the co-operation which we value. Thus he explicitly rejects what he calls the 'lifeboat model' of the national community, in which I am simply thrown together with others and can only make the best of the situation by participating in a collective response, on the grounds that the mutual obligations of members arise, not 'from the present fact of their co-operation', but from their 'historic identity' which stems from relationships into which they are born and raised (Miller 1995: 41–2). This has conservative consequences; for since co-operation springs from national identity, not vice versa, immigration can cause problems unless 'the immigrants come to share in a common national identity' (1995: 76) – a process Miller likens to marrying into a family and acquiring its culture (1997: 78).

A conservative conception of the family and the nation results from regarding the relationships involved as simply given, along with one's identity, and, furthermore, as structured by a system of *obligations* – the acceptability of which apparently derives from the sentiments that motivate them being, along Humean principles, natural ones. This again is a departure from the communal family model sketched earlier, in which commitments are freely entered into through an ethical appreciation of one's situation, not somehow forced on one by nature. Yet this difference raises a crucial question as to whether the sentiments within the family *can*, as Miller requires, be generalised to the nation. For within the family, as in the local community, it is, as I suggested, one's commitments to *particular* people that justify special treatment of them. But, as Benedict Anderson has famously observed (1991), the nation is not a face to face community in which I relate to others as particular individuals, but an 'imagined' one in which I relate to them on the basis of some supposed affinity. Yet, as I indicated in discussing the New Right's naturalistic conception of the nation, there is no good reason to postulate genuinely *natural* sentiments towards compatriots; and if they are merely sentiments we find ourselves entertaining should we not ask whether the supposed affinity which evokes them does actually justify the relationship? An over-conservative and over-naturalistic view of the family leads Miller, as it leads the New Right, to an insufficiently critical nationalism. Similarly, I suggest, the nationalism of New Labour shows that it has not sufficiently broken free from the assumptions of the New Right to embrace the consequences of a socialist communitarianism.

Acknowledgement

I should like to thank Kathleen Lennon and other members of the Hull Centre for Gender Studies for valuable suggestions on the original version, and the editors for indispensable advice on a penultimate draft.

Notes

1 For an appreciation of the importance of nationhood to the New Right I am greatly indebted to Bhikhu Parekh (1994).
2 For a discussion of the accommodation between family values and the minimal state under the New Right see Lorraine Fox Harding, this volume.
3 I take the consent theory to be what a liberal theory of legitimation consists in (see Beran 1987). This does not imply that a state otherwise legitimated cannot be a liberal state in the sense of maximising and protecting human freedoms other than the freedom of association expressed in consent.
4 Which I distinguish from the New Right as a form of liberalism.
5 This aspect of New Right thinking may be regarded as part of its Conservative organicism. But whereas earlier Conservatives treat the organic whole they take society to be in an analogical way, or, at most, under the influence of idealism in a spiritualised way, the New Right treats it as literally and materialistically as possible. This is why the New Right gravitates towards biological formulations. For an interesting example of the tension between old and new see Scruton (1990), especially 304–8.
6 The notion of what is a *natural* attraction is also at work here, oscillating between supposed statistical norms and normative judgements upon exceptions to them. The former gives rise to the idea of the range of our relationships with others (e.g. whom we are attracted to) being inexplicable and *therefore* natural; the latter to that of possible pathologies requiring special explanations (e.g. of excessive sexual drive). The result is that the nation is seen as the normal field of love relationships, i.e. of those proper to the formation of families.
7 See such works influential upon the New Right as Ardrey (1967) and van den Berghe (1981).
8 For an influential economic account of why this is so see Becker (1981). The classic, if idiosyncratic, British treatment is Mount (1982). For criticism of this view, which derives from Westermarck, see Coward (1983). For a general survey see Abbott and Wallace (1992).
9 See, for example, the papers by Shanley and Krause in Elshtain (1982).
10 Hobbes, 1651. The quotations are drawn from Chapters 13 and 20.
11 Even though the operation of the free market so justified in fact threatens such ways of life, in particular, family life.
12 The title of Lasch (1977), not itself New Right in its intent.

13 So Hume, always an inspiration to the New Right, observes: 'We blame a father for neglecting his child. Why? Because it shows a want of natural affection, which is the duty of every parent' (Hume 1740: 3.2.1). It is for this reason that 'clean break' settlements can be set aside by the Child Support Agency, since natural duties cannot be forsworn.

14 This idea is expressed by Hegel (see Blustein 1982: 90–6).

15 For an interesting elucidation of this paradox, see Poole (1991: 95–105).

16 On the notion of a social construction see Frazer and Lacey (1993: 107 ff).

17 The New Right, like Conservatives generally, would reply that 'ought' implies 'can', and that we cannot escape the constraints of nature. No doubt. But if that is the case my *believing* it is so is irrelevant, while the effect of New Right thinking on what I believe I should do is achieved by securing a belief as to what I can. Since this is so, no test has been provided as to what people *can* do from what they are, under the influence of the New Right and related ideologies, prepared to do.

18 Kathleen Lennon has pointed out to me that it seems difficult to account for this presumption without falling back into the liberal contractual account, which, of course, is not my intention. Rather what is intended is an account of the relationship as one that people will typically *find* themselves in, accepting its constraints. This does not imply that the mother's claim to support may not be withheld, when the presumption of such a relationship is cancelled.

19 I leave for consideration elsewhere the thorny question of the role of sexual relations between parenting adults in the family, making no assumption here as to its nature or existence.

20 This is a delicate notion: its paradigm is the arrival of a child in need of care. When a child is adopted, say, what is chosen is to be in such a situation, which may turn out quite differently than anticipated or intended.

21 The demands of the particular person are indefinitely extended within it: I cannot reply to them, 'But that is not the job of a father'.

22 Indeed, that they can and should be realised through *state* sponsored activities is what distinguishes the socialist view of community from that of the New Right.

23 Miller adds the requirement of a common culture, but this seems necessary only to secure mutual recognition, not to add to the value stemming from reciprocity and co-operation (see Miller 1988a: 654).

24 Miller sees the effects of this kind of politics in the low level of welfare provided in the USA (1988b: 246) and uses it as an argument against the 'radical multiculturalism' of Iris Marion Young (Miller 1995: 130–40).

25 Although Miller comments with apparent regret that 'the family seems, as our century advances, to be taking on more and more the characteristics of a voluntary institution' (1988a: 653).

Bibliography

Abbott, P. and Wallace, C. (1992) *The Family and the New Right*, London: Pluto.

Anderson, B. (1991) *Imagined Communities*, London: Verso.

Ardrey, R. (1967) *The Territorial Imperative*, London: Collins.

Becker, G. S. (1981) *A Treatise on the Family*, Cambridge, Mass.: Harvard University Press.

Beran, H. (1987) *The Consent Theory of Political Obligation*, London: Croom Helm.

Blustein, J. (1982) *Parents and Children*, Oxford: Oxford University Press.

Coward, R. (1983) *Patriarchal Precedents: Sexuality and Social Relations*, London: Routledge.

Elshtain, J. B. (ed.) (1982) *The Family in Political Thought*, Brighton: Harvester.

Frazer, E. and N. Lacey (1993) *The Politics of Community*, New York: Harvester.

Fukuyama, F. (1992) *The End of History and the Last Man*, Harmondsworth: Penguin.

Hobbes, T. (1651) *Leviathan* (many editions).

Hume, D. (1740) *Treatise of Human Nature* (many editions).

Lasch, C. (1977) *Haven in a Heartless World*, New York: Basic.

Miller, D. (1988a) 'The ethical significance of nationality', *Ethics 98*: 647–62.

—— (1988b) 'Socialism and toleration' in S. Mendus (ed.) *Justifying Toleration*, Cambridge: Cambridge University Press.

—— (1995) *On Nationality*, Oxford: Oxford University Press.

—— (1997) 'Nationality: Some Replies', *Journal of Applied Philosophy*, 14: 69–82.

Mitchell, G. D. (ed.) (1968) *A Dictionary of Sociology*, London: Routledge.

Mount, F. (1982) *The Subversive Family*, London: Cape.

Parekh, B. (1994) 'National identity and the ontological regeneration of Britain' in P. Gilbert and P. Gregory (eds) *Nations, Culture and Markets*, Aldershot: Avebury.

—— (1995) 'Ethnocentricity of the nationalist discourse', *Nations and Nationalism*, 1: 25–52.

Poole, R. (1991) *Morality and Modernity*, London: Routledge.

Scruton, R. (1990) 'In defence of the nation' in *The Philosopher on Dover Beach*, Manchester: Carcanet.

van den Berghe, P. L. (1981) *The Ethnic Phenomenon*, New York: Elsevier.

Walzer, M. (1983) *Spheres of Justice*, New York: Basic.

Zimmern, A. (1939) (ed.) *Modern Political Doctrines*, Oxford: Oxford University.

8 Unpicking political communitarianism

A critique of 'the communitarian family'

Elizabeth Frazer

Introduction

This chapter explores the connection between 'family' and 'community' in recent politics and policy. In speech and journalism the juxtaposition of 'family' and 'community' has an evident *rhetorical* effect. Avowedly 'communitarian' discourse makes a deeper *conceptual* connection between the two – the meanings of 'family' and 'community' are mutually constitutive. And for communitarians there is an *empirical sociological* connection between family and community. This putative empirical connection is under-theorised and under-substantiated – partly because political discourse generally is weak on sociology, and partly because of flaws in the conceptualisations of 'family' and 'community' the communitarians begin with. But, the state of the discourse being as it is, showing the conceptualisations to be flawed and the sociological theses to be mistaken, does not undermine the rhetorical and political power of the link between 'family' and 'community'. In this chapter I trace the structure of this circle.

These rhetorical effects, and the putative conceptual connection between family and community are, in part, mystificatory. The two concepts are in many contexts *code* for each other, and their constant reference to each other obscures how social institutions and social phenomena are related. For instance, the social policy 'community care' is actually 'family care': *community* care sets up a relationship between *state* and *family* which are intended to provide complementary sources of assistance (Finch 1989: 126). (Finch also points out that the old Poor Law was nothing like so mystificatory, as it was quite explicit about who was expected to do what for whom.) We shall see that in communitarian thought family is defined *as* community. It is this aspect of the discourse, where a term actually is code for another, that generates suspicions that talk of family and community are actually code for talk about gender – talk about the respective roles of women and men.

The close connection between family and community is, of course, imputed in speech from the right, the left and the centre left, conservative, liberal and social democratic. The development of policies such as 'community care' and 'community policing' command widespread assent among electorates and practitioners alike, although inevitably there are sceptical worries from sections of the public and professionals that there will not be adequate resources to realise these policies. Insofar as communitarianism is politically significant it is because it appeals to a potential, diverse, coalition. Unless individuals and groups are willing to go in for allegiance across difference, change cannot occur politically. But coalitions are frequently fragile, and invariably susceptible to a variety of destabilising forces. And importantly, critics are quick to denounce coalitions as unholy alliances, putting coalition members on the ideological defensive. This has certainly been the case with communitarians: liberals accuse them of conservatism; socialists accuse them of liberalism; and feminists accuse communitarians of patriarchalism.

A critical examination of communitarian political discourse turns our attention to the relationship between political speech and political theory. On the one hand, political speech often garbles political theory. On the other, political theory itself is inevitably a development of ideas, values, practices and projects that are immanent in practical political and social speech and practice. One point of political theory in its academic style is to explore the structure of political ideas, values, beliefs, and objectives, to see whether they are consistent, and to ask whether they could be realised in practice. (Of course, ideas, beliefs, etc. don't have to be strictly consistent to be viable, in the medium term at least.) Political theory is also prescriptive, and when issues are propelled onto the political agenda (as family and community have been recently) academics often act as entrepreneurs or parties to the debate and no clear distinction can be drawn between academic output and political intervention.

Thus, communitarianism consists of a continuum of output from the very abstract to the highly practical. For the purposes of this essay I have divided communitarian texts into two groups. The first I label *philosophical communitarian* – the major preoccupation of these texts are abstract questions of epistemology, metaphysics, the philosophy of mind, science and language, of ethics and methodology (MacIntyre 1981; Sandel 1982; Walzer 1983; Taylor 1985a, 1985b). This very abstraction means that, from the point of view of the philosophical communitarian, there can be no straightforward inference to what in this paper I call *political communitarianism* – the attempt to realise communitarian principles in political platforms (Etzioni 1993b; Mandelson and Liddle 1996; Tam 1995).

The presentation here inevitably simplifies communitarianism. Actually, the dominant voices of political communitarianism are challenged by critics with a more socialist starting point. And traditional British conservative thought features the ideal of community and other communitarian themes (Scruton 1991). So the communitarian coalition is decidedly not univocal. Further, communitarianism is party political indeterminate. For instance, 'community activism' as a distinctive political project and style is consistent with all kinds of party and theoretical political allegiances from Marxism, anarchism, liberalism, to green politics. Communitarianism can generate a critique of corporate capitalism as easily as a critique of broken down families (Bookchin 1995). It can generate an ideal of a fluid society, or an ideal of a settled society.

Certainly communitarianism shifts the focus in political analysis and social science from the state on the one hand, and the autonomous individual on the other, to the mediating institutions – like family, school, firm, neighbourhood – and overlapping networks of dependence, inter-dependence and independence in which individuals (adults and children) are located; and how these located individuals have unequal endowments and differing access to resources and power. However, far from developing this kind of understanding, what is heard from communitarians in popular political discourse is an insistent emphasis on 'the family' as *the* relevant and significant institution. Communitarians like Amitai Etzioni protest that this is a partial presentation of their complex view of social institutions. Perhaps it is not his fault that the British (left of centre) think tank Demos publishes *just* the chapter on the family from his book, rather than the chapter on communitarian institutions, or the public interest, or rights and responsibilities (Etzioni 1993b). Nevertheless, in their own textual practice the political communitarians put the family first – it is discussed in earlier rather than later chapters. And they explicitly put it first theoretically, as we shall see. Moreover, although other institutions like schools are discussed, the use of the term 'community' (as we shall also see) tends to obscure rather than illuminate their structure.

Communitarianism: philosophical and political

Philosophical communitarianism is best thought of as a coalescence of a number of established strands in the Western philosophical tradition (Frazer and Lacey 1993: 101–7). Communitarians' conceptions of social reality and knowledge are influenced by the phenomenological, hermeneutic or pragmatic traditions, rather than empiricism or rationalism. Strands from republican political philosophy, and from socialism, are discernible. In a brief account like this I can only note this complex genealogy, and try to avoid presenting communitarianism as a monolithic whole.

The three main tenets of philosophical communitarianism are strands of its key theme: anti-individualism. First, there is an ontological or *metaphysical thesis*: that it is not the case that all there is in the world are individuals. Communitarians like many other social philosophers, depending upon their philosophical commitments to one or other of the traditions mentioned above, are likely to argue for the existence and significance of relations, meanings, social institutions, collectives, and so forth. Second, there is an *ethical thesis*. Communitarians argue that what we might call the locus of value (the entity on which value is centred, or from which it proceeds) is not the individual as such, but rather the social individual, or the community. Separately, communitarians argue prescriptively for a range of values that have tended to be neglected in individualist philosophies: reciprocity, solidarity, trust, tradition and so on. Third, there is a *methodological thesis*: communitarians are inclined to subscribe to the view that the way to do ethics, and social science, is not to try to deduce and apply universally valid fundamental principles (or to discover invariant laws), but to interpret and refine values that are immanent in the ways of life of really living groups – societies, communities. This way, a social scientific understanding of how people live and the outcomes of their actions will reflect the understandings and decision making processes of the actors themselves. And in ethics, values and principles are likely to be accepted and owned by the social actors themselves. The addition of a critical focus in ethics and social science can ensure that such moral arguments and social scientific descriptions do not just confirm people in complacent (and perhaps harmful) ways of living (Walzer 1987; Taylor 1985b).

The weight given to these various strands, and the inferences for practical ethics, politics and social life drawn from them, vary from philosopher to philosopher. But we can summarise some of the inferences in the literature. First, these rather abstract theses can generate a rejection of the idea (the powerful idea in modern societies, and one that has been promoted in a number of important ways – notably in the development of modern legal systems, and welfare states) that the individual stands or should stand in a direct, unmediated relationship with the state and society as a whole. Second, they generate a rejection of the market as the key social institution, the particularly right or even natural pattern of human relationships and interaction. In place of the individual who has defensive rights against society, against social interference and pressure, who can make claims against the state in return for compliance with the laws, and who engages with other individuals in instru-mentally self-interested exchanges of value, communitarian philosophers focus on a variety of mediate institutions, and the variety of human relationships and interactions that both constitute and are constituted by those institutions. The communitarian literature is full of references to corporations, voluntary organisations, religious institutions such as temple, synagogue and church, neighbourhoods and localities, social networks of friendship, acquaintanceship and exchange, occupational groups, schools and families. In these institutions individuals enter into relationships that are governed by a variety of shared norms and practices; when we consider this range of social institutions in total it seems clear that instrumental self-interest cannot be said to be the dominant motivation of interaction (although, of course, it may have its place). Even markets, it is observed, are founded on trust, shared meanings and conformity to norms – which are the threshold that enables instrumental self-interest then to operate without complete social breakdown.

It is notable that the philosophical communitarians have not rushed to sign up to political communitarian platforms. Rather they have tended to reassert their commitment to liberal values and principles and to distance themselves from some other inferences that have been drawn from philosophical communitarianism – notably the valorisation of communal tradition, and the identification of groups such as ethnic formations, nations and kinship as surpassing the value of the individual's autonomy (Taylor 1989; Walzer 1990:

22; Rorty 1989). There can be no clear inference from communitarianism to a political programme. But we find themes that are recognisable from philosophical communitarianism in the writings of the political communitarians.

For instance, they promote the *social thesis* that insists that individuals are fundamentally connected to each other, that our relations are constitutive of our social identities and personalities, that the quality of our lives, judgements, and understandings of the world are causally connected to the institutions and networks within which we live, and that communities are valuable in themselves (Etzioni 1993a: 116–22). Second, communitarians mention the importance of *interpretivism* in ethics. The idea is that ethical principles or values are only powerful if they are in some sense already part and parcel of ordinary people's ideas in and about their daily lives. Communitarians appeal to people's tacit understandings that community really does matter, that our unchosen obligations to others are as important as our voluntaristic choices and freely entered into contracts. Ethical argument is then a combination of interpretation of the values and understandings that are implicit or explicit in ways of life, the refinement and development of certain aspects of these, together with a prescriptive analysis of what life could be like under ideal moral conditions (Etzioni 1993a: 101, 258–9).

But philosophical communitarianism is not the most important source for contemporary political communitarianism. Other important sources are *left Jewish thought* (the journal *Tikkun* in the US is significant), and *Christian socialism*, whose significance in British and other European polities, and in socialist thought more generally, tends to be under-estimated by contemporary political theorists. (Of course, ideas congenial to communitarianism are also found in other religious traditions.) The centrality of ideas of community in Christian socialism, and the connection between these and the socially informed critique of theology, and theological critique of economy and polity, are important – especially in light of Tony Blair's avowal that his 'new tough conception of community...where rights and responsibilities go hand in hand' (Mandelson and Liddle 1996: 3) is very closely linked to his religious commitment. A separate, third, source for political communitarianism is the *ethical socialist tradition* more generally. The central values of solidarity, co-operation and reciprocity have underpinned many socialist projects. More recently, socialist political theorists have argued that the egalitarianism that is prescribed in socialist, social democratic and left liberal thought must presuppose a particular quality of relationships between persons – a sense of common membership of some collective, a sense that our relations with other members are relations of reciprocity, fraternity, concern about the needs of others. Frequently, the term community is used to characterise such relationships, or clusters of such relationships (Miller 1989a: 57–60; Cohen 1994).

And, fourth, there are distinct sources of communitarianism which are anti-socialist. The *conservative* criticisms of liberal society, economy and polity that were generated at liberalism's inception frequently invoked the value of settled relationships and ways of life, in the face of liberalism's emphasis on individual freedom and voluntarism (Scruton 1991: 8–11). In response to the libertarian themes associated with the New Right the communitarian strand of conservatism has become, if anything, more loudly insistent in the last twenty years.

The content of political communitarianism can be summarised as three key themes. First is an approach to *markets* that emphasises the social conditions for successful and efficient market exchange and distribution; that is disbelieving of the power of states and bureaucracies to distribute goods successfully; and which asks that serious consideration should be given to placing distributive power elsewhere – in community networks and associations (Etzioni 1993b: 146; Mandelson and Liddle 1996: 28; Miller 1989a: 128ff). The second, and perhaps the central theme in communitarianism is the *poverty of rights* culture, and the insistence that rights must be correlated with duties, obligations and responsibilities. It is important to be aware of the very different rhetorical ring this kind of attack on rights has in the individualistic rights-based polity and legal system of the United States by contrast with less individualistic Europe. The third prominent theme is the need for institutions to grow out of, and remain rooted in, the *local community* (Mandelson and Liddle 1996: 34; Etzioni 1993a: 226ff). For Tony Blair, the relationship of party branches to their locality is of first importance – here communitarian ideas are exploited in the context of a rather specific intra-party dispute. But the rejection of state bureaucracy as the proper distributor of certain goods is also relevant here. This theme obviously meshes with the concerns of community workers and community activists who have long worked in practical ways to enable local people to 'own' and have the opportunity for meaningful participation in organisations, agencies and institutions that affect local life.

Community and family

A reader who is interested in analysis of the concept 'community' will be struck by its absence – absence of analysis, rather than absence of the concept itself – in the philosophical communitarian texts. By asking for analysis like this I do not intend to suggest that such complex abstract concepts have a definite reference or a determinate content – they are of course complex ranges of overlapping usages with a variety of reference and semantic connotation. But this does not usually prevent philosophers from exploring this complexity. Philosophical analyses of equality, liberty, authority, exploitation, for instance, run into millions of words – it is next to impossible for any socialist to ignore the complexity of the concept of equality. By contrast, community has rarely been explicitly analysed (see Plant 1978; Stacey 1969). The philosophical communitarians themselves invoke, rather than analyse, its meaning. The term is used somewhat in passing, and the reader has to work rather hard to interpret the concept's content and exact place in the philosophy.

Often it is deployed as a kind of umbrella term for all the social institutions and groupings that communitarians refer to – family, school, neighbourhood, firm, voluntary organisation and the like are all *instances of* community (e.g.

MacIntyre 1981: 221). Elsewhere it seems to be used in the very different sense of that which is constituted by all these institutions aggregated together and in relation to one another. Individuals in all these complex social groupings, all these various social institutions in relations with each other, add up to or are the *building blocks of* community (e.g. Selznick 1987: 449). Both of these usages suggest that community is a *kind of social formation* or an *entity.* Communitarians also seem to mean by community a particular *kind of social relation* between persons. Sometimes this relation is defined negatively: where people are not relating to each other just on the basis of their own instrumental interests, there we have the relation of community. Sometimes though we find a more positive definition: for instance where we relate to each other on the basis that we give each other service where it is needed, and that we understand that service to be intrinsically valuable. Or where we relate to each other on the basis of solidarity, altruism, or reciprocity, rather than self-interest. Or where we truly care about the other. Or where we share convictions about how our society should be organised. These have all been offered as characterisations of the relation of community (Cohen 1994; MacIntyre 1981: 236; Sandel 1982: 86–7; Dworkin 1986: 195–216).

In socialist non-conformism, in Christian socialism and, of course, in some strands of Jewish religious and social tradition, we find the conceptualisation of *community as voluntary settlement.* The point here for political theory is that people might remake the manner of their living and relating, in new settlements of collective life, where their environment is under the collective control of the members, where there can be an attempt to realise the communitarian and collective presumptions of religious life. Some thinkers though have not argued that this kind of community is the ideal model of social life for all – rather they have emphasised the role of the monastic, the special contribution to social life that can be made by individuals living in sacramental communities (Leech 1981). The second conceptualisation is *community as the site for the realisation of communion.* Communion and sacramental life more generally, in turn, give us a glimpse and a symbolic realisation of a generalisable ideal of social relations centred on friendship, fellowship and the like (MacMurray 1961).

These religious conceptions of community are not vague. However, they pose obvious difficulties as a practical political goal. The philosophical and political communitarians hesitate to deploy such a strong conception of community – and end up either with such weak conceptions that they might as well drop the vocabulary of community altogether (were it not for its rhetorical effect!) or with an ambivalent and contradictory conception. For instance, political communitarians are very ambivalent about *community as locality.* On the one hand there are numerous references to neighbourhoods, local communities and the like. On the other it seems important to disavow localism for fear of being accused of nostalgia (Etzioni 1993a: 30–2). So Etzioni both wants to conceive of community as transcending place – he emphasises the networks and associations made possible by modern and post-modern technology, voluntary organisations, and the non-geographical communities of ethnic groups and political and social movements (Etzioni 1993a: 116–18), and yet wants to insist on the importance of place: he conceptualises 'nested communities': families, neighbourhoods, village or town, nation, the international community of states (Etzioni 1993a: 32). Similarly, sometimes the political communitarians talk rather sensibly of community as a particular *set of relations* – the kind, specifically, that can support socially useful and desirable exchanges and distributions of goods, and resources like care for the ill and needy, emotional and social support, and so forth. And then they slip into a much less sensible way of talking – referring to the *community as a subject*. Etzioni stresses at length 'the moral voice of the community', the community as a moral subject (Etzioni 1993a: 54). We find the same idea in Blair's thought where we meet the view that the community, for instance, has the right to be safe from crime, as well as a responsibility to prevent it; or the view that parents' responsibility in matters of child care is to the community (Mandelson and Liddle 1996: 20).

When we turn to the concept 'family' we find a similarly mixed and muddled picture. The philosophical communitarians mention the *family as an instance of community* (MacIntyre 1981: 221). In the course of their discussions of what is wrong, or what is inadequate, about individualism, philosophers mention families as places of special and particular relationships – that is, family relations stand as a counter-example and alternative to the voluntary, rights-based, market exchanges and contracts that are privileged in liberal theory. The family is an exemplar of unchosen relations and obligations (Taylor 1985: 203), and is invoked as an inspiration or *model for community* – in the family there is a good greater than abstract justice, there are relations that are not based on self-interest (Sandel 1982: 33). In this vein the family is more than just an instance of community:

> Family is the original human community and the basis as well as the origin of all subsequent communities. It is therefore the norm of all communities, so that any community is a brotherhood....The more a society approximates to the family pattern, the more it realises itself as a community, or, as Marx called it, a truly human society.
>
> (MacMurray 1961: 155)

On the other hand, some communitarians resist this move, seeing the family as an imperfect model for political community and family relations as insufficient for civic virtue (Taylor 1985: 204).

The two senses of *family as community* and *family as the basis of community* are straddled in the concept of '*the communitarian family*' which is elaborated by both the US and the UK political communitarians. The communitarian family is characterised as one where both partners are actively and deeply involved in their children's upbringing, and where all members are collectively active and participatory in the community. Parents' moral responsibility to bring their children up is a responsibility to the community. The communitarians argue explicitly that the two-parent (different sex) family is best, and a variety of social scientific sources are cited in support of a variety of reasons why this is allegedly so. This use of social science data has met with a good deal of criticism (Crawford 1996; Stacey 1994). It must be said that Etzioni's, in particular, breezy presentation of the 'facts' is replete with contradiction and also features some breathtaking ambiguity of scope. For instance: 'In a *wide variety* of human societies (from the *Zulus to the Inuit*, from ancient Greece and ancient China to modernity) there has *never* been a society that did not have two parent families' (Etzioni 1993b: 60; my emphasis). He also insists that the communitarian family is not the traditional family and underlines this by stating that as he reads the social science findings it would be preferable for children to have three parents rather than two (Etzioni 1993b: 62). This ambivalence about the 'traditional family' is very marked in the speeches of Tony Blair. In response to questions from a BBC Radio 4 interviewer about whether 'the family' he wishes to support includes house-holds of same-sex couples, single people with children, several single people sharing a house, and so forth, Blair replied, more than once, that 'we all know what we mean by the family'. Evidently he felt it impossible to say that such households and domestic groups were excluded from his category 'the family'; he equally refused to say that they are included (BBC World at One 14 October 1996; *Guardian* 15 October 1996: 1; *Independent* 15 October 1996: 9).

Communitarianism, family values and sociological analysis

I have presented the content of philosophical and political communitarianism at some length. This is because I wish it to be clear that communitarianism is a complex ideological and programmatic position, although inevitably in a piece of this length there is no space to explore all the variations and disagreements within it. I have also wanted to show that the concept community is vaguely defined. In addition, a particular, moralised, conception of the family is important, and in this case there is ambiguity too, especially on the part of political communitarians, about the exact contours of the concept. Most important for our purposes are the empirical theses about family and commu-nity that are central to political communitarianism: that the family is the basis of community; that 'strong families make strong communities' (Mandelson and Liddle 1996: 196) and that communities can both sustain individuals and families in need, and have a legitimate interest in the individual's and the family's behaviour.

In this section I wish to make three points about this theory of family and community:

1   there is an invalid inference in communitarianism from the social thesis – which emphasises the embeddedness of individuals in associations, net-works and institutions – to a primary focus on 'the family' and 'the com-

munity'. The emphasised categories of 'the family' and 'the community' effectively obscure any detailed analysis of how social institutions work and interact with one another, and how they interact with individuals' quality of life.

2   many feminist critics and commentators have expressed their suspicion that communitarianism means the reinstatement of the traditional roles and relations that are believed to have contributed to a less disorderly society in the past – and that central among these are traditional gender roles. Now some of the political communitarians, notably Etzioni, and Blair, vehemently deny that they intend that women should be reconfined to the kitchen, or that they mean 'traditional femininity and masculinity' when they speak of 'family' and 'community'. Now actually I see no real reason to disbelieve either Etzioni or Blair when they say this (although it would be unwise to think that all political communitarians are automatically as right minded). But:

3   communitarianism as a social theory lacks a critical theory of power, and is ill equipped to identify, let alone analyse, the social conflict that is a systematic feature of life inside families, and life inside other social groups and formations like neighbourhoods, networks and associations (life inside the so-called community); and even less the conflict between 'communities'. So although Blair and Etzioni protest that they are not anti-feminist, the categories they work with have the consequence that feminist and other conflict will look – to them – anomalous or downright perverse, if they recognise it at all.

So, first, the invalid inference. As we have seen communitarians insist upon the social nature of the individual, and in their value commitments are guided by the principle that social relationships and networks must be such that they can support the circulation and exchange of crucial social goods – welfare, social order, individual flourishing and the like. Communitarians are aware, and make reference in their philosophy and theory, to the wide range of social institutions and groups that are relevant: voluntary associations, culturally embedded organisations and networks, institutions like churches and schools, etc. On the face of it, then, communitarianism (especially when contrasted with its major rivals, liberalism and libertarian conservatism) has a pronounced theoretical strength: it is sensitive to the variety of social groups and formations in which individuals are embedded and through which they move, and to the complicated inter-relationships between these collectives. Communitarians refuse to accept – whether for the purposes of social scientific modelling, for ethical reasoning, or for the purposes of practical politics – that all human relationships are just like market relations. This, we might think, should enable them better to see just what specific human relationships are like. Thus communitarians should be able to ask sensibly under what kinds of domestic arrangements, and in what kinds of social institutions and relationships, adults and children best flourish.

Of course, sociology and psychology are nowhere near to a definitive answer to this, and nor could they be in a changing world – but there are plenty of hints that loose ties of acquaintanceship and friendship are as important for certain purposes as the ties of kinship; that voluntary organisations are important for their social outcomes as well as for the individuals who are members of them; that children benefit from trusting relationships with a wide range of adults; that learning takes place in a wide variety of settings; and so on. We also know that many individuals lack the sociable ties that form a valuable buffer against loneliness; that voluntary organisations can be demobilised and disabled by lack of co-ordination and resources, or by powerful interests which do not stand to gain by their success; that adults cannot just automatically be trusted to care for children; that individuals can be silenced and crushed and stopped from learning.

Neither the theoretical framework of the social thesis, nor the data, licence the political communitarian emphasis on 'the family' and 'the community' – indeed, these undifferentiated categories skew communitarian approaches to evidence, and are barriers to analysis.

Second, the question of gender and sex roles. Are women the destroyers of community in recent times? Etzioni proposes a historical thesis: that first of all with the industrial revolution men left the community and family and went into waged work for long periods of each day. Second, with the post-war entry of married women into the labour market they too left the community and family. The identification of women with the local and with the community itself has a history. For instance, in the UK there were efforts to reinforce this identification during the debates about women's suffrage – with anti-suffragists arguing that local government was women's special sphere (Harrison 1978: 133–6; Phillips 1996). This identification of women and the local, therefore, poses a problem of justice and of politics. The identification can be vigorously rebutted by arguments that responsibility for our localities, where we live, where we work, and where we spend our time, should lie with everyone (Frazer 1996). This is not to refuse to recognise that relations in and with community are not frequently gendered in present society. For instance, Beatrix Campbell writes of women who have to live in run-down and disadvantaged localities, and who do try to build community. Far from being the destroyers of community, these women are its furious defenders in the face of men's hindrance (Campbell 1993: 144, 230).

Campbell's work, and that of many other sociologists, vividly depicts the conflict in community: a conflict which is often gendered, is frequently between generations, frequently over ethnic or racial identities. It is clear that the *descriptive connotations* of community as close knit, solid, characterised by shared values and meanings, can effectively conceal such conflicts, tensions and fractures. The concealment of these tensions and fractures by discourses of community is especially serious where, for instance, all people in a locality are dismissed as criminal because the conflicts and inequalities within the population are invisible to 'outsiders' like police, local councillors and officials

(Campbell 1993: 153, 170–8). Similarly, the *normatively positive connotations* of community conceal the consistency between community building and maintenance, and the production and circulation of social *bads*. 'Community' can be the site of subcultures of criminality, racism, sexism and so forth (Crawford 1996). Social relations in a locality can be such that bads like threats and reprisals can circulate efficiently. This circulation of bads (just like the patterns of circulation of goods) is constitutive of and part of a structure of inequality and antagonism, across fissures of generation, sex, race, ethnicity, etc.

Similarly, the conceptualisation of family as community is liable to obscure patterns and relations of conflict within families. Individuals within households and families are connected in complex ways: by the norms and motivations of kinship; by specific and variable affective relations (they like each other, or not); they are engaged in particular kinds of economic exchanges; they share or do not share political identification and antagonisms. As individuals they are socially mobile or immobile, and this will vary according to sex, age, occupation, domestic role, etc. Hence there is no preventing class, cultural, political, and economic antagonisms entering into family relations. This degree of complexity leads to great variation in the welfare of individuals. And, of course, social policy affects and can restructure these relationships: if parents are defined as responsible for children's behaviour, for example, this shifts power within the family and household towards the children (Jones and Wallace 1992: 152).

Such complexity means that questions about power, authority and governance will arise. Who gets what? Who does or gives what to whom? Who tells who what to do? Here are questions of justice. Both philosophical communitarians and philosophers from other traditions such as liberalism and socialism have tended to consider that the 'private' realm of the family and household is not and should not be governed by justice as such. Communitarians in particular are critical of the cultural dominance of rights discourse, and the social fragmentation that results when individual rights' claims over-ride co-operative effort, concern for others, and concern for the social whole. As we have seen, they gesture to 'the family' to show us another way of living: one where we are as concerned for others as for ourselves, where our own happiness and welfare is dependent upon the happiness and welfare of others, where the unit, not the individual, is the source and locus of value. Within the family, it is argued, individual rights and fair decision procedures are seldom appealed to, not because injustice is rampant, but because their appeal is pre-empted by a spirit of generosity in which I am rarely inclined to claim my fair share (Sandel 1982: 30–1, 33–4, 169).

This question of justice and the family is considerable, and there is no space here for an examination of all the problems and issues (Okin 1989; Bubeck 1995; Baier 1994). The one point I wish to make is that, when set beside research data, this picture seems to overlook the good deal of reasoning about justice that does go on in kin and household relations. We must not overlook the possibility that the spirit of generosity and disinclination to claim one's fair share may be unequally distributed, with women family and household members deploying it in greater quantities than men do. That the norm of family exchanges is 'sharing without reckoning' as Janet Finch puts it, is consistent with some members being ripped off (Finch 1989: 69). This norm may be in conflict with people's sense of justice, fairness and grievance.

It is indeed evident that where negotiations about responsibility and obligation are conducted between the sexes, male protagonists tend not to notice that their sisters are not claiming their fair share – precisely because assumptions about sexual difference intervene. By contrast, in intra-family exchanges between women there often is overt concern about justice – for instance, money payments from daughters to mothers in respect of child care, in order that the daughter does not exploit her mother (Finch 1989: 60). We cannot then assume that there are no conflicts of interest, or questions of justice and fairness arising within these conflicts between family and household members. Sociological evidence emphasises men's reluctance to co-operate in domestic regimes, and the strain that this engenders. Sometimes this strain leads to family or household breakdown. Often it leads to the construction and maintenance of myths that the domestic division of labour is more egalitarian than it actually is (Hochschild 1990). This enables women's conscious sense of injustice and resulting overt discontent to be minimised.

These awkward observations about the fractures and tensions within so-called communities and within families might be countered by an unabashed communitarian. 'I acknowledge all that', he or she might say, 'but you are making the mistake of muddling up our argument about how relations within the family and the community *ought* to be, and our attempts to think about how to get from the unhappy situation we are now in to a happier state of affairs in which the community and the family are put to rights, with a descriptive argument about how relations within the family and the community *are now*'. The difficulty with this view is that the communitarian is mistaken if s/he thinks that social conflicts and complications, across the fissures of gender, generation, class, and ethnicity, can be eliminated. It is crucial to acknowledge that neither shared values, solidarity, reciprocity, or the relation or entity of community itself can unambiguously be classified as good things in the abstract. Shared values among some group might result in violence to another. For this reason, it is a mistake to think that the concepts 'the community' and 'the family' will ever be adequate to capture the complexity of social institutions and formations – even as ideals. So the visionary politician who fixes on the concepts community and family will fail to realise his/her vision; the visionary politician needs to think about the shape of various and complex social institutions and networks – localities, associations, institutions – and to consider how goods can be distributed between these in an acceptable way.

The political communitarian might, at this point, rejoin that talk of 'the community' and 'the family' is just shorthand for the range of localities, associations, institutions, networks and all the rest in which the individual, and households, are embedded. The point of emphasising family and community is to counter the 'individuals and families' philosophy of the New Right, to insist that there is a social whole to be considered, a wider context that individuals must take into account when making decisions. To quibble about the sociological details is to miss the point. But this is to acknowledge that the point of communitarian discourses is mainly rhetorical. The beauty of using these categories, from the point of view of practical politics, is precisely their rhetorical power, their status as place-markers for whatever cherished ideals the particular listener wishes to project into them. They meet the politician's need to speak and appeal to all sides of the polity. Community activists can envision a society with properly funded community organisations; the socially conservative can envision a society with a reinstatement of proper patriarchal power.

For my part, I think that to quibble about the details is not, at all, to miss the point. Social policies that are built on the concepts 'the family' and 'the community' are likely to be ineffectual, or disastrous. We have seen that with right-wing governments' 'community care' and so on. Their centre and left challengers should recognise the need for more concreteness, and less rhetoric, in the policy making process.

Bibliography

Baier, Annette (1994) *Moral Prejudices: Essays on Ethics*, Cambridge Mass.: Harvard University Press.

Bookchin, M. (1995) *From Urbanisation to Cities: towards a new politics of citizenship*, London: Cassell.

Bubeck, Diemut (1995) *Care, Gender, and Justice*, Oxford: Clarendon Press.

Campbell, Beatrix (1993) *Goliath: Britain's Dangerous Places*, London: Methuen.

Cohen, G. A. (1994) 'Back to socialist basics', *New Left Review* 207: 3–16.

Crawford, Adam (1996) 'Review article: the spirit of community', *Journal of Law and Society* 23: 247–61.

Dworkin, Ronald (1986) *Law's Empire*, London: Fontana.

Etzioni, Amitai (1993a) *The Spirit of Community: Rights, Responsibilities and the Communitarian Agenda*, New York: Crown Publishers Inc.

—— (1993b) *Parenting Deficit*, London: Demos.

Finch, Janet (1989) *Family Obligations and Social Change*, Cambridge: Polity Press.

Frazer, Elizabeth and Lacey, Nicola (1993) *The Politics of Community: a Feminist Critique of the Liberal Communitarian Debate*, Hemel Hempstead: Harvester Wheatsheaf.

Frazer, Elizabeth (1996) 'The value of locality' in Desmond King and Gerry Stoker (eds) *Rethinking Local Democracy*, Basingstoke: Macmillan.

Harrison, Brian (1978) *Separate Spheres: the Opposition to Women's Suffrage in Britain*, London: Croom Helm.

Hochschild, Arlie (1990) *The Second Shift: Working Parents and the Revolution at Home*, London: Piatkus.

Jones, Gill and Wallace, Claire (1992) *Youth Family and Citizenship*, Bristol: Open University Press.

Leech, Kenneth (1981) *The Social God*, London: Sheldon Press.

MacIntyre, Alasdair (1981) *After Virtue*, London: Duckworth.

MacMurray, John (1961) *Persons in Relation*, London: Faber & Faber.

Mandelson, Peter and Liddle, Roger (1996) *The Blair Revolution: Can New Labour Deliver?*, London: Faber & Faber.

Miller, David (1989a) *Market State and Community: Theoretical Foundations of Market Socialism*, Cambridge: Clarendon Press.

—— (1989b) 'In what sense must socialism be communitarian?', *Social Philosophy and Policy* 6: 51.

Okin, Susan Moller (1989) *Justice, Gender and the Family*, New York: Basic Books.

Phillips, Anne (1996) 'Feminism and the Attractions of the Local' in D. King and G. Stoker (eds) *Rethinking Local Democracy*, Basingstoke: Macmillan.

Plant, Raymond (1978) 'Community: concept, conception and ideology' *Politics and Society* 8: 49–78.

Rorty, Richard (1989) *Contingency, Irony and Solidarity*, Cambridge: Cambridge University Press.

Sandel, Michael (1982) *Liberalism and the Limits of Justice*, Cambridge: Cambridge University Press.

Scruton, Roger (ed.) (1991) *Conservative Texts: an Anthology*, Basingstoke: Macmillan.

Selznick, Philip (1987) 'The idea of a communitarian morality', *California Law Review* 77: 445–63.

Stacey, Judith (1994) 'Scents, scholars and stigma: the revisionist campaign for family values', *Social Text* 40: 51–75.

Stacey, Margaret (1969) 'The myth of community studies', *British Journal of Sociology* 20: 134–47.

Tam, Henry (1995) *Citizen's Agenda for Building Democratic Communities*, Cambridge: Centre for Citizenship Development.

Taylor, Charles (1985a) *Philosophy and the Human Sciences*, Cambridge: Cambridge University Press.

—— (1985b) 'Interpretation and the sciences of man' in *Philosophy and the Human Sciences*, Cambridge: Cambridge University Press.

—— (1989) 'Cross purposes: the liberal communitarian debate' in N. Rosenblum (ed.) *Liberalism and the Moral Life*, Cambridge Mass.: Harvard University Press.

Walzer, Michael (1983) *Spheres of Justice*, New York: Basic Books.

—— (1987) *Interpretation and Social Criticism*, Cambridge Mass.: Harvard University Press.

—— (1990) 'The communitarian critique of liberalism', *Political Theory* 18: 6–23.

9 From modern nuclear family households to postmodern diversity?

The sociological construction of 'families'

Jo VanEvery

> The 'modern' family of sociological theory and historical convention des-
> ignates a family form no longer prevalent in the United States – an intact
> nuclear family household unit composed of a male breadwinner, his full-
> time homemaker wife, and their dependent children – precisely the form of
> family life that many mistake for an ancient, essential, and now-endangered
> institution....
> For better or for worse, the post-modern family revolution is here to stay.
>
> (Stacey, 1992: 93 and 110)

Although referring to trends in the US, Stacey's comments might equally apply
in the UK. The precise ways in which family life is changing may differ but the
overall pattern is certainly recognisable. Also recognisable are the public
anxieties and political debates about the causes and consequences of these
changes, and the legislative solutions aimed at halting the 'post-modern family
revolution'.

Family is not the only institution undergoing a postmodern revolution.
Sociology, too, is finding the 'modern' formula increasingly problematic. In a
highly theoretical body of work, the implications of a shift from 'modernity' to
'postmodernity' for both sociology and society are debated and discussed. One
key component of these debates is the relationship between sociology and
public debates and political actions.

> Post-modernism calls into question the belief (or hope) that there is some
> form of innocent knowledge to be had....By innocent knowledge I mean
> the discovery of some sort of truth which can tell us how to act in the
> world in ways that benefit or are for the (at least ultimate) good of all.
> Those whose actions are grounded or informed by such truth will also have
> *their* innocence guaranteed. They can only do good, not harm to others.
>
> (Flax 1992: 447)

Political events in the past thirty years have called this 'belief (or hope)'
into question.

The version of postmodernism that I find most compelling is that which engages productively with the critiques that feminists, anti-racists and other so-called new social movements have made of liberal and Marxist social theories and political projects. I agree with Linda Nicholson and Steven Seidman that 'at least certain strains of postmodern thinking are a key resource for rethinking a democratic social theory and politics' (1995: 7). The promise of postmodernism to recognise and accept diversity and difference seems a marked improvement on a 'modern' sociology which often treats diversity and difference as temporary, a 'problem' to be 'solved', or unimportant compared to the qualities which unite us.

Sociologists who study families and households are not immune to these wider debates. It is now rare to see articles begin with a universal definition of family such as this one from the height of 'modern' family sociology:

> we shall regard the family as a structural unit composed, as an ideal type, of a man and woman joined in a socially recognised union and their children. Normally, the children are the biological offspring of the spouses, but, as in the case of adopted children in our society, they need not necessarily be biologically related. This social unit we shall call the *nuclear family* or simply the *family*.
>
> (Bell and Vogel 1960: 1; emphasis in the original)

In fact, discussions of the difficulty of defining family are not uncommon. For example, Faith Robertson Elliot takes four pages to discuss the question 'What is the family?' reaching no firm conclusions (Elliot 1986: 4–8). Some researchers have chosen to focus on households precisely because, being defined by common residence, they appear to provide a clear research focus which potentially incorporates some of this diversity (Morris 1988: 2).

Yet despite moves to recognise and deal with diversity, my impression of the sociological literature on families and households is that remarkably little has changed. In 1990 I began research on anti-sexist living arrangements and discovered that very little had been written on 'alternative' families of any sort. What seemed to pass for 'alternative' were families and households where women were in full-time employment or those which contained divorced or remarried adults. From my particular feminist perspective, these did not seem very alternative at all.

The problem of definition is central to debates about postmodern sociology. Influenced by methodological debates in feminism which argued that sociological texts construct the reality they seek to study (e.g. Smith 1990), I interpreted my impression of the sociological literature on families and households as follows. Regardless of how individuals organise their lives, and which relationships are important to them, in the 'reality' constructed by this sociological research only 'modern nuclear family households' exist. All other living arrangements are at best transitional and as such are not worthy of study, and 'family' is more important than 'just friends'. Of course some researchers do study other forms of family. However, it was my impression that these studies were framed so as to reinforce, rather than challenge, the 'normality' of the modern nuclear family household. Reflecting upon my own research and my review of the sociological literature on 'families' and households, I realised that, despite all the sociological talk about the difficulty of defining families and the plurality and diversity of family forms in contemporary (postmodern?) societies, sociologists were helping to construct a 'normal' family which looked remarkably similar to that which an earlier generation of sociologists felt confident enough to define. This chapter results from a more systematic attempt to examine this impression.

Methods

The analysis on which this chapter is based is influenced by contemporary debates about the nature of knowledge and the status of objectivity. I start from the position that sociological research is a social practice and an element of (hierarchical) social relations. It is, therefore, a suitable object of study in its own right. The chapter should not be read as a critique of the individual studies cited (e.g. on the basis that they did not set out to do what I am criticising them for not doing) but rather as an analysis of 'family sociology' in the UK in the 1990s. Despite the intentions of the individual researchers, 'family sociology' as a body of research has certain characteristics and political implications that all sociologists with an interest in families or households need to consider.

This chapter is based on an analysis of articles in journals which published sociological research in the UK in 1993.[1] These include social policy and some interdisciplinary journals (see Table 9.1). The focus on UK journals is primarily due to what David Morgan describes as the 'marked contrast' between family sociology in the US and the UK (1996: 5). The 'sociology of the family' is hardly recognisable in the UK as such: there are no UK journals devoted to the family, and undergraduate courses explicitly on 'the family' or household are by no means a standard offering in UK departments of sociology. However, as Morgan argues forcefully, this does not mean that 'family sociology' does not exist in Britain.

> What has taken place, largely during the 1980s, is a weakening of the boundaries between family/household studies and other kinds of socio-logical studies. The real strength of 'family studies', theoretically and em-pirically, has come, and is likely to come in future, from this increasing fuzziness at the borders.
>
> (Morgan 1996: 12)

Because of this, as a first stage, titles, abstracts and skim reading of articles (usually the methods section) were used to determine how many articles in the chosen journals focused on the family or household. Articles were classified as having either a primary or secondary focus on family and household. A primary focus was understood as either a family or household research question or a sampling method involving a family/household component. A secondary focus was understood to include articles which mentioned family/household as elements in the relevant literature or components of another characteristic (see Table 9.1). The analysis focused on the forty-five articles with a primary focus on families and/or households.[2]

Table 9.1 Articles on family and/or household in UK sociology journals, 1993

Journal	Volume	Total articles	Primary focus	Secondary focus	% Primary
Sociological Review	41	21	7	3	33
British Journal of Sociology	44	26	2	3	8
Sociology	27	37	7	3	19
Sociology of Health & Illness	15	25	5	2	20
Economy & Society	22	27	2	1	7
Journal of Gender Studies	2	9	0	0	0
Women's Studies International Forum[a]	16	34	6	4	18
Work, Employment & Society	7	16	5	1	31
Human Relations	46	60	2	4	3
British Journal of Sociology of Education	14	23	0	0	0
Journal of Social Policy	22	16	4	2	25
Critical Social Policy	36–39	17	2	2	12
Theory, Culture & Society	10	30	0	1	0
Feminist Review[b]	43–45	17	3	2	18
grand total		358	45	26	13

Notes:

[a] One issue of 6 (Vol. 16(4)) missing, therefore total may be higher.
[b] Two articles had been torn out of one issue of the journal. Neither had the word 'family' in the title and have not been counted in the total.

I discovered that there was a group of articles analysing political and legal discourses which did not easily fit my categories of primary and secondary focus. Of the total of forty-five articles, six which treat 'family' as a largely symbolic element in a political or other discourse (Bell 1993; Milner 1993; Ram and Holliday 1993; Hassim 1993; Yeganeh 1993; McClintock 1993) have been excluded from the analysis. The analytic focus of these six articles differs substantially from the other thirty-nine and in some ways they indicate the political *effects* of the trend I identify below.

The analysis is primarily interpretive, treating journal articles as data comparable to interview transcripts. Since it is widely assumed that family/household research is no longer based on a restricted definition of 'family', a significant portion of this chapter is devoted to demonstrating that this is not the case. Although there are variations, particularly in the degree of awareness of the specificity of the family/household form being researched, the evidence demonstrates that my initial impression was well founded. As I will demonstrate, most of the articles with a primary focus on family and/or household published in UK journals in 1993 were about married couple households, often with young children. Very few articles even mention other kin, much less inter-household relationships or families/households based on close relationships other than those of 'blood' and marriage. Divorce and step-parenting are also notable absences.

'We shall regard the family as...'

Unlike Bell and Vogel (1960), none of the articles explicitly defines family although most articles use the term 'family' or 'household', some quite frequently. For example, Gray (1993: 102–3) uses the term 'family' or 'families' twelve times in his introduction without defining what he means. In most articles, the definition was implicit or was gradually specified during the course of the article. Many articles also use specific family relationships as criteria for selecting a sample for data collection, for delimiting the data they will analyse, or for choosing examples. These sampling criteria also function as definers of family within the research. Sampling methods were separated for purposes of analysis and the data are presented separately in Tables 9.2 and 9.3. The discussion of the issue of definitions will be divided into two sections based on the main issues that arose in the analysis: the composition of households and families; and the assumptions that are made about divisions of labour (including parenting).

Twenty-four of the thirty-nine articles analysed either described the sampling method of the study on which the article was based or described a method by which they chose examples used within the text. For the most part the sampling methods and criteria for selecting exemplary cases in the text constructed 'household' and/or 'family' as married (or cohabiting heterosexual) couples with children. Where there was variation this tended to be in the woman's employment status. Table 9.2 indicates which articles displayed the particular features discussed below.

More broadly, twenty-nine articles were identified as eliding terms referring to distinct sets of relationships or as taking particular relationships for granted in their analysis (Table 9.3). Twenty-one of these did so in ways which contribute to the construction of the 'modern nuclear family household' as the norm, while eight challenged such assumptions, usually in a critique of other studies (marked 'c').

Table 9.2 Criteria used in sampling and choice of exemplary cases

Article[a]	I				II		III	IV	
	i	ii	iii	iv	i	ii	i	i	ii
Aryee		x	x		x	x		x	
Brannen		x			x	j[b]		x	
Bytheway		x	x					x	
Callen *et al.*								x	
Cliff	x							x	x
Cuvillier		x	x					x	
Duncombe and Marsden		x	x		x				
Evetts				x				x	x
Giles		x						x	
Gray					x	j	x	x	
Gregson and Lowe		x				x		x	
Hunt and Annandale	x				x			x	x
Irwin and Morris		x						x	
Jones and Fletcher		x	x		x			x	
Lessor							x		
Mayall					x	j			
O'Connor	x				x	j		x	
Parsons and Atkinson					x	j	x		
Roberts *et al.*					x	j			
Vogler and Pahl	x				x			x	
Warde and Hetherington	x				x	x		x	
Watson				x	x	x		x	x
Whelan	x						x		
White	x				x		x	x	

Notes:
[a]All articles are 1993. The full reference can be found in the bibliography.
[b]'j' in this column indicates those articles for which such a sampling strategy seemed justified by the research question.

Headings

i	analysis of more diverse sample limited to (married) couples
ii	draws sample of (married) couples
iii	title clearly states focus on marriage/couples
iv	sample also includes single person households
II	Children
i	mentioned in description of sample
ii	used as a criterion of sampling
III	Other relatives
i	mentioned
IV	Employment status
i	mentioned
ii	focus of article is on employees' family/household circumstances.

Table 9.3 Assumptions made regarding family/household composition and domestic division of labour

Article[a]	Composition			Division of labour	
	i.	ii.	iii.	i.	ii.
Benenson				c[b]	c
Brannen	x	x	x		
Callan *et al.*				x	
Chisholm and duBois-Reymond	x	x	x	x	x
Cliff	x				
Duncombe and Marsden		x		x	
Edwards	c	c	c		
Evetts	x			x	
Ginn and Arber	x	x	x	x	x
Graham				c	c
Gray	x	x	x		
Gregson and Lowe	x				
Hayes and Miller	x			x	x
Irwin and Morris	x				
Jackson	c	c	c		
Leira	x	x	x	x	x
Mayall					x
McLaughlin	x	x	x		
Milner			x		
O'Connor			x[c]		
Parsons and Atkinson			x		
Pfau-Effinger				c	c
Richards	c	c	c		
Roberts *et al.*					x
Thomas				c	c
Vogler and Pahl	x				
Watson		x			
Watson-Franke				c	c
Whelan				x	

Notes:
[a] Articles are 1993. Full references can be found in the bibliography.
[b] Articles marked 'c' are critical of the pattern identified.
[c] More precisely, O'Connor elides wife and mother.

Headings;

Composition

i	elision of family and (married) couple
ii	elision of couple and married couple
iii	elision of family and parenthood

Division of labour

i	in marriage
ii	in parenthood

Family/household composition

The lack of explicit definitions could be seen as a response to an increasing awareness of the diversity of family and household forms and the consequent difficulty of defining 'family' on this basis. However, this interpretation is belied by a tendency to restrict samples to households resembling the 'modern nuclear family' (Table 9.2) and to elide terms which properly refer to distinct relationships (Table 9.3). I looked at three aspects of family/household composition in the analysis: marriage, children, and other relationships.

Sixteen articles indicate in the description of the sample that the analysis is of married couple households (which in some cases included couples 'living as married'). Only two articles describe the sample as also containing single women but the analyses focus on marriage and the articles provide much more information about this household/family form (Table 9.2, column I iv). The focus on marriage may arise from analysing only a portion of the total sample (Table 9.2, column I i) or from drawing a sample of (married) couple households (Table 9.2, column I ii). In only five cases is the focus on couple households clearly stated in the title of the article (Table 9.2, column I iii). The effect is to imply that 'households' are 'couple households'. That they are also *heterosexual* couple households is not even thought worthy of mention by most of these researchers. The increasing visibility of single-person households, single-parent households, same-sex households and households with more than two adults (related or unrelated) is not evident, nor is the number of divorced or remarried couples, the proportion of which are not identified.

Fourteen articles mention children in relation to sampling, ten of which also mentioned marriage (Table 9.2, column II i). Only one of these (Watson 1993) explicitly includes a childless woman in the sample (of three case studies). Ten used the existence of children as a sampling criterion, therefore explicitly defining 'family' as containing children (Table 9.2, column II ii). In six of these ten (marked 'j') this seems justified by a research question about mothering, parents, reproductive decisions or children (rather than more generally about families). However, in some articles this is part of a general construction of 'modern nuclear family households' as the 'norm'. For example, two articles are based on studies which use schools or day-care centres to recruit couple households (Aryee 1993; Warde and Hetherington 1993), but do not clarify this focus on couples *with children* (of a particular age) rather than couples *in general*. The other five articles which mention children focus on couples but describe the sample as containing some couples with children. In both cases, the fact that the analysis does not address the differences between households with and without children contributes to the construction of 'normal' households as those with children. At the very least, it does not allow us to determine what difference children make (if any).

Beyond issues of sampling there is an overall pattern of elisions from family or household to couple or partners to married couple or spouses to parents or mother and father. Though seventeen articles display some of these moves, only six display them all (Table 9.3). Gray (1993) is illustrative of the pattern (emphasis has been added to all quotations). The article begins, 'Any form of chronic illness represents a serious challenge, not only to the afflicted individual, but also to the individual's *family*' (Gray 1993: 102). Five pages later Gray specifies that 'the sample for this study consists of thirty-two *parents* of autistic children' but on the same page refers to these parents as both 'partners' and 'spouses' despite the fact that no mention has been made of marital status in the description of the sample. These terms all have distinct meanings and moving between them as if they described basically the same thing obscures these differences and gives the impression that 'households' are 'family households' and that 'family' is 'marriage and parenthood'. In addition to this pattern of elisions, the effect of variations in family/household composition is rarely analysed, thereby obscuring any significant differences between households composed differently.

Although there is an overwhelming concentration on families and households consisting of married couples, usually with children, it is not true to say that no other close relationships are considered. However, only five of the twenty-nine articles even mentioned other relatives or close relationships in the description of their samples (Table 9.2, column III i). One further article mentioned other relatives in the analysis (McLaughlin 1993). In two of these six articles (White 1993; Parsons and Atkinson 1993) kin outside the nuclear family are mentioned but are not discussed in the analysis. McLaughlin devotes a section to 'inter-household family life' (1993: 560–2) which is fully integrated in the subsequent discussion of 'the limits of matrifocality'; and Gray (1993: 112) provides a short discussion of the effects on grandparents of having an autistic grandchild. In the remaining two articles although wider kin relationships are central to the research questions, they are constructed as less important to relationships of marriage and children at some point in the analysis. Lessor is more aware of the cultural specificity of this and briefly discusses ethnic and cultural differences between the women in her study but still values sister relationships over other kin relationships and friendship.

Divisions of labour

The modern nuclear family household is premised on a particular gendered division of labour in which men work in the 'public' sphere earning enough to support the family, and women work in the 'private' sphere providing care for men and children. Of course, this model has never been a description of the reality of most families even in the West and in structural-functionalist approaches served mainly as an indicator of 'modernity' (Cheal 1991). Despite the widely held view that functionalism has been discredited, views very similar to those which are foundational to this theory survive and underpin large bodies of sociological work. For example, one article begins with a statement about the importance of studying the family to learn more about processes thought to be extra- or non-familial.

to summarise, the core of the traditional or 'conventional' view justifying
female exclusion is that stratification theory concerns itself with examining
inequalities that arise out of the occupational and economic structure of
society. Since women, it is argued, are peripheral to the occupational
structure because of both their intermittent employment patterns and their
primary responsibility for familial duties, their social class or prestige position is determined by the occupation of the bread-winner or the male head
of the household.

(Hayes and Miller 1993: 654)

Sociologists of work and employment have become interested in households
primarily because of an interest in the extent to which changes in the labour
market have affected this domestic division of labour (Morris 1990: 2). Not
surprisingly, therefore, several articles mention employment status in the
description of their sample (Table 9.2, column IV i). The use made of
employment status varies but is generally related to the 'modern' assumption
and includes examining the family or household circumstances of employed
individuals (Table 9.2, column IV ii), commenting on the employment status of
family members in the description of the sample, and limiting the analysis to
families/households containing a member with a particular employment status
(e.g. 'housewife'). The percentages of women in full-time employment vary
considerably between studies. The treatment of employment status in sampling
will be discussed in more detail in the next section.

Fifteen articles contained evidence of the assumption of a particular gendered division of labour in the analysis or the inappropriate use of gender
neutral language to describe activities or processes which are gendered (Table
9.3). Clear examples of the way an assumed 'modern' domestic division of
labour underpins the analysis of families/households are found in two articles
based on the same study. Callan *et al.* (1993), in their discussion of the
measurement of poverty, only consider one household characteristic in their
explanations – the employment/occupational status of the head of household.
This is based on the assumption that there is a breadwinner and home-maker
division of labour and ignores copious evidence that even women's part-time
work can be crucial for keeping households out of poverty. Whelan (1993),
using data from the same study, makes a similar assumption referring to 'The
information obtained from the head of household and household manager'
(1993: 91). Although the use of gender neutral terminology allows us to
consider 'role-reversed' households, the division itself is not thought amenable
to change in this operationalisation.

Of course, breadwinning is only half of the 'modern' story. The modern
nuclear family household also provides the central emotional support for adults.
Whelan embeds these assumptions about the importance of the nuclear family
household into his measure of emotional support.

Respondents were scored low on emotional support if they indicated that their spouse was not the person in whom they would choose to confide in relation to personal problems, or the best person to talk to when they were really upset.

(Whelan 1993: 91)

This same assumption, albeit in less obvious terms, provides the impetus for Duncombe and Marsden's (1993) work on 'the gender division of emotion and "emotion work" '. Although this article differs from Whelan's in that the authors are looking for ways of changing the emotional aspects of the gender division of labour, both articles are based on the assumption that nuclear families based on marriage provide emotional support in 'modern' societies.

Implications

'Modern' family sociology, as characterised by the structural-functionalist approach in particular, was based on a particular view of social change. The concentration on the relatively isolated nuclear family with a breadwinner– housewife division of labour was not due to the statistical predominance of this type of family in the post-war period in either the US or the UK. Rather it was theoretical considerations which highlighted this form as that most suited to the demands of modern industrial societies. Central to the 'modern' theoretical perspective is an emphasis on convergence rather than diversity (see Cheal 1991). Criticisms of this approach have been widely accepted but there appears to be a continued emphasis on the 'modern' family in UK 'family sociology', an emphasis which limits our understanding of social relations and of social change.

One form in which this emphasis manifests itself is in the tendency to assume that households and families composed differently will display differences on other dimensions, leading many researchers to limit their samples (or their analyses) to particular types of household, as in the following example.

The sample does not include single mothers; lesbian mothers or mothers of adopted children. Hence one might expect that there would be little varia- tion in the range of these women's experiences of motherhood. In fact, however, even within this relatively homogeneous sample, it will be shown this was not the case.

(O'Connor 1993: 350)

O'Connor's analysis demonstrates that her sample is not 'homogeneous'. However, the exclusion of those mothers *assumed* to be different means that there is no research evidence to *demonstrate* whether the categories 'single mother', 'lesbian mother', etc. would in fact correlate with heterogeneity of experience of motherhood or whether other factors are more salient. As the analysis above indicates, the limitation of the sample (either at the collection or the analysis stage) is common. Irwin and Morris (1993) provide an example where family composition is not a salient explanatory factor. Comparing their evidence of the constraints on *married* women's labour force participation to that found in studies of *lone mothers* indicated that what both groups of women 'manifest in their employment patterns is the inability to furnish household resourcing through a secondary wage' (1993: 368).

The emphasis on 'modern' families is also evident in the tendency to treat cohabiting heterosexual couples as married couples. Although these two family forms may indeed display similar characteristics, there is actually very little research which would allow us to make confident decisions about the similarity or dissimilarity of cohabitation and marriage. Burgoyne (1991) notes that while many cohabitees in her sample characterised their relationships as preludes to or similar to marriage, a significant minority saw cohabitation as different. As such it seems prudent to examine the evidence in each individual study and indicate to the reader on what grounds the decision to aggregate the two household types (or not) has been made.

In other circumstances family/household composition is ignored as an explanatory factor when it may indeed be relevant, for example in an article on genetic counselling and women's reproductive decisions (Parsons and Atkinson 1993). The authors focus on carrier risk as the principal explanatory factor in the reproductive decisions of individual women. The sample is not described in terms of marital status although husbands' influence on reproductive decisions is often referred to in passing. However, they describe one case in which a woman had two pregnancies, the first an 'unplanned teenage pregnancy', the second 'a planned conception in a stable relationship': 'the first was terminated without foetal sexing, the second she proceeded with untested' (1993: 697). Although the authors admit that biography is more important than carrier risk in this case, such family circumstances are not investigated for other women. The reader is left to assume that all the pregnancies in this study are the same, influenced only by carrier risk, except these two which are noted as exceptional.

Recent theoretical and methodological debates have highlighted the ways in which sociology as a 'textually mediated discourse' (Smith 1990) itself participates in the construction of social relations. This is evident in some of the articles examined when the categorisation of data and the operationalisation of concepts itself produces the 'modern' division of labour, characterised by the relative isolation of the nuclear family from wider kin, and the separation of family/household from the economic sphere. Whelan's operationalisation of emotional support illustrates the first dimension by privileging the 'isolated nuclear family' over '(a) relatives (children, parents, brothers, sisters, etc.) living outside the household; (b) neighbours; (c) friends' (1993: 92). It is impossible to judge to what extent the nuclear family is, in fact, the primary source of emotional support or to what extent social change might involve inter-household support.

Vogler and Pahl (1993) provide an example of the way employment status categories may be constructed such that only 'modern nuclear family households' are visible.

> Among the men, 87 per cent were in full-time employment, while 8 per cent were unemployed and 4 per cent non-employed, most of whom were retired. Among the women, 29 per cent were in full-time employment and 37 per cent in part-time employment, while 34 per cent were unemployed or non-employed, most of whom were housewives.
>
> (Vogler and Pahl 1993: 73)

This categorisation assumes that women are 'housewives' unless employed, negating the possibility that 'unemployment' and 'retirement' can have any meaning for women. Employed women appear not to be housewives and households in which men are not 'breadwinners' disappear into the 'retired' category. Radical renegotiations of the 'modern' sexual division of labour, such as both partners working part-time, are indescribable in these terms. Even in research which focuses on households which are not based on a breadwinner–housewife division of labour, the use of descriptors such as 'divergent' and 'new' serves to reinforce the 'normality' of the modern division of labour (e.g. Gregson and Lowe 1993; Aryee 1993).

Some of the articles in the sample provided a critical perspective on some of these issues and indicated some of the implications of the practices outlined above. Four articles provide a critical perspective on the treatment of family composition. Jackson's review of the sociological and feminist literature on love points out that 'The pervasiveness of love as a representational theme is related to its institutionalisation in marriage and family life' (1993: 202). Edwards (1993) argues that assumptions about marriage and the family contribute to the difficulty of defining 'lone-parent families', particularly for the purposes of targeting social provision. Richards (1993) addresses the gulf between professional and lay beliefs about heredity, pointing out the role of the latter in the active construction of kinship by individuals. McLaughlin (1993), although she elides 'family life' with marriage and parenthood,[3] addresses the meanings of these life events and the way that strong extended family networks concerned with 'respectability' powerfully constrain individual choices in family and household formation.

Five articles provide either a critique or an alternative to the 'modern' division of labour. Two (Thomas 1993; Graham 1993) address the impact such assumptions have had on concepts of 'care', highlighting that despite the important knowledge gained about patterns of caring in the UK, the 'experiences of those who are not tied into kinship structures based on marriage' remain unexplored (Graham 1993: 465). Pfau-Effinger (1993) and Benenson (1993) use historical and comparative studies to examine the diversity of women's labour market participation. Watson-Franke (1993) examines anthropological studies of matrilineal societies in order to show that a decline in paternal authority and rise in mother-headed families (the centrepiece of public and political debate over the 'breakdown' of the family) might be the basis for a less violent society.

These articles indicate in detail some of the consequences *for sociology* of the broad trend I am identifying. The implicit and explicit construction of 'modern nuclear family households' as the norm results in the development of concepts, explanations and theories of household and family processes which are of limited usefulness in understanding the complexities of family life in contemporary societies. The concepts that have been developed to understand these processes may only apply to this particular type of household. Graham (1993) has argued this quite forcefully in her analysis of 'concepts of care'. I have made a similar argument in the case of housework and the division of domestic labour (VanEvery 1997). In many cases we do not know whether marital status or the presence of children (of a particular age) is important or not in explaining certain patterns. Irwin and Morris (1993) suggest that it may not be relevant to understanding women's employment patterns. We also know very little about *how* marriage and children, and *women's* responsibility for domestic and family matters, come to appear 'inevitable' to such a large proportion of the population (even, it seems, sociologists, see Chisholm and duBois-Reymond 1993: 269). McLaughlin's (1993) analysis of the impact of close extended family networks seems useful in this respect.

The slippage between family/household, couple/marriage and marriage/parenthood which was identified above, also has important conceptual and explanatory consequences. A household is a residential group whose members usually share some basic tasks (like cooking). A family may or may not also be a household, but is usually distinguished by formal ties of 'blood' and marriage. However, 'family' also connotes ties of love and affection, commitment, and obligations whether these are formally recognised or not. Recent studies of lesbian and gay 'chosen' families (e.g. Weston 1991) extend our knowledge of these informal processes. When we take these relationships into account the term 'family building' can obviously involve much more than having children, and even in families based on marriage and childbearing, using 'family building' to denote childbearing implies that getting married is somehow separate from building a family.

Beyond these important conceptual issues are the political implications of sociological research. Judith Stacey's chapter indicates the direct impact some social scientists are having on political debate in the US. Most of the researchers whose work I have examined in this chapter do not have these political interests nor are they involved directly in this sort of political project. This is not to say that their work has no political implications. Sociologists can no longer take the 'innocent' position that our 'objective' research is above the fray. We can no longer believe the protestations of 'modern' social theorists that their work was objective and distanced from political debate. For example, Steven Seidman argues that Talcott Parsons 'envisioned sociology as a vehicle for a reconstructed social liberalism in the face of the failure of individualistic or utilitarian liberalism and the threat of socialism' (Seidman 1998: 115). Feminist, anti-racist, post-colonial, queer, and other 'new social movements' (including the intellectual projects associated with them) have demonstrated that this social liberalism, along with the predominant forms of socialism or social democracy, have been unable fully to recognise large sectors of society.

Taking a postmodern perspective, sociologists have different responsibilities.

> Social life becomes no longer, as it tended to be in much modern social theory, a relatively static field, understandable through the use of abstract categories. Rather, it becomes a field continually in shift where the very categories actors are using to depict it are productive of the shifts themselves. Following this understanding, the social theorist becomes, with the social worker, the state agent, the journalist, and the protester, one more social actor in the process of social production.
>
> (Nicholson and Seidman 1995: 24)

As an institutionalised form of knowledge, sociology carries a certain weight in public discourse. By not paying attention to the differences between terms and not specifying clearly what family/household forms we have researched, we contribute to the construction of a particular family/household form as the 'norm'. Even if it were specified more clearly, the 'modern nuclear family household' would still appear as the norm by virtue of the relative volume of research.

Perhaps more importantly, 'pro-family' discourse plays on people's insecurities. We are in a period of rapid social change. There have been major shifts in women's expectations of employment and family even if the changes in actual jobs and responsibilities have not met those expectations. Lesbian and gay lifestyles are more visible, even if discrimination and violence against lesbians and gay men are still rife. Single parenthood is increasing and many single mothers live in poverty. Violence and property crime are increasing and fear of violence and crime is high. The fact that we do not know very much about households and families that are *not* composed of married couples with children contributes to our collective insecurities. Even though we know a lot of negative things about modern nuclear families, we also know a lot of positive things about them. And at least we *know* the negatives and can try to prevent or cure them in our own relationships (witness the burgeoning of therapy, counselling, agony columns, talk shows, etc.) or pass legislation to deal with them more effectively (e.g. in the case of child abuse). But the lack of knowledge about other family and household forms makes them more threatening. Divorce rates might be high but we have no idea how stable cohabitation is. Your husband may not do much to help with housework and child care but 'lone mothers' *have to* do it themselves (or so it seems).

Sociological discourses are also implicated in the link made between the 'breakdown' of the family and the 'breakdown' of social cohesion. Without knowledge of the way diverse patterns of personal life (which we might call family) meet the emotional and physical needs of individuals or how those patterns of personal life connect with other social relations contributing (or not) to social cohesion, it is easy to fall back on those 'modern' theories which posited stable families (of a particular type) as a key element in stable societies. 'Family sociology' has not moved far enough in the direction of postmodernity to provide support for alternative explanations of the current social and political situation. We need a sociology that allows us to argue for *changing* family values in the face of the attack on the *lack* of family values in contemporary society.

Conclusions

I set out to determine if the evidence bore out my impression that the sociological literature on families and households was characterised by an overwhelming focus on the 'modern nuclear family household'. My analysis of articles published in UK journals in 1993 confirmed this impression. The authors of these articles are not known for their support of 'pro-family' politics and at least some of them would identify themselves with feminist and/or left politics. And yet, by analysing samples of married couples often with children; by eliding the terms 'family', 'household', 'partners', 'spouses', 'parents'; and/or by assuming a particular (gendered) division of labour, they contribute to the construction of 'family' as the 'modern nuclear family household' at the centre of current public anxieties.

In the sociology examined here, married couples with children living in households with no other members predominate. We know how they divide housework tasks, how they distribute financial resources, how they cope with an autistic child or poverty or stress, how they deal with (male) unemployment and early retirement, and numerous other aspects of the organisation of their daily lives. We know almost nothing about how these things get done in other forms of family or household.

Of course, sociologists could construct more diverse families and households. We could start from where people are and analyse 'how our everyday worlds are organised and how they are shaped and determined by relations that extend beyond them' (Smith 1988: 121). This conceptual process will not be simple. The concepts of family and household have an everyday currency. People define their living arrangements in relation to their understanding of these terms. In addition, concepts developed to understand data about particular types of families/households may not work for data on other types. If our concepts only work for dividing money or household tasks between two people and we discover that some people divide those things between more than two people (who perhaps do not even live in the same household), the concepts need to be revised. This is obviously more difficult than applying existing concepts to new data but is vital sociological work.

At the very least we need to be more specific about the generalisability of our findings. For example, if our research is about married couple households, we should say so. If there are unmarried couples in the sample, we should not refer to individuals as 'husbands' and 'wives'. The research I have reviewed for this paper is interesting and important research. I am not saying it should not be done in favour of examining other family and household forms. However, it should be clearer that these studies are of a *particular* type of household, usually at a *particular* stage of the life cycle. Of course it would be useful if researchers would *also* include other household forms, particularly where they have the data. If a focus on marriage means only analysing two-thirds of the data set (as in, for example, Vogler and Pahl 1993), perhaps researchers should consider what analysing the other third would do to their concepts and conclusions.

Some sociologists have begun to talk about these changes in terms of 'postmodernism'. This framework is contested, and many find it highly problematic. However, it does seem (to me) to be useful in at least some respects. 'Postmodern' sociology argues that the link between (social) science and politics assumed by 'modern' sociology is flawed, that science is itself political and that no political solution will have uniformly positive effects. In addition, 'postmodern' sociology attempts (with varying degrees of success) to account for and deal with diversity as a central aspect of social life. How does the sociological study of families and households engage in these debates? Have we moved from 'modern nuclear family households' to 'postmodern' diversity? And how would the social world look once we make such a conceptual shift?

Notes

1 When I began this research, 1993 was the most recent complete year. The gestation of this volume now makes it appear a bit out of date. I believe that the situation has not changed significantly since then. Although I am aware of research on other family forms, my impression is that this is still marginal to the discipline. I would welcome evidence to the contrary.
2 There were a few of these that I did not manage to get copies of for various reasons.
3 See especially the headings and sub-headings on pages 558–9.

Bibliography

Aryee, S. (1993) 'Dual-earner couples in Singapore: an examination of work and non-work sources of their experienced burnout', *Human Relations* 46 (12): 1441–68.
Bell, N. W. and Vogel, E. F. (eds) (1960) *A Modern Introduction to The Family*, London: Routledge & Kegan Paul.
Bell, V. (1993) 'Governing childhood: neo-liberalism and the law', *Economy & Society* 22(3): 390–405.
Benenson, H. (1993) 'Patriarchal constraints on women workers' mobilization: the Lancashire female cotton operatives 1842–1919', *The British Journal of Sociology* 44(4): 613–33.
Brannen, J. (1993) 'The effects of research on participants; findings from a study of mothers and employment', *Sociological Review* 41(2): 328–46.
Burgoyne, J. (1991) 'Does the ring make any difference? Couples and the private face of a public relationship in post-war Britain' in Clark, D. (ed.) *Marriage, Domestic Life and Social Change*, London: Routledge.

Bytheway, B. (1993) 'Ageing and biography: the letters of Bernard and Mary Berenson', *Sociology* 27(1): 153–65.

Callan, T., Nolan, B. and Whelan, C. T. (1993) 'Resources, deprivation and the measurement of poverty', *Journal of Social Policy* 22(2): 141–72.

Cheal, D. (1991) *Family and the State of Theory*, Toronto: University of Toronto Press.

Chisholm, L. and duBois-Reymond, M. (1993) 'Youth transitions, gender and social change', *Sociology* 27(2): 259–79.

Cliff, D. (1993) ' "Under the wife's feet": renegotiating gender divisions in early retirement', *Sociological Review* 41(1): 30–53.

Cuvillier, R. (1993) 'Equality of treatment for housewives in tax and benefit systems: a proposal', *Journal of Social Policy* 22(4): 439–60.

Duncombe, J. and Marsden, D. (1993) 'Love and intimacy: the gender division of emotion and "emotion work": a neglected aspect of sociological discussion of heterosexual relationships', *Sociology* 27(2): 221–41.

Edwards, R. (1993) 'Taking the initiative: the government, lone mothers and day care provision', *Critical Social Policy* 39: 36–50.

Elliot, F. R. (1986) *The Family: Change or Continuity?*, London: Macmillan.

Evetts, J. (1993) 'Careers and partnerships: the strategies of secondary headteachers', *Sociological Review* 41(2): 302–27.

Flax, J. (1992) 'The end of innocence', in J. Butler and J. W. Scott *Feminist Theorize the Political*, London: Routledge.

Giles, J. (1993) 'A home of one's own: women and domesticity in England 1918–1950', *Women's Studies International Forum* 16(3): 239–53.

Ginn, J. and Arber, S. (1993) 'Pension penalties: the gendered division of occupational welfare', *Work, Employment and Society* 7(1): 47–70.

Graham, H. (1993) 'Social divisions in caring', *Women's Studies International Forum* 16(5): 461–70.

Gray, D. E. (1993) 'Perceptions of stigma: the parents of autistic children', *Sociology of Health and Illness* 15(1): 102–20.

Gregson, N. and Lowe, M. (1993) 'Renegotiating the domestic division of labour? A study of dual career households in north east and south east England', *Sociological Review* 41(3): 475–505.

Hassim, S. (1993) 'Family, motherhood and Zulu nationalism: the politics of the Inkatha Women's Brigade', *Feminist Review* 43: 1–25.

Hayes, B. C. and Miller, R. L. (1993) 'The silenced voice: female social mobility patterns with particular reference to the British Isles', *The British Journal of Sociology* 44(4): 653–72.

Hunt, K. and Annandale, E. (1993) 'Just the job? Is the relationship between health and domestic and paid work gender-specific?', *Sociology of Health and Illness* 15(5): 632–64.

Irwin, S. and Morris, L. D. (1993) 'Social Security or economic insecurity? The concentration of unemployment (and research) within households', *Journal of Social Policy* 22(3): 349–72.

Jackson, S. (1993) 'Even sociologists fall in love: an exploration in the sociology of emotions', *Sociology* 27(2): 201–20.

Jones, F. and Fletcher, B. (1993) 'An empirical study of occupational stress transmission in working couples', *Human Relations* 46(7): 881–903.

Leira, A. (1993) 'Mothers, markets and the state: a Scandinavian "model"?', *Journal of Social Policy* 22(3): 329–47.

Lessor, R. (1993) 'All in the family: social processes in ovarian egg donation between sisters', *Sociology of Health and Illness* 15(3): 393–413.

McClintock, A. (1993) 'Family feuds: gender, nationalism and the family', *Feminist Review* 44: 61–80.

McLaughlin, E. (1993) 'Women and the family in Northern Ireland: a review', *Women's Studies International Forum* 16(6): 553–68.

Mayall, B. (1993) 'Keeping healthy at home and school: "it's my body, so it's my job" ', *Sociology of Health and Illness* 15(4): 464–87.

Milner, J. (1993) 'A disappearing act; the differing career paths of fathers and mothers in child protection investigations', *Critical Social Policy* 38: 48–63.

Morgan, D. H. J. (1996) *Family Connections: An Introduction to Family Studies*, Cambridge: Polity Press.

Morris, L. (1990) *The Workings of the Household*, Cambridge: Polity Press.

Nicholson, L. and Seidman, S. (1995) 'Introduction' in L. Nicholson and S. Seidman (eds) *Social Postmodernism: Beyond Identity Politics*, Cambridge: Cambridge University Press: 1–35.

O'Connor, P. (1993) 'Women's experience of the mother role', *Sociological Review* 41(2): 347–60.

Parsons, E. and Atkinson, P. (1993) 'Genetic risk and reproduction', *Sociological Review* 41(4): 679–706.

Pfau-Effinger, B. (1993) 'Modernisation, culture and part-time employment: the example of Finland and West Germany', *Work, Employment & Society* 7(3): 383–410.

Ram, M. and Holliday, R. (1993) 'Relative merits: family, culture and kinship in small firms', *Sociology* 27(4): 629–48.

Richards, M. P. M. (1993) 'The new genetics: some issues for social scientists', *Sociology of Health and Illness* 15(5): 567–86.

Roberts, H., Smith, S. and Bryce, C. (1993) 'Prevention is better...', *Sociology of Health and Illness* 15(4): 447–63.

Seidman, S. (1998) *Contested Knowledges* (2nd edn), Oxford: Blackwell.

Smith, D. E. (1988) *The Everyday World as Problematic*, Milton Keynes: Open University Press.

—— (1990) *The Conceptual Practices of Power: A Feminist Sociology of Knowledge*, Toronto: University of Toronto Press.

Stacey, J. (1992) 'Backward toward the postmodern family: reflections on gender, kinship, and class in the Silicon Valley' in B. Thorne and M. Yalom (eds) *Rethinking the Family: Some Feminist Questions* (2nd edn), Boston: Northeastern University Press.

Thomas, C. (1993) 'De-constructing concepts of care', *Sociology* 27(4): 649–69.

VanEvery, J. (1994) 'Anti-sexist living arrangements: a feminist research project', unpublished PhD thesis, University of Essex.

—— (1995) *Heterosexual Women Changing the Family: Refusing to be a 'Wife'!*, London: Taylor & Francis.

—— (1997) 'Understanding gendered inequality: reconceptualizing housework', *Women's Studies International Forum* 20(3): 411–20.

Vogler, C. and Pahl, J. (1993) 'Social and economic change and the organization of money within marriage', *Work, Employment and Society* 7(1): 71–95.

Warde, A. and Hetherington, K. (1993) 'A changing domestic division of labour? Issues of measurement and interpretation', *Work, Employment and Society* 7(1): 23–45.

Watson, I. (1993) 'Life history meets economic theory: the experiences of three working-class women in a local labour market', *Work, Employment and Society* 7(3): 411–35.

Watson-Franke, M.-B. (1993) 'The Lycian heritage and the making of men: matrilineal models of parenting', *Women's Studies International Forum* 16(6): 569–79.

Weston, K. (1991) *Families We Choose: Gays, Lesbians, and Kinship*, New York: Columbia University Press.

Whelan, C. T. (1993) 'The role of social support in mediating the psychological consequences of economic stress', *Sociology of Health and Illness* 15(1): 86–101.

White, C. (1993) ' "Close to home" in Johannesburg: gender oppression in township households', *Women's Studies International Forum* 16(2): 149–63.

Yeganeh, N. (1993) 'Women, nationalism and Islam in contemporary political discourse in Iran', *Feminist Review* 44: 3–18.

10 Virtual social science and the politics of family values in the United States

Judith Stacey

From the wild Irish slums of the 19th century Eastern seaboard to the riot-torn suburbs of Los Angeles, there is one unmistakable lesson in American history: a community that allows a large number of young men to grow up in broken families, dominated by women, never acquiring any stable relationship to male authority, never acquiring any set of rational expectations about the future – that community asks for and gets chaos. Crime, violence, unrest, unrestrained lashing out at the whole social structure – that is not only to be expected; it is very near to inevitable.

(Daniel Patrick Moynihan 1965)[1]

The way a male becomes a man is by supporting his children....What (the Democrats) cannot accept is that government proposals have failed. It is the family that can rebuild America....The dissolution of the family, and in particular, the absence of fathers in the lives of millions of America's children is the single most critical threat (to our future).

(Dan Quayle 8 September 1994)[2]

That is a disaster. It is wrong. And someone has to say again, 'It is simply not right. You shouldn't have a baby before you're ready, and you shouldn't have a baby when you're not married'.

(President Clinton 9 September 1994)[3]

I am flattered by Judith Stacey's view that my colleagues and I at the Institute for American Values are 'central players' in a successful effort to 'forge a national consensus on family values and to shape the family politics of the "new" Democratic Party'. As I understand it, we stand accused of persuading many people, including many in the media and in the Clinton Administration to pay more attention to the problem of fatherlessness and the importance of the two-parent home. I believe that we are guilty as charged.

(David Blankenhorn July 1994, unpublished letter to *Nation* magazine)

The discourse of family crisis in the USA has a history as long as that of the republic, but as the twentieth century draws to a close, its outpourings proliferate in terms more urgent, fractious and ubiquitous than ever before.

David Blankenhorn, president of the Institute for American Values and director of the National Fatherhood Initiative, quoted above, figures prominently in the most recent, and least anticipated, development in this discursive history – a cultural campaign for 'family values' waged primarily by social scientists operating outside the academy. The campaign claims the legitimacy of social science in a crusade to restore eroded privileges and prestige to fathers and the heterosexual, married-couple nuclear families it wishes them to head (Stacey 1994a; 1994b). From the Institute for American Values, the Council on Families in America and the American Family Panel of research scholars, to the Communitarian Network and the Progressive Policy Institute, social scientists in the US lead a concerted effort to promote centrist family ideology and policies. Among the most visible of these academic, family-values activists are William Galston (until 1995, Deputy Assistant to President Clinton), Amitai Etzioni, David Popenoe, Jean Bethke Elshtain and Senator Daniel Patrick Moynihan, the forefather of late twentieth-century family-crisis discourse.

On 26 December 1992, this discourse 'hailed' me, by name, from the editorial pages of the *New York Times*.[4] Cast in the role of a dissident respondent, I began to map its institutional, rhetorical and political frameworks (Stacey 1994a; 1994b). Extending that cartographical project, I offer here a reflexive sociology of knowledge treatment of political and intellectual developments inside and outside the US academy that drive and configure this eleventh-hour twentieth-century campaign. After identifying historical forces that motivate some of the principal figures who produce and disseminate this family-crisis talk, I assess the campaign's implications for emergent realignments of knowledge and power.

No geographer of family-values discourse can survey the domain from disinterested epistemological and political locations. Fair disclosure principles prompt me to acknowledge my position as an increasingly active participant in contemporary representational struggles over family politics, particularly those operating at the boundaries of social science, the media, and political discourse. Indeed, hostile attention attracted by *Brave New Families* (Stacey 1990), my feminist ethnography about postmodern family life, drew me away from an ethnographic project on cultural studies and into the fray of public intellectual combat over family research and politics.[5] From this engaged, and inevitably partial, stance I survey the shifting borderlines and fissures of fin-de-si cle family-values terrain.

My overlay will suggest that a widely recognised, but largely untheorised, postmodern family condition has created genuine representational, material, and moral crises in the practice, knowledge and politics of family life in the US. Everyone in the US, as in most other post-industrial societies, experiences this postmodern family condition, which, in turn, impinges on virtually all significant domains and axes of power.[6] There is no longer popular or scholarly consensus on how to define the boundaries of what constitutes a legitimate family. But neither does consensus exist to grant legitimacy, or even tolerance, to the implicitly pluralistic definition of family by which the nation's inhabitants, in fact, presently live. This gaping gorge between practice and consciousness signals the collapse of a once-shared family culture rooted in religious and naturalist narratives.

The popular representational crisis of family authority reverberates in the academy where the ruling paradigms of 1950s sociology – structural-functionalism, modernisation theory, and empiricism – have lost prestige and power, but where most sociologists remain aloof from challenges posed by debates about postmodern theory and cultural studies disturbing the peace in adjacent disciplinary corridors. Feminism, however, has had a profoundly unsettling impact on the field, one which almost no sociologist has been able to ignore. Some, like David Popenoe, have nearly abandoned academic sociology to feminists and liberal demographers, while creating independent institutions through which to deploy their academic status (and more than compensate for some of its decline) in circuits of power and knowledge with far greater reach and weight than engage most feminist, postmodernist or cultural studies scholars. The gap in the degree of prestige that functionalist sociology enjoys in popular, as compared with professional, domains is also considerable, and growing.

Moreover, fin-de-si cle politicians of disparate ideological hues in the US also have come to perceive significant rewards in family-values discourse, as the two excerpts above from back-to-back, and nearly interchangeable, 1994 election season speeches by former vice-president Dan Quayle and President Clinton indicate. A peculiar conjuncture of material, political and academic dislocations has opened the door for collaboration between mainstream social scientists and electoral politicians. Revisionist family-values scholars are supplying substantial ideology, rhetoric and legitimacy to post-Cold War politicians in both major political parties.

Playing hookey from besieged and tarnished ivory towers, numerous social scientists, now including myself, are waging public cultural combat, for weighty political stakes, over the sources of and remedies for the fall of the modern family system. As the US approaches the third Christian millennium, its populace inhabits a world of contested family life whose everyday practices and conditions of social and material decline are increasingly at odds with a mythic discourse of virtual family values that envelops us.[7]

A virtual bedtime fable for the American century

Once upon a fabulised time, half a century ago, there was a lucky land where families with names like Truman and Eisenhower presided over a world of wholesome, middle-class families. Men and women married, made love and (in that proper order), produced gurgling, Gerber babies. It was a land where, as God and Nature had ordained, men were men and women were ladies. As epitomised in the mythic 1950s US sitcom characters Ozzie and Harriet, fathers worked outside the home for pay to support their wives and children, and mothers worked inside the home without pay to support their husbands and to cultivate healthy, industrious, above-average children. Streets and neighbour-hoods were safe and tidy. This land was the strongest, wealthiest, freest and fairest in the world. Its virtuous leaders, heroic soldiers, and dazzling technology defended all the freedom-loving people on the planet from an evil empire which had no respect for freedom or families. A source of envy, inspiration and protection to people everywhere, the leaders and citizens of this blessed land felt confident and proud.

And then, as so often happens in fairytales, evil came to this magical land. Sometime during the mid-1960s, a toxic serpent wriggled its way close to the pretty picket fences guarding those Edenic gardens. One prescient Jeremiah, named Daniel Patrick Moynihan (1965), detected the canny snake and tried to alert his placid country*men* to the dangers of family decline. Making a pilgrimage from Harvard to the White House, he chanted about the ominous signs and consequences of 'a tangle of pathology' festering in cities that suburban commuters and their ladies-in-waiting had abandoned for the crabgrass frontier. Promiscuity, unwed motherhood and fatherless families, he warned, would undermine domestic tranquillity and wreak social havoc. Keening only to the tune of black keys, however, this Pied Piper's song fell flat, inciting displeasure and rebuke.

It seemed that, overnight, those spoiled Gerber babies had turned into rebellious, disrespectful youth who spurned authority, tradition and conformity, and scorned the national wealth, power and imperial status in which their elders exulted. Rejecting their parents' grey flannel suits and Miss American ideals, as well as their monogamous, nuclear families, they generated a counter-culture and a sexual revolution, and they built unruly social movements demanding student rights, free speech, racial justice, peace, liberation for women and for homosexuals. Long-haired, unisex-clad youth smoked dope and marched in demonstrations shouting slogans like, 'Question Authority', 'Girls Say Yes to Boys Who Say No', 'Smash Monogamy', 'Black is Beautiful', 'Power to the People', 'Make Love, Not War', 'Sisterhood is Powerful', and 'Liberation Now'. Far from heeding Moynihan's warning, many young women drew inspiration from the 'black matriarchs' he had condemned and condemned Moynihan instead for blaming the victims.

Disrupting families and campuses, the young people confused and divided their parents and teachers, even seducing some foolish elders into emulating their sexual and social experiments. But the thankless arrogance of these privileged youth, their unkempt appearance, provocative antics and amorality also enraged many, inciting a right-wing, wishful, 'moral majority' to form its own backlash social movement to restore family and moral order.

And so it happened that harmony, prosperity, security and confidence disappeared from this once most fortunate land. After disturbing Black communities, the serpent of family decline slithered under the picket fences, where it spewed its venom on white, middle-class families as well. Men no longer knew what it meant to be men, and women had neither time nor inclination to be ladies. Had the Ozzie and Harriet Show still been running,

Ozzie would have had trouble finding secure work. He'd have been accused of neglecting, abusing or oppressing his wife and children. Harriet would no longer have stayed home with the children. She too would have worked outside the home for pay, albeit less pay. Ozzie and Harriet would have sued for divorce. Harriet would have decided she could choose to have children with or without a marriage certificate, with or without an Ozzie, or perhaps even with a Rozzie. After all, as front page stories in her morning newspaper would have informed her, almost daily, 'Traditional Family Nearly the Exception, Census Finds' (Shogren 1994).

As the last decade of the century dawned, only half the children in the land were living with two married parents who had jointly conceived or adopted them. Twice as many children were living in single-parent as in male breadwinner, female home-maker, families. Little wonder few citizens could agree over what would count as a proper family. Little wonder that court chroniclers charted the devolution of the modern family system in books with anxious titles like, *The War Over the Family* (Berger and Berger 1983), *Embattled Paradise* (Skolnick 1991), *Disturbing the Nest* (Popenoe 1988), *Brave New Families* (Stacey 1990), *The Way We Never Were* (Coontz 1992), *Fatherless America* (Blankenhorn 1995) and *Families on the Faultline* (Rubin 1994).

The era of the modern family system had come to an end, and few felt sanguine about the postmodern family condition which had succeeded it. Unaccustomed to a state of normative instability and definitional crisis, the populace split its behaviour from its beliefs. Many who contributed actively to such postmodern family statistics as divorce, remarriage, blended families, single parenthood, joint custody, abortion, domestic partnership, two-career households, and the like still yearned nostalgically for the 'Father Knows Best' world they had lost. 'Today', in the United States, as historian John Gillis (1994) so aptly puts it, 'the anticipation and memory of family means more to people than its immediate reality. It is through the families we live *by* that we achieve the transcendence that compensates for the tensions and frustrations of the families we live *with*'. Not only have the fabled modern families we live *by* become more compelling than the messy, improvisational, patchwork bonds of postmodern family life, but, as my bedtime story hints, because they function as pivotal elements in a distinctive national imaginary, these symbolic families are also far more stable than any in which future generations ever dwelled.

Similar evidence of the decline of the modern family system appears throughout the advanced industrialised world, and for similar reasons, but thus far, in no other society has the decline incited responses so volatile, ideological, divisive nor so politically mobilised and influential as in the US.[8] Only there, where the welfare state was always under-developed and is now devolving, where religious fervour and populist movements flourish and organised labour languishes, has the beloved bedtime fable begun to evoke so many nightmares. Now the popular representational crisis of family order incites acrimonious conflicts in every imaginable arena – from television sitcoms to Congress, from the Boy Scouts of America to the United States Marines, from local school boards to multinational corporations, from art museums to health insurance underwriters, and from political conventions to social science conferences.

Social science marching on

> Contrary to expectations many of you may have of historians, I'm not here to tell you that we have seen it all before. The current obsession with family values seems to me, if not entirely new, then peculiar to the late twentieth century, and I will argue that what we are experiencing is yet another dimension of what David Harvey has called the 'postmodern condition', an example of what Anthony Giddens has identified as the late twentieth-century capacity for intimacy at a distance.
>
> (John Gillis 1994)[9]

> What lies behind the family values debate is that the family is in big deal trouble. No child would understand John Gillis's talk. A child wants to know will my mommy and daddy still be there....I'm working to help make putting children at the very highest level of personal and public priority (sic). And it's been gratifying seeing this liberal intelligentsia gradually shift. Most recently Donna Shalala even said yes when she was asked if Dan Quayle was right. I urge you to join in this new national bandwagon for the family.
>
> (David Popenoe 1994)[10]

> The essential integrity of at least a large proportion of American family social scientists is evidenced by the fact that as the evidence accumulated on the effects of family changes, the originally sanguine views of the changes began to change to concern.
>
> (Norval Glenn, 1994)[11]

Just as no new family system has yet succeeded in attaining the kind of hegemonic status which the modern male-breadwinner nuclear-family order enjoyed at mid-century, likewise the ruling paradigms of 1950s sociology have been dethroned, but not supplanted. Probably no discipline felt the disruptive impact of the social movements of the 1960s and early 1970s more strongly than sociology. Seeking to understand and critique their own society and to explore alternatives, militant students with left-wing commitments, including draft resistors in search of student deferments, entered sociology in droves. Infatuated with romantic versions of Marxism, Leninism, Trotskyism, Maoism, and Frankfurt School theory, radical, young sociologists rejected positivism, Parsonian structural-functionalism and modernisation theory as apologias for US racism and imperialistic ventures and for the conformity and 'false promises' of the Cold War era.

A feminist onslaught on the discipline pursued the left-wing attacks on modernisation theory and on the 'functionalist' theories of Talcott Parsons which had justified the gender order of the modern family as 'functional' for a modern industrial society. During the late 1960s and early 1970s, the grass roots women's movement spurred a wave of feminists to enter academic careers, where the liberal cast and the diffuse intellectual boundaries of sociology attracted many, like myself, to the discipline.

Marxist and feminist interventions challenged value-free empiricist pretensions throughout sociology, but few sub-fields were quite so dislocated as family sociology. During the mid-1970s, sociology of the family experienced what Canadian sociologist David Cheal (1991: 8) terms, 'a Big Bang in which feminism played a conspicuous part'. I share Cheal's view that the, 'explosion blew the field apart, and the separate pieces have been flying off in different directions ever since'. Parsonian sociology had posited the universality of the nuclear family and theorised that the gender structure of its male breadwinner–female home-maker genus evinced an ideally evolved 'functional fit' with modern, industrial society and political democracy (Parsons and Bales 1955). In 1963, William J. Goode's *World Revolution and Family Patterns* predicted that modernisation would accomplish the global diffusion of the superior Western variety of family life and, thereby, of the democratic society it was thought to nurture.

Feminist scholars, however, rapidly subjected 1950s families and family sociology alike to trenchant critique. Influenced by demo*graphic* evidence of rapid family transformations in the US, by counter-cultural communal experiments and by the anti-housewife ethos of the early women's liberation movement, feminist scholars exposed ethnocentric and androcentric foundations of functionalist and modernisation theories of family life. Betty Friedan's scathing attack on 'the functionalist freeze' in *The Feminine Mystique* (1963) had directly launched such a project, and it was but a short leap from there to Jessie Bernard's academic work on His and Her marriages (1972), or from incendiary movement classics like Pat Mainardi, 'The politics of housework' (1970) and Ann Koedt, 'The myth of the vaginal orgasm' (1970), to scholarly treatments like Ann Oakley, *The Sociology of Housework* (1974) and Gayle Rubin, 'The traffic in women' (1975).

Meanwhile, outside the embattled groves of academe, a right-wing pro-family movement rapidly polarised popular discourse on family change into feminist v. anti-feminist, left v. right, and fundamentalist v. 'secular humanist' camps. This forced the largely liberal ranks of mainstream family scholars, many of them predisposed to sympathise with Moynihan's earlier, ill-timed critique of Negro family decay, to confront uncomfortable ideological choices.[12] Initially most accommodated their work to liberal feminist values, but the conditions under which they did so implanted an embryo of resentment that would come full-term in the backlash against 'political correctness' of the 1990s. While remaining firmly wedded to an empiricist, value-free paradigm that failed to engage the theoretical challenges of feminist and materialist critiques of family sociology, during the 1960s and 1970s most scholars in the sub-field supported liberal feminist critiques of the modern nuclear family. Embracing a relativistic tolerance of family experimentation as well as elements of the sexual revolution, many in the functionalist lineage produced research findings on subjects like divorce, maternal employment, day care, single parenthood, and sexual experimentation that gave comfort to the rising numbers of people involved in such practices.

Norval Glenn (1994), a prominent senior family sociologist in the US and a member of the Council on Families in America, surveys this disciplinary history as participant-observer:

> Social scientists in the United States generally took a sanguine view of the family changes that started or accelerated in the mid-1960s. Although the label of 'family decline' was often attached by social scientists to the family changes that occurred early in the century, the prevailing view in the 1960s and 1970s was that the family was only adapting to new circumstances, not declining.
>
> (Glenn 1994: 2)

For example, sociologists promoted a Pollyanna-ish assessment of rising divorce rates, interpreting the trend both, 'as a sign that marriage had become more, not less, important', to adults, because they were no longer willing to settle for unhappy unions, and as beneficial in the long run for children released from the hostile environment of an unhappily-married parental home (Glenn 1994: 3). Glenn confesses that he and his colleagues felt, 'strongly inclined to express positive views of recent family changes', then, because the changes coincided with a feminist movement which, 'viewed family change and the trend toward gender equality as parts of the same bundle. Being human', Glenn explains, sociologists sought 'the approval of those whose opinions matter to them, and those persons are largely liberals' who embrace, 'the ideal of male–female equality' (Glenn 1994: 4–5). Andrew Cherlin, a prominent demographer and family sociologist who does not support the family-values campaign, confirms Glenn's assessment of feminist influence on family sociologists: 'It is above all the wish to avoid sounding like an antifeminist, I think, that causes liberals to downplay the costs of the recent trends' (Cherlin 1992: 138).

Since the late 1970s, however, the ideological force field within which scholars investigate the consequences of family change has veered decidedly rightward. Glenn demonstrates that his own views have kept pace. Speaking in conjunction with the United Nations International Year of the Family in 1994 to prominent governmental, religious and academic bodies in Australia, Glenn (1994) applauded social scientists for a voluminous 'second thoughts' literature recanting earlier, uncritical stances on family change, especially concerning the social effects of divorce, fatherlessness, and single motherhood. Psychologist Judith Wallerstein's widely-popularised work (Wallerstein and Blakeslee 1989), which finds that divorce inflicts substantial, lasting and harmful effects on children, has been particularly influential, as has demographer Sara McLanahan's revised assessment that single-parent families harm children (McLanahan 1994; McLanahan and Bumpass 1988) . Adding his voice to, 'most of the more prominent family social science researchers', who, he claims, now evaluate such changes, 'in distinctly negative terms', Glenn (1994: 10) recounts his personal conversion to what he considers to be the now, 'virtually unanimous', social scientific view that, 'the best family situation for children and adolescents is one in which there is a successful, intact marriage of the biological (or adoptive) parents', and that single-parent and stepfamilies are 'far less than ideal'.

Whereas Glenn perceptively identifies the ideological context informing earlier, uncritical social scientific appraisals of family change, he shifts to an 'objectivist', scientific narrative to account for current pessimistic verdicts. His tribute to 'the essential integrity' of family social scientists (included in an epigraph above), claims that the weight of cumulative data compelled this intellectual conversion. I believe, in contrast, that just as was true during the 1960s and 1970s, reconfigurations of power and knowledge provide more illuminating explanatory pathways than does the autonomous march of (social) science. The metamorphosis occurred as a New World Order of global capitalism and economic crisis brought the glory days of sociology as a discipline to a halt, while the modernist liberal theories that had sustained its humanitarian, progressivist ethos began to falter in postmodernist, neo-liberal and post-feminist currents.

If feminism unleashed a 'Big Bang' in family sociology, postmodernism and cultural studies have yet to provoke much more than a whimper in the US. Even though most family scholars are enmeshed in an ideological crisis of representation over the meaning of 'family' under postmodern conditions of patchwork intimacy, most remain wedded to a realist epistemology, to empiricism and to an unproblematic view of the transparency of discourse, texts and representation. Feminist sociologists, European theorists, like Foucault, Giddens and Bourdieu, and infrequent visits from colleagues in other disciplines, like historian John Gillis who spoke at a session on the family-values debate at the 1994 meetings of the American Sociological Association, provide mainstream sociologists with their principal, still marginal, and often defensive, exposure to such questions.[13]

Fending off the intellectual challenge of Gillis's (1994) reading of postmodern family developments and discourse on the ASA panel, for example, Popenoe (1994), resorted to an anti-intellectual, populist rhetorical mode pervasive in family-values discourse.[14] Amidst lingering echoes of appreciative applause for Gillis's paper, Popenoe (1994) mounted the podium and declared, 'I guess I'm the right wing here, but that's not true outside of sociology'. Popenoe positioned himself against the elite world of academia and with, 'most Americans [who] agree with what I just said, except for the liberal intelligentsia I've been battling'.

A singular lack of reflexivity about the changed historical conditions for knowledge production in which we operate renders many family social scientists, particularly senior white males, like Popenoe and Glenn, responsive to the rewards of the revisionist campaign. Since the 1970s, the discipline of sociology in the US has become increasingly feminised, but the massive feminist sex and gender section remains a female ghetto – alien, unfamiliar territory to

most mainstream family scholars.[15] Academic feminism has been institutionalised and, thereby, has become both intellectually respectable, and, as any
student familiar with Weber's (1946) analysis of the routinisation of charisma
might have predicted, partly defanged. It is unsurprising that displaced male
scholars might now feel freer to expel feminist perspectives they once had been
force-fed and never fully digested.

Moreover, the collapse of communism has provoked a crisis in Marxism and
a loss of faith in materialist explanations for social change, with particularly
strong effects in sociology. The nation's generalised right-wing political shift,
the diffusion of post-feminist culture (Rosenfelt and Stacey 1987) and the
organised movement against 'political correctness' in higher education have
offered family scholars compelling inducements to hopscotch over challenges to
academic family theory posed by the postmodern family condition, to land
directly in the public political fray.

The centrist campaign for family values allows displaced, formerly liberal,
scholars an opportunity to reclaim positions of intellectual authority without
appearing to be anti-feminist. Adopting the power-evasive, post-feminist
rhetoric of 'a new familism', the campaign distances itself from reactionaries
intent on restoring Ozzie and Harriet to the frayed upholstery of their
suburban throne. New familism, in Glenn's (1994) formulation, represents

> a return to the belief that stable marriages, two-parent families, and putting
> children's needs before those of adults are desirable and important. It
> differs from the older familism in its espousal of male–female equality and
> the rejection of economic dependence as a basis for marital stability.
>
> (Glenn 1994: 12)

Migrating ideologically from Moynihan (1965) to Friedan (1963) and then
even farther back than Friedan (1981) herself has since travelled, revisionists
applaud phantom signs 'at the mass level' of a 'return toward more traditional
family values (excluding the ideal of male dominance)' (Glenn 1994: 12).[16]

A few social scientists have found the centrist campaign a route to considerable public influence, media celebrity, and even academic attention. David
Popenoe is a good example. Speaking at a symposium in April 1994, Popenoe
acknowledged that his book, *Disturbing the Nest* (1988), which criticises the
impact of social democratic policies on family change in Sweden, had received a
chilly response from the Swedes: 'My book did not start a dialogue in Sweden.
I wasn't even invited back'. As if to confirm Popenoe's self-report, prominent
Scandinavian scholars and officials in attendance gave his critical analysis of
Scandinavian family policy a dismissive response. Karin Stoltenberg, the
Director General of the Norwegian Ministry of Children and Family Affairs, for
example, termed 'insane' Popenoe's belief that welfare state policies were the
source of rising divorce rates in the Nordic nations (see also, Sandqvist and
Andersson 1992). Likewise, an anti-intellectual polemic that Popenoe delivered
'from the heart' at the August 1994 American Sociological Association

Meetings mentioned above confronted a nearly solid wall of disapproval from co-panellists and the audience. Session organiser, Frank Furstenberg, a prominent demographer and family sociologists in the US, publicly chastised Popenoe's 'unhelpful us/them approach' to sociologists and the family-values debate. In response, Popenoe portrayed most sociologists as out of touch with popular concerns and invited listeners sympathetic with his views to accompany him to a nearby conference sponsored by the Communitarian Network.

Yet since Popenoe became a major organiser of the centrist family-values campaign, he has been 'invited back' again and again to deliver his lament for family decline in venues that range from national TV broadcast networks to the US Department of Transportation, from the *New York Times* to the *Chronicle of Higher Education*, in addition to academic conferences and meetings such as at UC, Berkeley and the American Sociological Association.

Blankenhorn, who often claims the mantle of social science despite his lack of an advanced degree in any of the social science disciplines, has achieved even greater celebrity with the National Fatherhood Tour he launched in conjunction with the release of his book, *Fatherless America* (1995). From daytime TV talk shows like *Oprah* to evening TV debates like CNN's *Talkback*, from the cover pages of *Time* magazine to syndicated feature stories in hundreds of local newspapers, Blankenhorn has blazed an extra-mural trail to academic podiums.[17]

The rhetoric of the few women scholars, like Jean Bethke Elshtain and Sylvia Hewlett, who are visibly active in the revisionist campaign suggests that they harbour more personalised resentments against academic feminists. Hewlett (1986) has blamed the anti-maternalist ethos of second-wave feminism for compounding the tribulations she suffered with her pregnancies when she was an Assistant Professor of economics at Barnard College in the 1970s. Elshtain complains, more plausibly, that she is, 'hooted out of the room' by feminists whenever she talks, 'about not ceding the issue of family values to the right' (quoted in Winkler 1993: A7). It is true that few academic feminists sympathise with Elshtain's support for heterosexual marital privilege or her disapproval of single motherhood. Feminists have personal and political stakes in these judgements as profound as Elshtain's, and thus few respond to her public challenges with scholarly dispassion.

It seems ironic, and in my view unlucky, that challenges to knowledge induced partly by radical family changes and by feminism, which de-centred mainstream family social scientists within the academy, propelled quite a few of them into centre stage in the public sphere where they speak to the broad audiences feminists used to address. There, aloof from even the modest constraints of peer review, they deploy social scientific authority to influence political responses to postmodern family struggles by disseminating selective readings of the very kind of modernist research on family change that feminist and other critical sociologists imagined we had discredited. Family sociology, after all, never had been the site of too many power lunches within the academic arena, not even for feminists, let alone for postmodern or cultural studies theorists. In an era of academic retrenchment it should not be surprising that dining halls outside the ivy pastures beckon with more gratifying fare. Modernist family social scientists (and pretenders, like Blankenhorn) can often enhance their academic status in the public domain, where they enjoy much more intellectual esteem and influence than do most post-positivist or feminist theorists.

Unfazed by late century epistemological quagmires, they have developed an extra-mural social science apparatus with which they wage their cultural crusade for centrist family values. Through interlocking networks of think tanks, organisations, periodicals, and policy institutes, these social scientists have been constructing a 'virtual' scholarly and popular consensus in the media supporting the very narrative about universal family values that succumbed to feminist and other forms of deconstructive scrutiny in academia. Saturating the media and policy world they now inhabit with this virtual new familism, they misleadingly maintain that social science has confirmed Moynihan's warning about the socially destructive effects of single motherhood, 'illegitimacy' and fatherless families. In reality, scholars do not now, and likely will not ever, achieve consensus on the relative significance that family structure, material circumstances, the quality of parental relationships, and psychological factors play in shaping children's lives. While it is true that most family sociologists in the US do express some uneasiness over mounting rates of single motherhood, the predominant scholarly view is that single-parent families are more often the consequence than the cause of poverty, unemployment, emotional distress and other negative correlates (e.g. Cherlin 1981; Furstenberg and Cherlin 1991; and even McLanahan 1994). Ironically, a book about the history of family policy in Sweden by a right-wing historian and family-values champion, Allan Carlson (1990), criticises Gunnar and Alva Myrdal for their 'use and abuse of social science' in promoting the kinds of social democratic family policies in their nation of which Carlson disapproves. Yet Carlson's critique of this practice applies at least as well to the contemporary family-values campaign in the US that he actively supports:

> In short, it is difficult to see social science in this episode as little more than a new tool for rhetorical control and political advantage. Weak and inconsistent data, confusion over cause and effect, and avoidance of experimentation proved to be no obstacles to the construction and implementation of policy.
>
> (Carlson 1990: 194)

The contemporary family-values campaign in the US admixes a flawed modernist framework with an untheorised notion of culture. It presumes that the truth about the relative merits and effects of diverse family structures – be they intact married-couple families, stepfamilies, single-parent families, extended families, adoptive families, not to mention gay families – is singular, knowable and extricable from its social, economic and political context.

Although some revisionists, like Glenn, concede that at times (always past times), ideological and cultural convictions interfere with the capacity of social scientists to perceive this truth and temporarily distort social scientific knowledge, still truth and virtue triumph in the end. In this view, most social scientists are sufficiently scientific to listen when 'the data' speak to them in robust and uniform tones.

A second dubious assumption of the neo-family values campaign is that truth is timeless as well as singular – a happy marriage in the 1990s is the same as one in the 1950s, and divorce has the identical, negative effects. 'Culture' intervenes simply to affect the frequency of these structures by rendering each more or less attractive or despised and by sustaining or subverting individual submission to a regime of duty, propriety and self-sacrifice. Culture functions as an untheorised, grab-bag category – a black hole ready to absorb all messy, unexplained causes and consequences. Here it trumps material circumstances, collective struggles and institutional constraints as the source of the decline of stable and 'happy' marriages and families documented by rising rates of divorce, unwed motherhood and 'deadbeat dads'. Culture becomes an unproblematic, remarkably flexible category from which individuals, like savvy shoppers, can select timeless garments – like marital commitment, fidelity, responsibility – and discard their unfashionable accessories – like male dominance.

Somewhat regretfully, perhaps, most of the social scientists active in the centrist campaign have accepted the demise of the 1950s-style, male breadwinner family and the likely permanence of a level of postmodern family instability, diversity and change.[18] Recognising that working mothers, at least, are 'here to stay', they promote a new (post)familism that evades power and justice conflicts embedded in family transformation.[19] However, revisionists have not conceded the decline of positivism, if they have even noticed its infirmity. Instead, following the successful example set by right-wing intellectuals (Messer-Davidow 1993), some modernist family social scientists have regrouped outside the academy to provide a middle course between ideologies of the religious right on one side and feminism and gay liberation on the other. They proffer eager politicians a social science narrative to compete with naturalist and divine justifications for the contested modern gender and family regime.

Sitcom sociology for a disaffected electorate

Post-Cold War politicians from both moribund parties in the US have compelling cause to grasp at this outstretched academic hand. With a shrinking, increasingly cynical, electorate, one described in a study by the Times Mirror Center for the People and the Press (Berke 1994b) as, 'angry, self-absorbed and politically unanchored', the volatile balance of electoral power rests in the hands of those elusive, 'neglected, middle-class' voters, who are disproportionately white (Yoachum 1994).[20] The Democratic Party, weakened by the erosion of its traditional liberal and working-class base, has particularly urgent need to court this constituency. The neo-family-values campaign offers 'New Democrats' a way to exploit the ideological stranglehold that religious, right-wing, pro-family crusaders have secured on the Republican Party in their efforts to lure Reagan Democratic defectors back to the party fold. As one political journalist (Brownstein 1994) quipped, 'Democrats Find the Right's Stuff: Family Values'.

During the 1994 US election season, many prominent Republicans, for their part, worked to shed the unpopular, intolerant, pro-family image emblazoned on the national unconscious by their televised 1992 national convention. Republican luminaries like Dan Quayle, William Bennett, and even leaders of the right-wing Christian Coalition, retreated from the militant pro-family rhetoric they had imposed on the 1992 party platform, such as uncompromising opposition to abortion and gay rights. Asked for his views on abortion and homosexuality just before he addressed the Christian Coalition in September 1994, Quayle told reporters, 'That's their choice' (Berke 1994a: A8). Bennett's speech to the Christian conference advised participants to constrain their homophobic passions:

> I understand the aversion to homosexuality. But if you look in terms of damage to the children of America, you cannot compare the homosexual movement, the gay rights movement, what that has done in damage to what divorce has done to this society.
>
> (Berke 1994a: A8)

Quayle defended this political regression towards the mean in explicitly instrumental terms: 'The political situation has changed in this country. There's not the political support to make it illegal, so we should focus on reducing the number of abortions, and we want to change attitudes' (Berke 1994a: A8).

Mirror-image speeches delivered during the 1994 election season by Quayle and Clinton previewed campaign rhetoric that was to dominate the last presidential election of the millennium, when the electorate was treated to prime-time combat for the family-values crown. Ultimately this is a riskier game show for the Democrats than for the Republicans. Richard Sennett (1994: 490) suggests that, 'the popular language of "family values" and of "values" per se is a barely disguised language of sexual prohibitions', which imagines, 'the breakdown of family values and community standards to be synonymous with sexual explicitness'. Voters in the US overwhelmingly view Republicans rather than Democrats as defenders of this symbolic domain.[21]

The rhetoric of family values provides an infinitely malleable semiotic resource that is understandably irresistible to politicians from both major parties in the age of corporate-sponsored mass media politics. A floating signifier, the language of family values functions more like potent, subliminal images than like verbal communications subject to rational debate. Little wonder, therefore, that TV sitcom heroine Murphy Brown (but not Candice Bergen), enjoyed star billing in the 1992 presidential campaign when Quayle castigated her for glamorising unwed motherhood. In a moment of supreme irony, anchorwoman

Murphy took to the sitcom airwaves to chastise the former vice president for being out of touch with the problems of 'real' families. Millions of US voters watched this well-hyped episode and the ensuing responses to Murphy's sermon provided by Quayle and the small group of single mothers he had selected to join him in viewing this electoral spectacle, on camera (see Fiske 1994). Most political commentators at the time echoed the sitcom heroine's scorn for the vice president's inability to distinguish virtual from actual families. Because the Quayle–Brown spectacle underscored the message of the Republicans' 1992 nominating convention that the grand old party was 'out of touch' with ordinary families, it assisted Clinton's slim margin of victory.

Breathtakingly soon, however, Dan Quayle began to enjoy the last laugh-in, as even President Clinton joined the 'Dan Quayle was Right' brigades (Stacey 1994b). Quayle's campaign against single mothers scored such a dramatic comeback victory over Clinton, the reputed comeback king, because the former vice-president's campaign scriptwriters were quick to grasp the virtual rather than factual character of contemporary family-values talk. They recognised that Murphy Brown could function symbolically as a wayward stepdaughter of Ozzie and Harriet Nelson, the mythic couple who lodge, much larger than life, in collective nostalgia for the world of 1950s families.

The 1950s was the originary moment of the fable of virtual family values. Those halcyon days of the modern nuclear family were also the years when television became a mass medium, indeed an obligatory new member of 'the family'. From its hallowed living room perch, the magic box broadcast the first generation of domestic sitcoms, emblazoning idealised portraits of middle-class family dynamics into the national unconscious. From 'Ozzie and Harriet' to 'Murphy Brown', from 'Amos and Andy' to 'The Cosby Show', from 'The Life of Riley' to 'Roseanne', the world of TV sitcoms saturates popular imagery of family life in the US. Ozzie and Harriet and their kin serve as the Edenic families of our century's bedtime fable, because the apogee of the modern family system coincided with television's own originary Golden Age.

Family sitcom programming was created in the post-Second World War period to construct a mass viewing audience for the nascent television industry and its corporate sponsors. The programmes did not simply reflect, nor even just romanticise, the existing structure and values of the family audience they sought to entertain. Rather, as cultural historians have demonstrated (Spigel 1992, 1995; Taylor 1989), the introduction of television played an active role in constructing, and later in deconstructing, the boundaries of the isolated nuclear family it depicted in such sentimental tones. Because the 1950s was also the first Cold War decade, the years when the US emerged as the dominant global superpower, images of an invincible family and nation mingle inextricably in the national imaginary of the 'good old days' (see May 1988). Clinton, Quayle, Newt Gingrich, the primary constituencies of the electorate they address, as well as many of their academic counsellors, all were reared in the first generation of families who learned to spend their evening hours huddled alone together in their families, watching family TV, in their newly-conceived, 'family rooms', designed as small shrines for the magic box.

This semiotic history of family sitcom TV, which evolved while the modern family it celebrated devolved, renders the idiom of family values a potent, inescapably visual and emotional register. Addressing psychic rather than cognitive frequencies, family-values discourse offers politicians and populace a brilliant defence mechanism with which to displace anxieties over race, gender, sexual, and class antagonisms that were unleashed as the modern family regime collapsed (see Stacey 1994b). No wonder that as the century ends, 'it's all in the family'.

During the 1994 and 1996 political seasons, the most popular sitcom social science plot furnished simple, emotionally resonant motivations and resolutions for those spectacles of normative fin-de-si cle violence, crime, and social decay that the networks broadcast nightly, in Technicolor, for the pleasure and edification of home viewers. Serial killers, crack babies, gang rapists, car-jackers, dope dealers, drive-by shooters, school dropouts, welfare queens, arsonists, wife-beaters, child abusers, sex offenders, kidnappers, runaways, pregnant teens, gang warriors, homeless vagrants, terrorists – all social pathologies begin in a broken home. Her parents divorced, or they never married. His mother was hooked on welfare and drugs, or she dumped him in day care. No one taught them family values. We need to stop coddling these criminals and con artists. From the punitive, anti-crime fervour of, 'three strikes and you're out' to 'two tykes and you're out' welfare caps, family-values ideology plays to the privatistic, anti-government sentiments and the moralistic and vindictive appetites of a dismal, late millennial political culture.

An unholy alliance of academic and political networks produce and sponsor this sitcom sociology, which, ironically enough, is increasingly discordant with the diverse and even postmodern images of family life that now routinely appear on TV domestic sitcoms. Fending off competing political networks on the channels to their right and their left, mainstream family scholars and electoral candidates hope to keep the public tuned to the centre of the political dial. Unwilling or unable to analyse the social sources of postmodern family and civic disorder, or to address the manifold injustices these upheavals expose and intensify, they resort to reruns of old family favourites. Religious and naturalist treatments of virtuous family order continue to play to substantial numbers of viewers in their specialised market niches. However, ageing scholars, allied with New Democrats and moderate Republicans alike, have hitched their hopes for robust ratings to narratives featuring a prodigal society returning to conjugal family virtue after suffering the painful consequences of self-indulgent rebellions. The production company has assembled a postmodern pastiche of social science, fable, advanced technology and (dis)simulation to script and enact the serial melodrama. The plot-line, imagery and production values owe more to television archives, and to power and knowledge shifts in the academy, economy and polity, than they do to ethnographic or analytical acumen. This is the season for sitcom sociology – an effort to distract a disaffected public from the dire familial and social realities that the United States confronts as an ignoble century expires.

Notes

1 Senator Moynihan quoting his 1965 work in a fundraising letter mailed in October 1994.
2 Quayle quoted in Susan Yoachum, 'Quayle talks tough on fatherhood', *San Francisco Chronicle* 9 September 1994: A1, 6.
3 President Clinton quoted in, 'In Baptist talk Clinton stresses moral themes', *New York Times* 10 September 1994; A1, 6.
4 A widely-circulated editorial by David Popenoe (1992), 'The controversial truth: the two-parent family is better', identified me as an ideological exception to an emergent consensus among social scientists that two-parent families are superior.
5 I had been collaborating with Judith Newton in a study of male cultural critics (see Newton and Stacey 1993; 1995; and forthcoming) when the editorial mentioned above appeared, followed quickly by other articles by family-values advocates (see Popenoe 1993a; 1993b; Wilson 1993) that identified *Brave New Families* as an example of misguided liberalism.
6 The postmodern family condition has generated new controversies and challenges that bear on all five of the domains George Marcus (1993) identified in his proposal for the Santa Fe seminar which generated the volume in which this chapter first appeared. For example, political struggles over gender, sexuality and family policy affect local school boards, workplaces, international population conferences, immigration policies, and funding for public broadcasting and the NEA.
7 John Gillis (1996) is one of the first to employ the concept 'virtual family values'.
8 However, recently politicians in Britain and elsewhere in Europe have initiated efforts to stir public concern over single motherhood, divorce and family instability (see Gordon 1994; Millar 1994). For example, the headline story run by London's *Daily Express* on 23 June 1994, Paul Crosbie, 'The crumbling of family life', seems a direct replica of US rhetoric.
9 John Gillis, 'What's behind the debate on family values?', paper delivered at American Sociological Association Meetings, Los Angeles, 6 August 1994.
10 David Popenoe, 'What's behind the debate on family values?', paper delivered at American Sociological Association Meetings, Los Angeles, 7 August 1994.
11 Norval Glenn, 'The re-evaluation of family change by American social scientists', unpublished paper delivered in Australia, 1994, available from author.
12 After all, Moynihan's analysis of Black family decline (1965) had built quite directly on the sociological work of E. Franklin Frazier (1939), and even *Tally's Corner*, Elliot Liebow's (1967) decidedly liberal and sympathetic ethnography of urban Black families, supported the thesis of Black family pathology.
13 For example, on an evening plenary session attended by more than 1,000 sociologists at the American Sociological Association meetings in Los Angeles in August 1994, Patricia Hill Collins delivered a polemical assault on postmodern theory and was rewarded with rapturous applause.
14 For a discussion of this populist rhetorical device, see Stacey (1994b). For additional examples of it, see Wilson (1993) and Elshtain (quoted in Heller 1995).
15 While the proportion of doctoral degrees awarded to women in all fields in the US rose only from 30 per cent in 1980 to 36 per cent in 1990 (National Research Council 1991), in sociology, women's share of PhD degrees rose much more substantially, from 33 per cent in 1977 to 51 per cent in 1989 (National Science Foundation 1991). These data on completed degrees understate feminisation trends evident among currently-enrolled graduate students in sociology departments.

16 Friedan's *The Second Stage* (1981) celebrated the reappearance of familism among feminists. For an early critical discussion of the emergence of this perspective within feminism, see Stacey (1983; 1986).
17 For example, he co-convened an academic conference on family change at Stanford University and then co-edited the resulting conference volume (Blankenhorn, Elshtain and Bayme 1990). Blankenhorn also spoke at a Santa Clara University conference, 'Ethics, public policy and the future of the family', on 18 April 1995.
18 Glenn (1994: 11–12), for example, depicts himself as 'among the relatively small number of American family social scientists who believe that some of the changes can be halted if not reversed. Reconstitution of the American family of the 1950s – a goal of some conservatives – is indeed unrealistic and, in my view, undesirable'.
19 *Here To Stay* (Bane 1976) is the title of an early, misleadingly optimistic assessment of nuclear family stability in the US that is a frequent foil for the family-values campaign.
20 In California, whites constituted only 57 per cent of the adult population in the state, but they cast 83 per cent of the votes in the 1994 election.
21 Indeed, survey data indicate an alarming anomaly. On the one hand, since the 1980s 'the electorate as a whole moved in a clearly liberal direction on three issues besides gay rights: abortion, the role of women, and, to a lesser extent, on the role of government in guaranteeing jobs and living standards' (Strand and Sherrill 1993: 9). Nonetheless, in a November 1994 poll sponsored by the Democratic Leadership Council more voters identified the Republicans than the Democrats as the party that 'would do a better job strengthening families' (Greenberg Research 1994).

Bibliography

Bane, Mary Jo (1976) *Here to Stay: American Families in the Twentieth Century*, New York: Basic Books.

Berger, Brigette and Peter Berger (1983) *The War Over the Family*, New York: Anchor Press/Doubleday.

Berke, Richard L. (1994a) 'Two top Republicans soften their tone', *New York Times* 17 September: A8.

—— (1994b) 'US voters focus on selves, poll says', *New York Times, 21 September: A12.*

Bernard, Jessie (1972) *The Future of Marriage*, New York: World Publishing.

Blankenhorn, David (1995) *Fatherless America: Confronting Our Most Urgent Social Problem*, New York: Basic Books.

Blankenhorn, David, Jean Bethke Elshtain and Steven Bayme (eds) (1990) *Rebuilding the Nest: A New Commitment to the American Family*, Milwaukee: Family Service America.

Brownstein, Ronald (1994) 'Democrats find the Right's stuff: family values', *Los Angeles Times* 1 August: A1, A23.

Carlson, Allan (1990) *The Swedish experiment in family politics: the Myrdals and the interwar population crisis*, New Brunswick: Transaction.

Cheal, David (1991) *Family and the State of Theory*, New York: Harvester Wheatsheaf.

Cherlin, Andrew J. (1981) *Marriage, Divorce, Remarriage*, Cambridge, Mass.: Harvard University Press.

—— (1992) *Marriage, Divorce, Remarriage* (revised edn), Cambridge, Mass.: Harvard University Press.

Coontz, Stephanie (1992) *The Way We Never Were: American Families and the Nostalgia Trap*, New York: Basic Books.

Fiske, John (1994) *Media Matters: Everyday Culture and Political Change*, Minneapolis: University of Minnesota Press.

Frazier, E. Franklin (1939) *The Negro Family in the United States*, Chicago: University of Chicago Press.

Friedan, Betty (1963) *The Feminine Mystique*, New York: Norton.

Friedan, Betty (1981) *The Second Stage*, New York: Summit Books.

Furstenberg, Jr, Frank and Andrew J. Cherlin (1991) *Divided Families: What Happens to Children When Parents Part*, Cambridge, Mass.: Harvard University Press.

Gillis, John (1994) 'What's behind the debate on family values?', paper delivered at American Sociological Association Meetings, Los Angeles: 6 August.

—— (1996) *A World of Their Own Making: Myth, Ritual and the Quest for Family Values*, New York: Basic Books.

Glenn, Norval D. (1994) 'The re-evaluation of family change by American social scientists', paper presented to the Committee for the International Year of the Family of the Catholic Archdiocese of Melbourne.

Goode, William J. (1963) *World Revolution and Family Patterns*, New York: Free Press.

Gordon, Tuula (1994) 'Single women and familism: challenge from the margins', *European Journal of Women's Studies* 1(2): 165–82.

Greenberg Research (1994) Poll Sponsored by Democratic Leadership Council, 8–9 November, Roper Center Public Opinion Online Database.

Heller, Scott (1995) 'Finding a common purpose', *Chronicle of Higher Education* 31 March: A10, A16.

Hewlett, Sylvia Ann (1986) *A Lesser Life: The Myth of Women's Liberation in America*, New York: William Morrow.

Koedt, Anne (1970) 'The myth of the vaginal orgasm' in *Liberation Now! Writings From the Women's Liberation Movement*, New York: Dell: 11–20.

Liebow, Elliot (1967) *Tally's Corner*, Boston: Little, Brown and Co.

McLanahan, Sara (1994) 'The consequences of single motherhood', *The American Prospect* 18.

McLanahan, Sara and Larry L. Bumpass (1988) 'Intergenerational consequences of family disruption', *American Journal of Sociology* 94: 130–52.

Mainardi, Pat (1970) 'The politics of housework' in Robin Morgan (ed.) *Sisterhood is Powerful: An Anthology of Writings from the Women's Liberation Movement*, New York: Vintage: 447–53.

Marcus, George (1993) 'Power/knowledge shifts in America's present fin-de-si cle', a proposal for a School of American Research Advanced Seminar.

May, Elaine (1988) *Homeward Bound: American Families in the Cold War Era*, New York: Basic Books.

Messer-Davidow, E. (1993) 'Manufacturing the attack on liberalized higher education', *Social Text* 36: 40–80.

Millar, Jane (1994) 'State, family and personal responsibility: the changing balance for lone mothers in the United Kingdom', *Feminist Review* 48: 24–39.

Moynihan, Daniel Patrick (1965) *The Negro Family: The Case for National Action*, Washington, DC: US Department of Labor.

National Research Council (1991) *Summary Report 1990: Doctorate Recipients from United States Universities*, Washington, DC: National Academy Press.

National Science Foundation (1991) *Science and Engineering Degrees: 1966–1989, A Source Book*, NSF 91–314, Washington, DC: NSF.

Newton, Judith and Judith Stacey (1992–93), 'Learning not to curse, or feminist predicaments in cultural criticism by men: our movie date with Stephen Greenblatt and James Clifford', *Cultural Critique* 23: 51–82.

—— (1995) 'Ms representations: feminist dilemmas in studying academic men' in Ruth Behar and Deborah Gordon (eds) *Women Writing Culture/Culture Writing Women*, Berkeley: University of California Press.

—— (forthcoming) 'The men we left behind us' in Elizabeth Long (ed.) *Sociology and Cultural Studies*, New York: Basil Blackwell.

Oakley, Ann (1974) *The Sociology of Housework*, New York: Pantheon.

Parsons, Talcott and Robert Bales (1955) *Family, Socialization and Interaction Process*, Glencoe, IL: Free Press.

Popenoe, David (1988) *Disturbing the Nest: Family Change and Decline in Modern Societies*, New York: Aldine de Gruyter.

—— (1992) 'The controversial truth: the two-parent family is better', *New York Times* 26 December: 13.

—— (1993a) 'American family decline, 1960–1990: a review and appraisal', *Journal of Marriage and the Family* 55(3): 527–44.

—— (1993b) 'Scholars should worry about the disintegration of the American family', *Chronicle of Higher Education* 14 April: A48.

—— (1994) 'What's behind the family values debate?', American Sociological Association Meetings, Los Angeles, 7 August.

Rosenfelt, Deborah and Judith Stacey (1987) 'Second thoughts on the second wave', *Feminist Studies* 13(2): 341–61.

Rubin, Gayle (1975) 'The traffic in women: notes on the "political economy" of sex' in Rayna Reiter (ed.) *Toward an Anthropology of Women*, New York: Monthly Review: 157–210.

Rubin, Lillian (1994) *Families on the Faultline: America's Working Class Speaks about the Family, the Economy, Race, and Ethnicity*, New York: HarperCollins.

Sandqvist, Karin and Bengt-Erik Andersson (1992) 'Thriving families in the Swedish welfare state', *Public Interest* 109: 114–17.

Sennett, Richard (1994) 'The new censorship', *Contemporary Sociology* 23(4): 487–91.

Shogren, Elizabeth (1994) 'Traditional family nearly the exception, census finds', *Los Angeles Times* 30 August: A1, A28.

Skolnick, Arlene (1991) *Embattled Paradise: The American Family in an Age of Uncertainty*, New York: Basic Books.

Spigel, Lynn (1992) *Make Room for TV: Television and the Family Ideal in Postwar America*, Chicago: University of Chicago Press.

—— (1995) 'From the dark ages to the golden age: women's memories and television reruns', *Screen* 36(1): 14–31.

Stacey, Judith (1983) 'The new conservative feminism', *Feminist Studies* 9(3): 559–83.

—— (1986) 'Are feminists afraid to leave home? The challenge of profamily feminism' in Juliet Mitchell and Ann Oakley (eds) *What is Feminism?*, London: Basil Blackwell: 219–48.

—— (1990) *Brave New Families: Stories of Domestic Upheaval in Late Twentieth Century America*, New York: Basic Books.

—— (1994a) 'The new family values crusaders', *The Nation* 25 July–1 August: 119–22.

—— (1994b) 'Scents, scholars and stigma: the revisionist campaign for family values', *Social Text* 40: 51–75.

Strand, Douglas Alan and Kenneth Sherrill (1993) 'Electoral bugaboos? The impact of attitudes toward gay rights and feminism on the 1992 presidential vote', paper delivered at American Political Science Association Meetings, Washington, DC.

Taylor, Ella (1989) *Primetime Families: Television Culture in Postwar America*, Berkeley: University of California Press.

Wallerstein, Judith S. and Sandra Blakeslee (1989) *Second Chances: Men, Women, and Children a Decade After Divorce*, New York: Ticknor & Fields.

Weber, Max (1946) 'The sociology of charismatic authority' in Hans Gerth and C. Wright-Mills (eds) *From Max Weber: Essays in Sociology* (1958 edn), New York: Oxford University Press: 245–64.

Wilson, James Q. (1993) 'The family-values debate', *Commentary* 95(4): 24–31.

Winkler, Karen (1993) 'Communitarians move their ideas outside academic arena', *Chronicle of Higher Education* 21 April: A7.

Yoachum, Susan (1994) 'Small minority voter turnout a product of apathy and anger', *San Francisco Chronicle* 22 September: A4.

Name index

Subject index